MILKMAN

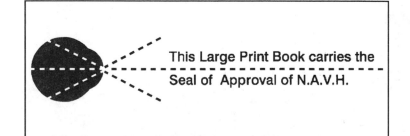

This Large Print Book carries the
Seal of Approval of N.A.V.H.

MILKMAN

ANNA BURNS

THORNDIKE PRESS
A part of Gale, a Cengage Company

GALE
A Cengage Company

Farmington Hills, Mich • San Francisco • New York • Waterville, Maine
Meriden, Conn • Mason, Ohio • Chicago

Copyright © 2018 by Anna Burns.
Thorndike Press, a part of Gale, a Cengage Company.

ALL RIGHTS RESERVED
Thorndike Press® Large Print Basic.
The text of this Large Print edition is unabridged.
Other aspects of the book may vary from the original edition.
Set in 16 pt. Plantin.

LIBRARY OF CONGRESS CIP DATA ON FILE.
CATALOGUING IN PUBLICATION FOR THIS BOOK
IS AVAILABLE FROM THE LIBRARY OF CONGRESS

ISBN-13: 978-1-4328-6329-6 (hardcover)

Published in 2019 by arrangement with Graywolf Press

Printed in the United States of America
2 3 4 5 6   23 22 21 20 19

For Katy Nicholson, Clare Dimond
and James Smith

ONE

The day Somebody McSomebody put a gun to my breast and called me a cat and threatened to shoot me was the same day the milkman died. He had been shot by one of the state hit squads and I did not care about the shooting of this man. Others did care though, and some were those who, in the parlance, 'knew me to see but not to speak to' and I was being talked about because there was a rumour started by them, or more likely by first brother-in-law, that I had been having an affair with this milkman and that I was eighteen and he was forty-one. I knew his age, not because he got shot and it was given by the media, but because there had been talk before this, for months before the shooting, by these people of the rumour, that forty-one and eighteen was disgusting, that twenty-three years' difference was disgusting, that he was married and not to be fooled by me for there were plenty of quiet, unnoticeable people who took a bit of watching. It had been my fault too, it seemed, this affair with the milkman. But I had not been having an affair with the milkman. I did not like the milkman and had been frightened and confused by his pursuing and attempting an affair with me. I did not like first brother-in-law either. In his compulsions he made things up about other people's sexlives. About my sexlife. When I was younger, when I was twelve, when he appeared on my eldest sister's rebound after her long-term boyfriend got dumped for cheating on her, this new man got her pregnant and they got married right away. He made lewd remarks about me to me from the first moment he met me — about my quainte, my tail, my contry, my box, my jar, my contrariness, my monosyllable — and he used words, words sexual, I did not understand. He knew I didn't understand them but that I knew enough to grasp they were sexual. That was what gave him pleasure. He was thirty-five. Twelve and thirty-five. That was a twenty-three years' difference too.

So he made his remarks and felt entitled to make his remarks and I did not speak because I did not know how to respond to this person. He never made his comments when my sister was in the room. Always, whenever she'd leave the room, it was a switch turned on inside him. On the plus side, I wasn't physically frightened of him. In those days, in that place, violence was everybody's main gauge for judging those around them and I could see at once he didn't have it, that he didn't come from that perspective. All the same, his predatory nature pushed me into frozenness every time. So he was a piece of dirt and she was in a bad way with being pregnant, with still loving her long-term man and not believing what he'd done to her, disbelieving he wasn't missing her, for he wasn't. He was off now with somebody else. She didn't really see this man here, this older man she'd married but had been too young herself, and too unhappy, and too in love — just not with him — to have taken up with him. I stopped visiting even though she was sad because I could no longer take his words and facial expressions. Six years on, as he tried to work his way through me and my remaining elder sisters, with the three of us — directly, indirectly, politely, fuck off-ly — rejecting him, the milkman, also uninvited but much more frightening, much more dangerous, stepped from out of nowhere onto the scene.

I didn't know whose milkman he was. He wasn't our milkman. I don't think he was anybody's. He didn't take milk orders. There was no milk about him. He didn't ever deliver milk. Also, he didn't drive a milk lorry. Instead he drove cars, different cars, often flash cars, though he himself was not flashy. For all this though, I only noticed him and his cars when he started putting himself in them in front of me. Then there was that van — small, white, nondescript, shapeshifting. From time to time he was seen at the wheel of that van too.

He appeared one day, driving up in one of his cars as I was walking along reading *Ivanhoe*. Often I would walk along reading books. I didn't see anything wrong with this but it became something else to be added as further proof against me. 'Reading-while-walking' was definitely on the list.

'You're one of the who's-it girls, aren't you? So-and-so was your father, wasn't he? Your brothers, thingy, thingy, thingy and thingy, used to play in the hurley team, didn't they? Hop in. I'll give you a lift.'

This was said casually, the passenger door already opening. I was startled out of my reading. I had not heard this car drive up. Had not seen before either, this man at the wheel of it. He was leaning over, looking

Aurora Public Library
(905)-727-9494
www.aurorapl.ca

User ID: 23164001383147

Date: 23 November 2022 12:49
Title: Milkman
Barcode: 33164300604951
Date due: 14 December 2022
23:59

Date: 23 November 2022 12:49
Title: Milkman : a novel
Barcode: 33164300615098
Date due: 14 December 2022
23:59

Total checkouts for session:2
Total checkouts:2

The amount of money you saved
today using APL is: $48.00

Download the APL app for
quick access to your library

out at me, smiling and friendly by way of being obliging. But by now, by age eighteen, 'smiling, friendly and obliging' always had me straight on the alert. It was not the lift itself. People who had cars here often would stop and offer lifts to others going into and out of the area. Cars were not in abundance then and public transport, because of bomb-scares and hijackings, was intermittently withdrawn. Kerb-crawling too, may have been a term recognised, but it was not recognised as a practice. Certainly I had never come across it. Anyway, I did not want a lift. That was generally speaking. I liked walking — walking and reading, walking and thinking. Also specifically speaking, I did not want to get in the car with this man. I did not know how to say so though, as he wasn't being rude and he knew my family for he'd named the credentials, the male people of my family, and I couldn't be rude because he wasn't being rude. So I hesitated, or froze, which was rude. 'I'm walking,' I said. 'I'm reading,' and I held up the book, as if *Ivanhoe* should explain the walking, the necessity for walking. 'You can read in the car,' he said, and I don't remember how I responded to that. Eventually he laughed and said, 'No bother. Don't you be worryin'. Enjoy your book there,' and he closed the car door and drove away.

First time that was all that happened — and already a rumour started up. Eldest sister came round to see me because her husband, my now forty-one-year-old brother-in-law, had sent her round to see me. She was to apprise me and to warn me. She said I had been seen talking with this man.

'Fuck off,' I said. 'What's that mean — *been seen*? Who's been seein' me? Your husband?'

'You'd better listen to me,' she said. But I wouldn't listen — because of him and his double standards, and because of her putting up with them. I didn't know I was blaming her, had been blaming her, for his long-term remarks to me. Didn't know I was blaming her for marrying him when she didn't love him and couldn't possibly respect him, for she must have known, how could she not, all the playing around he got up to himself.

She tried to persist in advising me to behave myself, in warning me that I was doing myself no favours, that of all the men to take up with — But that was enough. I became incensed and cursed some more because she didn't like cursing so that was the only way to get her out of a room. I then shouted out the window after her that if that coward had anything to say to me then he was to come round and say it to me himself. That was a mistake: to have been emotional, to have been seen and heard to be emotional, shouting out the window, over the street, allowing myself to be pulled into the momentum. Usually I managed not to fall into that. But I was angry. I had just so much anger — at her, for being the wee wife, for doing always exactly what he told her to, and at him, for trying to put his own contemptibleness over onto me. Already I could feel my stubbornness, my 'mind your own business' arising. Unfortunately whenever that happened, I'd pretty much turn perverse, refuse to learn from experience and cut off my nose to spite my face. As for the rumour of me and the milkman, I dismissed it without considering it. Intense nosiness about everybody had always existed in the area. Gossip washed in, washed out, came, went, moved on to the next target. So I didn't pay attention to this love affair with the milkman. Then he appeared again — this time on foot as I was running in the parks with the lower and upper waterworks.

I was alone and not reading this time, for I never read while running. And there he was, again out of nowhere, this time falling into step beside me where he'd never been before. Instantly we were running together and it looked as if always we were running together and again I was startled, as I would be startled by every encounter, except the last, I was to have with this man. At first he didn't speak, and I could not speak. Then he did and his talk was mid-conversation as if too, always we were mid-conversation. His words were brief and a little strained because of my pace of running, and it was of my place of work that he spoke. He knew my work — where it was, what I did there, the hours, the days and the twenty-past-eight bus I caught every morning when it wasn't being hijacked to get me into town to it. Also he made the pronouncement that I never caught this bus home. This was true. Every weekday, rain or shine, gunplay or bombs, stand-off or riots, I preferred to walk home reading my latest book. This would be a nineteenth-century book because I did not like twentieth-century books because I did not like the twentieth century. I suppose now, looking back, this milkman knew all of that as well.

So he spoke his words as we were going along one of the sides of the top-end reservoir. There was a smaller reservoir near the child's playground down at the bottom end.

He looked ahead, this man, as he spoke to me, not once turning towards me. Throughout this second meeting he didn't ask one question of me. Nor did he seem to want any response. Not that I could have given one. I was still at the part of 'where did he come from?' Also, why was he acting as if he knew me, as if we knew each other, when we did not know each other? Why was he presuming I didn't mind him beside me when I did mind him beside me? Why could I just not stop this running and tell this man to leave me alone? Apart from 'where did he come from?' I didn't have those other thoughts until later, and I don't mean an hour later. I mean twenty years later. At the time, age eighteen, having been brought up in a hair-trigger society where the ground rules were — if no physically violent touch was being laid upon you, and no outright verbal insults were being levelled at you, and no taunting looks in the vicinity either, then nothing was happening, so how could you be under attack from something that wasn't there? At eighteen I had no proper understanding of the ways that constituted encroachment. I had a feeling for them, an intuition, a sense of repugnance for some situations and some people, but I did not know intuition and repugnance counted, did not know I had a right not to like, not to have to put up with, anybody and everybody coming near. Best I could manage in those days was to hope the person concerned would hurry up and say whatever it was he or she thought they were being friendly and obliging by saying, then for them to go away; or else to go away myself, politely and quickly, the very moment I could.

I knew by this second meeting that the milkman was attracted to me, that he was making some move on me. I knew I didn't like him being attracted and that I did not feel the same way towards him myself. But he uttered no direct words by way of forwarding on this attraction. Still too, he asked nothing of me. Nor was he physically touching me. Not once so far in this second meeting had he even looked at me. Plus he was older than me, far older, so could it be, I wondered, that I was getting this wrong, that the situation was not as I imagined? As for the running, we were in a public place. This was two conjoined large parks during the day, a sinister environment at night, though during the day also it was sinister. People didn't like to admit to the day section being sinister because everyone wanted at least one place where they could go. I

16

didn't own this territory so that meant he was allowed to run in it just as much as I was allowed to run in it, just as much as children in the Seventies felt entitled to drink their alcohol in it, just as slightly older children would later in the Eighties feel justified sniffing their glue in it, just as older people again in the Nineties would come to inject themselves with heroin in it, just as at present the state forces were hiding in it to photograph renouncers-of-the-state. They also photographed renouncers' known and unknown associates, which was what then happened just at this point. An audible 'click' sounded as the milkman and I ran by a bush and this was a bush I'd run by lots of times without clicks coming out of it. I knew it had happened this time because of the milkman and his involvement, and by 'involvement' I mean connected, and by 'connected' I mean active rebellion, and by 'active rebellion' I mean state-enemy renouncer owing to the political problems that existed in this place. So now I was to be on file somewhere, in a photograph somewhere, as a once unknown, but now certainly known associate. This milkman himself made no reference to the click even though it was impossible he had not heard it. I dealt with it by picking up my pace to get this

17

run over with, also by pretending I had not heard the click myself.

He slowed the run down though, right down, until we were walking. This was not because he was unfit generally but because he was no runner. He had no interest in running. All that running along the reservoirs where I had not ever seen him run had never been about running. All that running, I knew, was about me. He implied it was because of pacing, that he was slowing the run because of pacing, but I knew pacing and for me, walking during running was not that. I could not say so, however, for I could not be fitter than this man, could not be more knowledgeable about my own regime than this man, because the conditioning of males and females here would never have allowed that. This was the 'I'm male and you're female' territory. This was what you could say if you were a girl to a boy, or a woman to a man, or a girl to a man, and what you were not — least not officially, least not in public, least not often — permitted to say. This was certain girls not being tolerated if it was deemed they did not defer to males, did not acknowledge the superiority of males, might even go so far as almost to contradict males, basically, the female wayward, a species insolent and far too sure of herself. Not all boys and men though, were like that. Some laughed and found the affronted men funny. Those ones I liked — and maybe-boyfriend was one of that lot. He laughed and said, 'You're having me on. Can't be that bad, is it that bad?' when I mentioned boys I knew who loathed each other yet united in rage at the loudness of Barbra Streisand; boys incensed at Sigourney Weaver for killing the creature in that new film when none of the men in that film had been able to kill the creature; boys reacting against Kate Bush for being cat-like, cats for being female-like, though I didn't tell about cats being found dead and mutilated up entries to the point where there weren't many of them left in my area anymore. Instead I ended on Freddie Mercury still to be admired just as long as it could be denied he was in any way fruity, which had maybe-boyfriend setting down his coffee pot — only he and his friend, chef, out of everybody I knew had coffee pots — then sitting down himself and laughing all over again.

This was my 'almost one year so far maybe-boyfriend' whom I met up with on Tuesday nights, now and again on a Thursday night, most Friday nights into Saturday, then all Saturday nights into Sunday. Sometimes this seemed steady dating. Other times not at all dating. A few over his way saw us as a proper couple. Most though, saw us as one of those non-couple couples, the type who might meet regularly but who couldn't be designated a proper pairing for all that. I would have liked to have been a proper pairing and to have been officially dating and said so at one point to maybe-boyfriend, but he said no, that that wasn't true, that I must have forgot and so he'd remind me. He said that once we tried — with him being my steady boy and me being his steady girl, with us meeting and arranging and seemingly moving, as did proper couples, towards some future end. He said I went peculiar. He said he also went peculiar, but that never had he seen me with so much fear in me before. Vaguely, as he spoke, I remembered something of what he was recounting. Another part of me though, was thinking, is he making this up? He said he'd suggested, for the sake of whatever it was we did have, that we split up as steady girl and steady boy which, in his opinion, had just been me anyway attempting that 'talking about feelings' which, given my freak-out when we did, given too, I spoke of feelings even less than he spoke of feelings, I mustn't have believed in any of that all along. Instead he put forward that we go back to the maybe territory of not knowing whether or not we were dating. So we did and he said I calmed down and that he calmed down as well.

As for that official 'male and female' territory, and what females could say and what they could never say, I said nothing when the milkman curbed, then slowed, then stopped my run. Once again, least not intentionally, he didn't seem rude, so I couldn't be rude and keep on running. Instead I let him slow me, this man I didn't want near me, and it was at that point he said something about all the walking I did whenever I wasn't running and these were words I wished he hadn't spoken or else that I hadn't heard at all. He said he was concerned, that he wasn't sure, and all the while still he did not look at me. 'Not sure,' he said, 'about this arunning, about all of that awalking. Too much arunning and awalking.' With that, and without another word, he went round a corner at the edge of the parks and disappeared. As with last time with the flashy car, this time too — with the sudden appearance, the proximity, the presumption, the click of the camera, his judgement upon my running and walking then once again that abrupt departure — there was confusion, too much of being startled. It seemed a shock, yes, but shock over something that must be too small, unimportant, even too normal to be really truly shocked over. Because of it though, it was only hours later when back home that I was able to take in he knew about my work. I didn't remember how I got home either because after he left, at first I attempted running again, trying to resume my schedule, to pretend his appearance had not happened or at least had not meant anything. Then, because I was lapsing in attention, because I was confused, because I wasn't being truthful, I slipped on glossy pages that had worked loose from some discarded magazine. They were a double-page spread of a woman with long dark, unruly hair, wearing stockings, suspenders, something too, black and lacy. She was smiling out at me, leaning back and opening up for me, which was when I skidded and lost balance, catching full view of her monosyllable as I fell down on the path.

TWO

The morning after that run session, and earlier than usual, and without telling myself why, I walked out of my way to the other side of the district to catch a different bus into town. Also I got that same bus home. For the first time ever I did not do my reading-while-walking. I did not do my walking. Again I did not tell myself why. Another thing was I missed my next run session. Had to, in case *he* reappeared in the parks & reservoirs. If you're a serious runner though, and a distance runner, and of a certain persuasion from a certain part of the city, you pretty much had to incorporate that whole stretch of territory into your schedule. If you didn't, you were left with a curtailed route owing to religious geography, which meant repeatedly going round a much smaller area in order to get a comparable effect. Although I loved running, the monotony of the wheelrun told me I didn't

love it that much, so no running went on
for seven whole days. Seemed too, no running ever again was to go on until my
compulsion to do so got the better of me.
On the evening of the seventh day of no
running, I decided to return to the parks &
reservoirs, this time in the company of third
brother-in-law.

Third brother-in-law was not first brother-
in-law. He was a year older than me and
someone I'd known since childhood: a mad
exerciser, a mad street fighter, a basic all-
round mad person. I liked him. Other
people liked him. Once they got used to him
they liked him. Other things about him were
that he never gossiped, never came out with
lewd remarks or sexual sneers or sneers
about anything. Nor did he ask manipulative, nosey questions. Rarely, in fact, did he
ask questions. As for his fighting, this man
fought men. Never did he fight women.
Indeed, his mental aberration, as diagnosed
by the community, was that he expected
women to be doughty, inspirational, even
mythical, supernatural figures. We were supposed also to altercate with him, more or
less too, to overrule him, which was all very
unusual but part of his unshakeable women
rules. If a woman wasn't being mythical and
so on, he'd try to nudge things in that direc-

tion by himself becoming slightly dictatorial towards her. By this he was discomfited but had faith that once she came to with the help of his improvised despotism, she would remember who she was and indignantly reclaim her something beyond the physical once again. 'Not particularly balanced then,' said some men of the area, probably all men of the area. 'But if he has to have an imbalance,' said all women of the area, 'we think it best he proceed in it this way.' So with his atypical high regard for all things female, he proved himself popular with the females without any awareness he was popular with them — which made him more popular. Of beneficial significance also — I mean for me with my current problem with the milkman — was that all the women of the area viewed brother-in-law this way. So not just one woman, or two women, or three or even four women. Small-numbered women, unless married to, mother of, groupie of, or in some way connected with the men of power in our area — meaning the paramilitaries in our area — would have gotten nowhere in directing communal action, in influencing to their advantage public opinion here. Local women en masse, however, did so command, and on the rare occasions when they rose up against some civic, social or local circumstance, they presented a surprising formidable force of which other forces, usually considered more formidable, had no choice but to take note. Together then, these women were appreciative of their champion which meant they'd be protective of this champion. That was him and the women. As for him and the men of the area — and perhaps to their astonishment — most men liked and respected third brother-in-law too. Given his superb physicality and instinctive understanding of the combative male code of the district he had the proper credentials, even if his behoving to women, in the eyes of the men, had reached extreme bananas stage. In the area therefore, he was all-roundly accepted, as by me too, he was accepted, and in the past I did used to run with him but then one day I stopped. His tyrannous approach to physical exercise overtook my own tyrannous approach to physical exercise. His way proved too intense, too straitened, too offensive of reality. I decided though, to resume running with him, not because the milkman would be intimidated physically by him, harbouring fears of brother-in-law fighting with him. Certainly he wasn't as young or as fit as brother-in-law, but youth and fitness don't count for everything, often not even for anything. You don't need to be young and able to run to fire a gun for example, and I was pretty sure the milkman could do that all right. It was his fanbase that cross-gender esteem third brother-in-law was held in — that I thought might prove a deterrent to the milkman. Should he take exception to brother-in-law accompanying me, he'd encounter not only the opprobrium of the entire local community, but his reputation in it as one of our highranking, prestigious dissidents would plummet to the point where he'd be put outside any and all safe houses, into the path of any and all passing military patrol vehicles, exactly as if he wasn't one of our major influential heroes but instead just some enemy state policeman, some enemy soldier from across the water or even one of the enemy state-defending paramilitaries from over the way. As a renouncer heavily reliant upon the local community, my guess was he wouldn't alienate himself for me. That was the plan then, and it was a good plan, and I took confidence from it, regretting only that it hadn't occurred to me seven days and six nights earlier. But it had occurred now so next thing was to launch it into action. I put on my running gear and set off for third brother-in-law's house.

Third brother-in-law's house was en route to the parks & reservoirs and as I approached everything was as expected: brother-in-law on his garden path, in his gear, warming up. He was muttering curses and I didn't think he knew himself he was muttering them. 'Fuckin' fuckin'' issued softly from him as he stretched his right gastrocnemius muscle then his left gastrocnemius muscle, then more 'fuckin's' during the right and left soleus muscles, then he said from profile, because stretching was a focused business, also without indication that here I was, returning to run with him after a considerable breach since last running with him, 'We're doing eight miles today.' 'Okay,' I said. 'Eight miles it is.' This shocked him. I knew I'd been expected to frown, to assert that eight miles certainly was what we were not doing, then in one of those imperialistic, goddess fashions, to assert how many miles we were doing. My mind though, was on the milkman so I didn't care how many miles we did. He straightened up and looked at me. 'Did you hear me, sister-in-law? I said nine miles. Ten. Twelve miles is what we're doing.' Again this was my cue to take issue and pick bone. Normally I'd have obliged but at that moment I didn't care if we ran the length and breadth of the country till we reached the point where the littlest cough — even someone else's should cause our legs to fall off. But I tried. 'Ach no, brother-in-law,' I said. 'Not twelve miles.' 'Yeah,' he said, 'fourteen miles.' Clearly then, I hadn't tried hard enough. Worse, my throwaway attitude, given the nature of my sex, now had him properly agitated. He looked intensely at me, maybe as he wondered was I sick or something. I didn't ever know what brother-in-law wondered but I did know it wasn't that he didn't want to do fourteen miles or wasn't capable of fourteen miles. To him — in his need to be gainsaid — as to me — in my preoccupation with the milkman — the mileage was the most irrelevant thing in the world. It was that I hadn't browbeaten him and, 'I'm no browbeater,' he began, which meant we were in for a prolonged bout of one-sided haggling, but then his wife, my third sister, stepped out onto their path.

'Runnin'!' she grunted, and this sister was standing in her drainpipes and flip-flops with every toenail painted a different colour. This was before the years when people except in Ancient Egypt painted toenails different colours. She had a glass of Bushmills in one hand and a glass of Bacardi in the other because she was still at that stage of working out what to have for her first drink. 'You two are fuckers,' she said. 'Uptight control freaks. Obsessive, anally retentive nutcases of — Anyway, what class of bastard goes runnin'?' Then she left off because five of her friends turned up at their door. Two used their feet to shove open the tiny house's little gate, for their arms couldn't do the shoving because their arms were piled with alcohol. The others went through the hedge which meant yet again that hedge was made a mess of. This was a miniature hedge, a foot high, 'a feature' as my sister called it, but it hadn't been able to feature because of people forgetting it was there and pushing through it or falling over it, which was what three of the friends now did. As a verdure therefore, it was distressed again, pulled out of shape again as these women made their way through it out onto the grass. Before they squashed into the tiny house, as usual they mocked the two of us as runners. This they did in passing, nudging us out of our stretches — the tradition whenever they came across us in any solemn, warming-up stance. Finally, before they closed the front door and we two had jumped the hedge to set off on our running, already I could smell the cigarettes and hear the laughter and bad language from the living room; could hear too, the glug of a long liquid being poured into a long glass.

We ran along the top reservoir, which was seven days after I'd last run along it with the milkman, with third brother-in-law continuing quietly to curse to himself. I myself was keeping a look-out for the disturbance even though I did not want that person in my head. I wanted maybe-boyfriend in my head, for there he'd been, all cosy, until uneasiness about the milkman had pushed him out of it. This was Tuesday and I was meeting him later that evening after I'd finished this run and he'd finished tinkering on his latest beat-up car. I called the present one grey and he called it a silver zero-x-something and he'd set aside his fixed-up white one to get in this beat-up grey one to start resuscitation immediately, but when I walked into his living room last Tuesday he had a completely different bit of car on the floor. I said, 'You got car on the carpet,' and he said, 'Yeah I know, isn't it brilliant?' Then he explained that all of them — meaning the guys at work — had been overcome with orgasms because some super-special motor vehicle, built by some high-dream carmaker, was dumped — *'For fuck all! For nothin'! They wanted nothin' for it!'* he cried into the middle of their garage, — into the middle of their laps. 'Can you imagine?' he said. 'No beans! No sausages!' meaning money, meaning the owners not wanting any. He seemed in shock so I was unclear if this encounter with the dream car had been a good thing or a bad thing. I was about to ask but still he hadn't finished. 'The people who brought it in,' he said, 'also said, "You fellas can have our broken cooker, our bit of fridge, our mangle, some ratty carpet that's okay really just a bit smelly so give it a wash then put it in your toilet, plus you can have all our broken glass and breezeblocks and bags of rubble for to make a conservatory hardcore foundation with as well." So then we thought,' said maybe-boyfriend, 'that these poor auld people think we're a boneyard and not a car mechanics and so maybe it wouldn't be right to take the Blower off them because they're mentally confused and don't know what they're doing, don't know either maybe, what that car — even in the state it's in — is worth. Some of us though, nudged others of us and hissed, *"Don't be sayin' anything. They want rid of it, so we'll just take it,"* but some of us did say something — rephrasing the mental bit so as not to hurt feelings of course.' He said the couple then rounded and said, 'Are you saying we're stupid or something? Are you saying we're poor or something? What is it you're saying? What something?' Then they got insulting. 'If you fuckers think we're mad, then we'll leave and take our white furnitures, our rubbles, our lumbers, our Blower Bentley, our carpet, all our excellent material that we brought for you with goodwill with us. So take it or leave it, see if we care.' 'Of course we took it,' said maybe-boyfriend. At this point I opened my mouth to ask what was a — but he preempted by saying 'racing car', supposedly to make it easier for me. Normally he didn't make it easier — not deliberately, but because he'd get carried away even though once again he was ill-judging his audience whenever he talked car and I was his audience. He'd talk on, giving technical exposition to the last hyphen and punctuation mark which was more than needful, indeed helpful, but I understood he had to make use of me because he was excited by the car and I was the only one in the room. Of course he wouldn't intend me to remember, just as I wouldn't intend him to remember *The Brothers Karamazov, Tristram Shandy, Vanity Fair* or *Madame Bovary* just because once, in a state of high excitement, I told him of them. Even though ours was a maybe-relationship, not a proper committed, going-somewhere relationship, each was allowed in heightened moments to give full coverage, with the other making an effort to take in at least a part. Besides, I wasn't completely ignorant. I could see now he was happy about what had happened at the garage. I knew too, that a Bentley was a car.

And now he was doting on it, on the bit that was currently on the living-room carpet. He stood beside it, gazing down, a big smile on his face, beaming away. And that was what he did — the way I'd get turned on, the way he'd turn me on, when he was engrossed, unstudied, unself-conscious, working on the old heaps, his face full of love and concentration, telling himself these were serious dilemmas from which the poor auld car mightn't recover if he didn't tinker conscientiously, also when some people might shrug and say in life, about life, *'Oh well, there's no point in trying, probably it won't work so we must just not try and instead prepare ourselves for bitterness and disappointment'* but maybe-boyfriend would say, *'Well, it might work, I think it will work, so how about we try?'* and even if it didn't work at least he didn't downgrade himself to misery before having a go. After he'd weathered his disappointment if it hadn't worked, once again, with renewed vigour, with that mindset of 'can' even when he couldn't, he'd be straight on to the next thing. Curious and engaged and eager — because of passion, because of plans, because of hope, because of me. And that was it. With me too, he was uncalculated, transparent, free from deception, always was what he was, with none of that coolness, that withholding, that design, those hurtful, sometimes clever, always mean, manipulations. No conniving. No games-playing. He didn't do it, didn't care for it, had no interest in it. 'Those are crazy things,' he'd say, brushing aside flank movements as protections for his heart. Strong therefore. Chaste too. Uncorrupted in the little things, which held fast for the bigger things. That was singular. That was why I was attracted to him. That was why standing there, looking at him looking at his car, doing his out-loud wondering and pondering, I was getting wet and —

'You are listening to me, aren't you?' he said. 'Yes,' I said. 'Heard everything. You were talking of inside-car.'

I meant the bit on the carpet but he said he'd tell again because it seemed I hadn't grasped the fundamentals. This was when I learned that this inside bit was an outside bit, that it went at the front of the vehicle. He said too, that the car it had come from had been a complete wreck when it turned up at the garage. 'Guess what! It was a write-off, a total terrible, due to some idjit blowing up the engine by not putting enough oil in. Vital bits missing, differential missing, pistons through the tappet cover, almost all of it, maybe-girlfriend, a tragedy.' From what I could gather — because the bit on the floor looked nothing special, just more of the usual — this car had been some coveted, early twentieth-century, cheery, brutish, speedy, noisy, not-good-at-stopping car. 'Beyond redemption,' said maybe-boyfriend, meaning beyond repair, yet still he was smiling down at it. He said he and the others, after much arguing, dissension and finally, a casting-of-votes, had decided to disassemble what was left. So they split it up, then they drew lots with maybe-boyfriend ending up with this bit on the carpet, a bit too, that was presently causing him transportations of pure joy.

'Supercharger,' he said and I said, 'Uh-huh,' and he said, 'No, you don't under-stand, maybe-girlfriend. Few cars were supercharged then so this was advanced technology. It decimated the competition —

all because of this' — he indicated the bit on the floor. 'Uh-huh,' I said again, then I had a thought. 'Who got the car seats?' which made him laugh and say, 'That's not a proper question, darlin'. C'mere' — and he brought his fingers — *oh God* — over to the nape of my neck. This was dangerous, always dangerous. Any time the fingers were there — between my neck and my skull — I'd forget everything — not just things that happened moments before the fingers, but everything — who I was, what I was doing, all my memories, everything about anything, except being there, in that moment, with him. Then, when he'd rub them in, into the groove, that crook, the soft bit above the bumpy bone, that was even more dangerous. At that point my mind would fall behind owing to deliciousness and to muddles with chronology. Belatedly I'd think, *oh, but what if he begins to rub his fingers there!* I'd go to jelly which meant he'd have to put his arms around me to stop me from falling which meant I'd have to let him. Even then though, within moments, we would be crashing to the ground.

'Forget the seats,' he murmured. 'Seats important but not most important. This is what's important.' I was unclear if still he was on 'car' or had moved his attention now to me. I suspected it was car but at some moments you can't stop to have an argument, so we kissed and he said he was getting turned on and was I not turned on and I said could he not look how I was looking, then he murmured what's this and I murmured what's what and he prodded something in my hand which I'd forgotten which turned out to be Gogol's 'The Overcoat' so he said he'd just set it there, meaning the table, which he did which was okay and we were about maybe to go to the carpet or to the settee or somewhere when there were voices. They were coming up his path and were followed by raps on his door.

On the doorstep were men, his neighbours. They had come to the house because word had spread about the Blower Bentley, with everyone not believing and wanting to see for themselves. Given their number and insistence, this was not one of those 'Kinda busy, can you not come back later?' moments. It seemed their excitement was higher, more unbrookable, more intense than ours. As they were explaining their presence, they kept nudging forward on the doorstep, going on tip-toes, trying to juke over maybe-boyfriend's shoulders to catch a glimpse of the precious motor vehicle. Maybe-boyfriend had to explain — for everybody knew he kept cars on his premises and cars *in* his premises — that in this case it wasn't the whole car but the supercharger from the car, but that too, seemed to make for awesome, incredible news. They wanted in definitely then, just for a moment, just for to peek at this amazing, uncommon development. He let them in and their eagerness fell to silence as they filled up the living room, staring in reverence at the bit on the floor.

'Extraordinary!' someone then said — which meant it must have been for that was not a word ever to be used in our lexicon. As with others like it — *'marvellous!'*, *'tremendous!'*, *'stupendous!'*, *'stunning!'*, *'sensational!'*, *'topper!'*, *'super!'*, *'crikey!'*, *'let's!'*, *'smashing!'*, *'diamondiferous!'*, *'bizarre!'*, *'exceedingly!'* — even *'however'* and *'indeed'* though I myself and wee sisters said *'however'* and *'indeed'* — it was an emotional word, too much of a colorant, too high-flying, too posturing; basically it was of that quintessential 'over the water' language, with *'quintessential'* being another of those words. Almost never were they used here without ruffling or embarrassing or frightening local people, so someone else said, *'Fuck, who would have thought!'* which toned things down, being more in keeping

39

with societal toleration here. This was followed by further societal tolerations, then there were more raps on windows and further knocks at the door. Soon the house was packed and I was shoved to the corner with the car-nuts talking classic cars, historic cars, enigmatic cars, performance cars, muscle cars, soft-skinned cars, cars with a lot of flash or pretty rough cars that should never be tidied up but always look as they were supposed to look. Then there was horsepower, distinct lines, big bangs, raw acceleration, extra-acceleration, lack of braking (a good thing), fantastic jolts (another good thing) that pinned one with 'a brilliant cracker feeling!' back to the back of one's seat. As this talk continued with no hint of stopping, I looked at the clock and thought, where's my Gogol? Then, when they moved to the harsh consonants, those number names, the alpha-numerical names — the NYX, the KGB, the ZPH-Zero-9V5-AG — which names maybe-boyfriend himself was partial to, I couldn't take the overload and had to get myself and 'The Overcoat' out of the room. As I was about to make my way through, someone, a young guy, a neighbour of maybe-boyfriend's, stopped me, stopped all of us, with a comment choicely dropped during a pause in this fight for airspace. 'It's all very well, neighbour,' said this neighbour, 'having this so-called classic bit and all, and it's not like I'm trying to be funny or anything but' — here all breath was held, everyone alert for an attack movement. Then it came — 'which among you at the garage then, drew the bit with that flag on?'

At this time, in this place, when it came to the political problems, which included bombs and guns and death and maiming, ordinary people said 'their side did it' or 'our side did it', or 'their religion did it' or 'our religion did it' or 'they did it' or 'we did it', when what was really meant was 'defenders-of-the-state did it' or 'renouncers-of-the-state did it' or 'the state did it'. Now and then we might make an effort and say 'defender' or 'renouncer', though only when attempting to enlighten outsiders, for mostly we didn't bother when it was only ourselves. 'Us' and 'them' was second nature: convenient, familiar, insider, and these words were off-the-cuff, without the strain of having to remember and grapple with massaged phrases or diplomatically correct niceties. By unspoken agreement — which outsiders couldn't grasp unless it should come to their own private expedien-

41

cies — it was unanimously understood that when everybody here used the tribal identifiers of 'us' or 'them', of 'their religion' or 'our religion', not *all* of us and not *all* of them was, it goes without saying, to be taken as read. That summed it up. Naïveté? Tradition? Reality? War going on and people in a hurry? Take your pick though the answer mainly is the last one. In those early days, those darker of the dark days, there wasn't time for vocabulary watchdogs, for political correctness, for self-conscious notions such as 'Will I be thought a bad person if', or 'Will I be thought bigoted if', or 'Am I supporting violence if' or 'Will I be seen to be supporting violence if' and everyone — *everyone* — understood this. All ordinary people also understood the basics of what was allowed and not allowed, of what was neutral and could be exempted from preferences, from nomenclature, from emblems and from outlooks. One of the best ways to describe these unspoken rules and regulations would be to home in for a second on the subject of names.

The couple who kept the list of names that weren't allowed in our district didn't decide themselves on these names. It was the spirit of the community going back in time that deemed which names were allowed and which were not. The keepers of the banned list were two people, a clerk and a clerkess, who catalogued, regulated and updated these names frequently, proving themselves efficient in their clerkiness but viewed by the community as mentally borderline aberrational for all that. Their endeavour was unnecessary because we inhabitants instinctively adhered to the list — abiding by it without going deeply into it. It was also unnecessary because this list, for years before the emergence of the missionary couple, had been excellently capable of perpetuating, updating and data-holding its own information itself. The couple who guarded it were called some ordinary man's name and some ordinary woman's name but were referred to in the community as Nigel and Jason, a joke not lost upon the good-natured pair themselves. The names not allowed were not allowed for the reason they were too much of the country 'over the water', with it no matter that some of those names hadn't originated in that country but instead had been appropriated and put to use by the people of that land. The banned names were understood to have become infused with the energy, the power of history, the age-old conflict, enjoinments and resisted impositions as laid down long ago in this country by that country, with the original nationality of the name now not in the running at all. The banned names were: Nigel, Jason, Jasper, Lance, Percival, Wilbur, Wilfred, Peregrine, Norman, Alf, Reginald, Cedric, Ernest, George, Harvey, Arnold, Wilberine, Tristram, Clive, Eustace, Auberon, Felix, Peverill, Winston, Godfrey, Hector, with Hubert, a cousin of Hector, also not allowed. Nor was Lambert or Lawrence or Howard or the other Laurence or Lionel or Randolph because Randolph was like Cyril which was like Lamont which was like Meredith, Harold, Algernon and Beverley. Myles too, was not allowed. Nor was Evelyn, or Ivor, or Mortimer, or Keith, or Rodney or Roger or Earl of Rupert or Willard or Simon or Sir Mary or Zebedee or Quentin, though maybe now Quentin owing to the filmmaker making good in America that time. Or Albert. Or Troy. Or Barclay. Or Eric. Or Marcus. Or Sefton. Or Marmaduke. Or Greville. Or Edgar because all those names were not allowed. Clifford was another name not allowed. Lesley wasn't either. Peverill was banned twice.

As for girl names, those from 'over the water' were tolerated because the name of a girl — unless it should be Pomp and Circumstance — wasn't politically contentious, therefore it had leeway with no decrees or edicts being drawn up on it at all. Wrong girl names did not connote the same taunting, long-memory, backdated, we-shall-not-forget, historical-distaste reaction as was the case with wrong boy names, but if you were of the opposite persuasion and from 'over the road' you would entirely allow yourself all of our banned names. Of course, you would not allow yourself a single name that was in flourishment in our community but given your own community's equally prescribed knee-jerk reaction, it is unlikely you would lose sleep over any of that. So with the names Rudyard, Edwin, Bertram, Lytton, Cuthbert, Roderick and Duke Of being the last of the names, on our side, on our list, which weren't allowed, all these names were guarded by Nigel and Jason. But there was no list of the names that were allowed. Every resident was supposed to know what was permitted based on what was not permitted. You gave your baby a name and if you were adventurous, avant-garde, bohemian, simply an unforeseen human factor going out on a limb to try a new name that wasn't an already established, legitimised name even if not on the banned list, then you and your baby would find out in due course whether you had made a mistake or not.

As regards this psycho-political atmosphere, with its rules of allegiance, of tribal identification, of what was allowed and not allowed, matters didn't stop at 'their names' and at 'our names', at 'us' and 'them', at 'our community' and 'their community', at 'over the road', 'over the water' and 'over the border'. Other issues had similar directives attaching as well. There were neutral television programmes which could hail from 'over the water' or from 'over the border' yet be watched by everyone 'this side of the road' as well as 'that side of the road' without causing disloyalty in either community. Then there were programmes that could be watched without treason by one side whilst hated and detested 'across the road' on the other side. There were television licence inspectors, census collectors, civilians working in non-civilian environments and public servants, all tolerated in one community whilst shot to death if putting a toe into the other community. There was food and drink. The right butter. The wrong butter. The tea of allegiance. The tea of betrayal. There were 'our shops' and 'their shops'. Placenames. What school you went to. What prayers you said. What hymns you sang. How you pronounced your 'haitch' or 'aitch'. Where you went to work. And of course there were bus-stops. There was the fact that you created a political statement everywhere you went, and with everything you did, even if you didn't want to. There was a person's appearance also, because it was believed you could tell 'their sort from over the road' from 'your sort this side of the road' by the very physical form of a person. There was choice of murals, of traditions, of newspapers, of anthems, of 'special days', of passport, of coinage, of the police, of civic powers, of the soldiery, the paramilitary. During the era of not letting bygones be bygones there was any number of examples and many nuances of affiliation. Inbetween was the neutral and the exempted and what had happened at maybe-boyfriend's house was that his neighbour — with all other neighbours present — had homed in on the protocol and inflammatory symbolism of all that.

He'd homed in on that flag issue, the flags-and-emblems issue, instinctive and emotional because flags were invented to be instinctive and emotional — often pathologically, narcissistically emotional — and he meant that flag of the country from 'over the water' which was also the same flag of the community from 'over the road'. It was not a flag greatly welcomed in our community. Not a flag at all welcomed in our community. There weren't any, not any, this side of the road. What I was gathering therefore, for I was not up on cars but was up on flags and emblems, was that those vintage, classic Blower Bentleys made in that country 'over the water' came with the flag on from that country 'over the water'. Reading between the lines therefore, of maybe-boyfriend's neighbour's comment — what was maybe-boyfriend doing, he implied, not only partaking in a raffle in which he might have won the bit with the flag on, but what was he doing, partaking in a raffle to win any bit — flag or no flag — of such a patriotic, nation-defining, 'over the water' symbol at all? Historical injustice, he said. Repressive legislation, he said. Practice of and pacts for, he said. Artificial boundaries, he said. Propping up of corruption, he said. Arrest without charge, he said. Declaration of curfews, he said. Imprisonment without trial, he said. Proscription of meetings, he said. Prohibition of inquests, he said. Institutionalised violation of sovereignty and territory, he said. Hot and cold treatments, he said. Anything, he said. In the name of law and order. All that was what he said though even then that wasn't what he meant. What he meant — underneath all the interpretation of that flag business was the driving home of the other business which was that the flag from 'over the water' was also that same flag from 'over the road'. 'Over the road' was viewed in our community as more 'over the water' than actual 'over the water', with the flag perceived to be flown there with more proximity and grandiosity than ever could muster — try as it might — the territory it came from in the first place. To come from this side of the road — *our* side — and to bring that flag in then, was divisive, indicative too, of a traitorous kowtowing and a betrayal most monstrous over which even informers and those who marry-out would be held in higher esteem. This of course was all part of the political problems here which I, for one, didn't like to get into. Amazing it was though, how much inflammatory suggestion could be gotten over in a few comments. Even so, yer man hadn't finished yet.

'I mean like I mean,' he said, 'don't get me wrong or anything, and obviously I'm saying this from a place of humility, and it's not that I've got experience in desiring to take part in anything disloyal to my own community, something that might involve winning something that had that flag on, then bringing it home, then being proud to have it in my area instead of being ashamed to have it my area. Far be it from me too, to asperse anything or anybody, to sow seeds of rancour. I'm not a stirrer-upper of rules or a summariser of conclusions and no expert am I either, or inciter, or bigot; in fact, ignorant as I am and gingerly as I hesitate to voice an opinion but . . .' — then he repeated all that about no matter how famous and coveted was the thing with the flag on, he himself wouldn't deign to legitimate such an ensign of oppression, of tragedy, of tyranny, not to mention the bad taste left in the mouth of losing face, not so much to the country 'over the water' as to that community 'over the road'. More to the point, he said, someone bringing that flag into a staunchly anti-establishment district could open himself to accusations of traitorship and of informership. So yes, flags were emotional. Primevally so. At least here.

So that was what he was about — that maybe-boyfriend was a traitor — and it was at this point maybe-boyfriend's friends started in on his defence. 'He doesn't have that bit with the flag on,' they said. 'Anyone can see that that supercharger has no flag on it.' They were angry rather than dismissive in that, no matter how unlikely that flag would appear on 'this side of the road' on 'this side of the water', thing was, these were paranoid times. These were knife-edge times, primal times, with everybody suspicious of everybody. You could have a nice wee conversation with someone here, then go away and think, that was a nice, wee unguarded conversation I just had there — least until you start playing it back in your head later on. At that point you start to worry that you said 'this' or 'that', not because 'this' or 'that' were contentious. It was that people were quick to point fingers, to judge, to add on even in peaceful times, so it would be hard to fathom fingers not getting pointed and words not being added, also being judged in these turbulent times, resulting too, not in having your feelings hurt upon discovering others were talking about you, as in having individuals in balaclavas and Halloween masks, guns at the ready, turning up in the middle of the night at your door. By now maybe-boyfriend's friends were pointing to the supercharger and it was clear there was no flag on it. 'Anyway,' they said, 'those cars didn't always come with flags on.' 'Besides,' ventured a neighbour — and this was one brave neighbour considering the others, in contrast to their earlier enthusiasm, had now grown silent — 'would it not be okay, because of what it is and all, of how rare it is, to take it if you won it even if it did come with that flag on, then to bring it home and cover the flag with a bomber aircraft sticker — say, a B29 Superfortress *Joltin' Josie* sticker, or a Superfortress *Girl Dressed In Not Very Much* sticker, or *A Bit o' Lace* B17 Flying Fortress sticker, or a sticker of Minnie Mouse or Olive Oyl or the planet Pluto or even a wee photo of your ma or a bigger one of Marilyn Monroe?' He was trying hard, this diplomat, stressing reference to the exceptions, to those dispensations, the individuals and situations here that were afforded exemption from bigotry, from prejudice, from exclusion. These would be the rock stars, the film stars, the culture stars, sports people, those of exceptional fame or of some highest personal endeavour. Might it not be the case, he intimated, that this crossover category also include superchargers from Blower Bentleys? Could not desire and rarity, he urged, be sufficient for the supercharger to be granted leeway, or was it to be the case that that flag was too big an impediment for one side of the divide —

our side in this instance — to be overlooked and let through?

He didn't know the answer, and I felt nobody else did except one person. I looked at him. Everyone was looking at him. 'All I'm saying is,' he said, 'is that I'm not sure I'd capitulate, that I'd want a bit of car, no matter how unique, if it sported national self-gratifying connotations, if it meant subsumption of the right to my own sovereign, national and religious identity, even if that particular car didn't sport those connotations and demands for subsumption on all its models and range. It's that I'm bewildered,' he stressed, 'that anyone from "our side of the road" would let their proclivity for car bits override what should be an instinctual recoil from the other side's symbolism and badges. And if the local boys should get to hear' — here he meant the renouncers which meant they would get to hear because he was going to make it his duty to tell them — 'the one who brought that flag in might find himself facing some hefty street justice. And what of the dead people — all those killed so far in these political problems? Is it to be the case then, that all of them died in vain?'

It seemed, listening to him, that if a person was determined, they could make an argument out of anything, and here he was, making it out of it not being normal to bring that flag in. Well, that was true, it wasn't normal. Then again, maybe-boyfriend hadn't brought it in. During all this, maybe-boyfriend wasn't saying anything. There was a cloud on his face though, a shadow, and maybe-boyfriend rarely had shadows. Instead he had agility, mobility, playfulness which was something else attractive about him, such as twenty minutes earlier, when there'd only been me and him in the room. Then, he'd been pleased with the supercharger, had shown he was pleased, and even later with these others, still he'd shown pleasure, if without the same display of pride and elation he'd felt safe to show me about it earlier. Instead, with them, he'd been cautious — not just to be polite and not boastful, but because of envy when people can suddenly turn on you and want revenge just because they do. It was trophy time, yes, but also humility with the trophy which was why maybe-boyfriend, with his neighbours, toned all his euphoria down. I could see though, that there was stubbornness, that again he was doing that thing which periodically he did when in the company of someone he didn't respect and so wouldn't offer explanations. I thought him foolish in this instance, given the seriousness of this flags-and-emblems issue which was why I was glad when his friends had spoken up. He himself was not naturally argumentative and nor did he link with the punch-up mentality. The only occasions really, when he'd get angry and involve himself in fighting would be when others picked on chef, his longest friend from primary school. But now he was looking at his neighbour who was shrugging and bad behaviour on the part of that neighbour — coming into maybe-boyfriend's house, inviting himself into the house along with the others, then talking like that, breaking rules of hospitality, stirring up trouble, being jealous. No wonder then, at the start of another 'far be it from me', he got himself punched on the nose. One of maybe-boyfriend's friends — the impetuous one, the one who objected to being called hotheaded though everybody knew he broke into fights even over things he was happy about — he punched him. Yer man himself though, didn't retaliate. Instead he rushed out in one of those adrenalin runs, throwing behind him something of maybe-boyfriend having brought the slur of that flag onto himself as well as onto the community. Hardly could it be surprising, he shouted, that consequence would follow upon that. Then he disappeared, colliding on the doorstep with chef who, looking set-upon and harried, had just that moment arrived at maybe-boyfriend's after work.

There was now a feeling in the room to which nobody was admitting: unpleasant, ominous, grey. Impossible to get the room back too, for the energy had shifted, killing off the car talk. Although a few tried, nobody was able to get it off the ground again. Maybe-boyfriend's longest friend, as usual with him, then cleared the room in seconds. This was chef — truly a man of nerves. Here I mean pure nerves, total nerves, dramatic nerves, nerves up to high doh, a hundred per cent not average. He was driven, unsmiling, sunken-eyed, also perpetually exhausted and he'd been these things even before the idea to become a chef had ever entered his head. As it was, he didn't become a chef, though often when drunk, he'd speak of going to cooking-school for to become one. In his working-life he was a brickie and had started getting called chef on the sites as part of a joke about his liking cooking when a man shouldn't like cooking and the name after that stuck. So did other insults — his fine palate, his going to bed with cookbooks, being obsessed with the innermost nature of the carrot, being a woman of fastidious over-refinement. They could never tell though, these workmates, if they'd managed to wind him up because from the moment he'd arrive in the morning until going home in the evening, chef seemed wound up as a matter of course anyhow. Even before starting work, and going back to schooldays, and again for reasons of his seeming unmanliness, certain boys would want to fight with him. It seemed a rite of passage to fight with him. This tended to happen until one day maybe-boyfriend in the schoolyard took him under his wing. Chef didn't know he'd been taken under a wing and gained no understanding, even after numerous beatings, that he'd needed to be. After maybe-boyfriend got involved though, and by extension maybe-boyfriend's other friends, those looking to fight with chef mostly then backed off. From time to time, even now, there'd be the odd outbreak of 'How's your artichokes?' followed by a violent encounter. I'd turn up at maybe-boyfriend's to find chef in the kitchen — sometimes on his own but most oftener with maybe-boyfriend — tending to the latest of his queer-bashed wounds. As for the idea of chefness itself, there existed in maybe-boyfriend's area, also in my area, a sense that male chefs — especially of little pastries and *petit fours* and fancies and dainties to which one could level the criticism 'desserts' and which chef here was a maker of — were not in demand and not socially acceptable. Contrary to other chef parts of the world, a man here could be a *cook,* though even then he'd better work on the boats, or in a man's internment camp or in some other full-on male environment. Otherwise he was a *chef* which meant homosexual with a drive to recruit male heterosexuals into the homosexual fold. If they existed therefore, these chefs, they were a species hidden, few in number, with chef here — even though he wasn't — being the only one I knew in a radius of a million miles. There was too, his borderline, compound emotional state which he'd exhibit without embarrassment or provocation — and over silly things such as measuring jugs and spoons. When he wasn't on the touchiness brink over food and kitchen things generally, he could be found, usually late at night and more so at the weekend, murmuring *'pomegranate molasses, orange flower water, crème caramel, crepe Suzette, bombe Alaska'* softly and with drink taken in some corner to himself. So he talked food, read food, lent food books (which freaked me out) to maybe-boyfriend who (also freaking me out) read them. And he experimented with food, thinking all the time he was an average guy, with no average guy, not even his mates, who did like him, thinking him this also. And now here he was, walking into the uncomfortable silence of maybe-boyfriend's living room, adding to the edgy atmosphere just by the force of his personality being there.

On the other hand, maybe not. This time, for the first time, it started with the usual, *'Oh no — not chef!'* with people about to dash off, but then realising it was a relief to see him. Definitely he was preferable to that former contentious flag affair. Before he'd come in maybe-boyfriend's neighbours had shifted from the carefreeness of car talk to that old political 'us and them' trajectory. Increasingly too, they were distancing themselves from maybe-boyfriend because, although there were superchargers, there were also kangaroo courts and collusion and disloyalty and informership. Chef though, immediately helped snap everybody into place. As usual he didn't notice the atmosphere, nor did he glance at the super-charger or at the specks of blood from maybe-boyfriend's neighbour's nose which were now about the supercharger. Instead he looked around, alarmed at what he did see. His eyebrows rose an octave. 'Nobody told me there was this many. How many are you? Easily a hundred. I'm not counting. There's no way,' he shook his head, 'no way, I'm plating up for all of you.' But he was mistaken. If that neighbour hadn't brought up the problems, probably it would have been prolonged car talk, followed by a drink session, then a music session, then a drunken carry-out from the chip shop or curry house session. Culinariness and little cakes from chef would not have been required. But chef was well into the *amuse-bouches* he was not going to make them, the detailed main course he was not going to make them, the dessert that definitely he was not going to make them and so the neighbours stood up and started in at once. 'You're all right there, chef,' they said and this was as jovial as they could feign it. 'No worries. No problem. We're leaving. Gotta go anyway.' At this they cast a last look, now more of an ambivalent look, towards the supercharger. Bit too quintessential after all, perhaps? Unsurprisingly, there came no more offers to buy. Instead they said good-bye to maybe-boyfriend, then goodbye to his mates who were staying on a bit longer.

Then some, as an afterthought, remembered and nodded goodbye into the corner, to me.

Toe-rag. Twerp. Pishpot. Spastic. Dickhead. Cunning-boy-ballocks. No offence or anything but. I'm only sayin' but. No harm to you like but. These were some of the words said by maybe-boyfriend's friends about his troublesome neighbour after that neighbour and the others had gone. Chef, maybe-boyfriend, three other of maybe-boyfriend's friends and myself had remained in the room. Chef said, 'Where'd they go but? Why'd they go? Who are they? Were they expecting me —' 'Forget it, chef,' said maybe-boyfriend, but he spoke distractedly because he was annoyed at the others offering excuses and placations to that neighbour for him. Especially I knew he'd be annoyed at their trying to smooth away the flag comments. In doing so they had played, he would think, right into that neighbour's hands. The others were saying 'Forget it' to chef as well by now, then the impetuous one warned maybe-boyfriend to watch himself. 'He's gonna meddle, that scuddy bastard, gonna brew some story.' The others nodded and maybe-boyfriend at first nodded too. Then he said, 'All the same, you shouldn't have hit him, and you three shouldn't have let him needle you or told him my business. My business isn't his business. I don't have to win him over or wheedle to get his approval. Don't need you either, to convince him of me.' The others didn't like this and more likely from hurt, they started an argument, the gist being that maybe-boyfriend needed to catch himself on. Of course he should have explained himself, they said, not so much to yer man for, after all, he'd just been jealous. It was that he should have spoken up for the benefit of the others, to stop rumour being launched big time. Maybe-boyfriend said that as for rumour, words didn't have to be disputed or undisputed, didn't even have to be spoken. 'It's that you made me lose power,' he said, and so the argument continued until one of them said, 'This won't be the end.' He meant none of them should be surprised if the issue of the supercharger got dropped amidst the scandal of maybe-boyfriend bringing countless flags from 'over there' in. Here they laughed, which didn't mean they thought such talk wouldn't happen. He shouldn't have been stubborn, they said, and I, not included in this, and without saying anything, agreed. Chef meantime, who'd been up in the clouds, checking the inventory of some imaginary pantry, came back with, 'Who? What?' and the others began to shove him about. 'Auld mucker,' they said. 'Missed the boat as usual,' but already no longer listening, chef went upstairs to wash before getting everybody something to eat. After a final few jokey disparagements of *it's all very well but, far be it from me but, no expert am I but,* and with more things tribalist left unsaid than probably were said, least in my earshot, the others got busy too, moving bits of car upstairs.

This was business as usual because maybe-boyfriend stored car everywhere — at the garage at work, here at his home, indoors, outdoors, in front, out the back, in cupboards, tops of cupboards, on furniture, on each stair, at the top of the stairs and all along the landing; as doorstops too, in all the rooms too, except for the kitchen and his bedroom — least not on the nights when I stayed there. So his house was less a house and more a beloved work-from-work environment, and now he and his friends were re-arranging, which in translation meant 'making room for more car'. 'New car coming?' I asked. 'Cars plural, maybe-girl,' said maybe-boy. 'Just a few carburettors and cylinders, bumpers, radiators, piston rods, side panels, mudguards, that sort of thing.' 'Uh-huh,' I said. 'Back in a minute,' he said, indicating some chunks of car in transit, 'shifting these for now into one of the brothers' rooms.' Maybe-boyfriend had three brothers, none of whom were dead, none either, living in this house with him. They had used to live in it with him but had drifted through the years to living elsewhere. And now maybe-boyfriend and the others got busy, and chef downstairs, from the sound of things, also was busy in the kitchen. He was talking to himself which was not rare. Often he'd do this, I'd hear him do it, because chef stayed over at maybe-boyfriend's perhaps even more nights than I did myself. As usual I could hear him describing to some imaginary person who appeared to be serving an apprenticeship under him, everything he was doing regarding the making of the meal. Often he'd say something like, 'Just do it this way. There's an easier way, you know. And remember, we can develop a unique style and technique without histrionics and drama' and whenever he did this, he'd sound so soft and much more accommodating than when he was interacting with real people in real life. He liked this acolyte who, from the sound of chef's praise and encouragement, was a good, attentive learner. 'We're just going to add this. No, this. Then we'll do that, *that.* We want finesse, remember — clean, precise stacking, so leave off that leaf. Why that leaf? It adds nothing to the texture and dimension or the elements. Here now — taste. Do you want to try some?' Once I peeked in when he was inviting his invisible apprentice to try some, and there he was, all alone, raising a spoon to his own lips. At that time, which was the first time I'd witnessed chef doing this, he put me in mind of me during the times I did my mental ticking-off of landmarks which I'd do peripherally whilst also doing my reading-while-walking. I'd pause after a page or so, to take stock of my surroundings, also occasionally to be specific and helpful to someone in my head who'd just enquired directions of me. I'd imagine myself pointing and saying, 'Well, orientation is there,' meaning the person needed to go round such-and-such a corner. 'Go there,' I'd say. 'Just round that corner. See this corner? Go round it and when you get to the junction by the letterbox at the start of the ten-minute area you head up by the usual place.' The usual place was our graveyard and this directing would be my way of helping some lost but appreciative person. And here was chef in his kitchen doing much the same thing. No hysterical fits, no tantrums, just meditation, absorption, relaxation. This was playfulness in the company of his very own appreciative person. So I left them to it, not wanting to shame chef out of his imagination, for there was an awful lot of shaming for playing, shaming for letting your guard down that went on in this place. That was why everybody read minds — had to, otherwise things got complicated. Just as most people here chose not to say what they meant in order to protect themselves, they could also, at certain moments when they knew their mind was being read, learn to present their topmost mental level to those who were reading it whilst in the undergrowth of their consciousness, inform themselves privately of what their true thinking was about. So, with maybe-boyfriend and the others upstairs, and with chef and his apprentice out in the kitchen, I stretched out on the settee to consider next steps. What I meant were my living options, for maybe-boyfriend had asked recently if I wanted to move in with him. At the time I had three objections as to why that might not be feasible. One was, I didn't think ma could cope on her own with rearing wee sisters though I myself took no active role in the rearing of wee sisters. It just seemed I had to be there, on call, as some sort of background buffer to help prevent their precocity, their uncontained curiosity, their sense of readiness for anything spinning way out of control. My second objection was the possible destruction that moving in might pose to my and maybe-boyfriend's already delicate, easily to be shattered maybe-relationship. And the third objection was, how could I move in, given the state of this place?

I saw a programme on TV years after I had been split from maybe-boyfriend, about people who hoard things but didn't consider they hoarded things, and although nobody was hoarding car, I couldn't help noticing a similarity between what these individuals were doing all these years forward during what is now the era of psychological enlightenment, and what maybe-boyfriend was doing, way back when enlightenment didn't yet exist. One couple consisted of a hoarder (him), and then there was her (not a hoarder). Everything was divided in half and his half dominated and was a mountain from carpet to ceiling, covering the mass of half the space in each room. After a while, some of his stuff began to slide down the mountain and spill over into her stuff, which was inevitable as he couldn't stop adding to it which meant he ran out of space and inclined himself necessarily into hers. As for maybe-boyfriend's house, the hoarding was nowhere as compressed and restricting as certainly it was on those later TV entertainment programmes. There was no doubt, however, that he was adding to it. As for my reaction, I could bear the cluttered state of *'Come in and welcome, but you're going to have to squeeze a little'* during times I stayed over because of the normality of the kitchen and of his bedroom and the half normality of the bathroom. Mainly though, I could bear it because of the 'maybe' level of our relationship, meaning I didn't officially live with him and wasn't officially committed to him. If we were in a proper relationship and I did live with him and was officially committed to him, first thing I would have to do would be to leave.

So this was maybe-boyfriend's house and it was a whole house, which at that time for a twenty-year-old man or woman — and especially an unmarried man or woman — was unusual. Not just in his area. It would have been unusual in my area too. It had come about because one day when he'd been twelve and his brothers had been fifteen, seventeen and nineteen, his parents had left home to dedicate themselves fully to professional ballroom-dancing careers.

At first their sons hadn't noticed they were gone because the parents were always taking themselves off unannounced, successfully to compete in ruthless, to-the-death, ballroom-dancing competitions. But one day, when the two elder came home from work and had rustled up dinner from the chip shop as usual for the four of them, second eldest, sitting on the settee, his plate on his lap, turned to eldest beside him and said, 'Something's wrong. Something's maybe missing. Do you not think something's missing, brother?' 'Yeah, something is missing,' agreed the eldest. 'Hey, you two' — this was to the younger brothers — 'Is something maybe missing?' 'It's the parents,' said second youngest. 'They've gone away.' Second youngest then resumed his dinner and watching of the TV, as did youngest, who seven years later was to become my 'almost one year so far maybe-boyfriend'. Eldest brother then said, 'When did they go but? Was it to another of them dancing things that always they're entered into?' But it wasn't just *one* dancing thing. Eventually the brothers had it from the neighbours that the parents had left for good some weeks previously. They had written a note, said the neighbours, but had forgotten to leave it; indeed primarily they had forgotten to write it and so had written it then forwarded it back from their undisclosed destination when they reached it, not deliberately undisclosed but because they hadn't time or memory or understanding to put a sender's address at the top. According to the postmark it was not just a country over a water, but a country over many, many waters. Also, they forgot their former address, the house they'd lived in for twenty-four years ever since getting married until twenty-four hours earlier when they left. In the end they'd hazarded the address in the hope the street itself might sort things out for them and, thanks to the resourcefulness of street, it managed to do just that. It forwarded the letter to their offspring and this letter, after it had done the rounds of the neighbours before reaching the hands of the brothers, said: *'Sorry kids. Seeing things in right relation we should never have had children. We're just off dancing forever. Sorry again — but at least now you're grown up.'* After this, there was an afterthought: *'Well, those of you who aren't grown up can be brought up and finished by those of you who are — and look, please have everything — including the house.'* The parents insisted their boys take the house, that they themselves didn't want it; that all they wanted was what they had with them — each other, their choreomania and their numerous trunks of fabulous dancing clothes. The letter ended, *'Goodbye eldest sone, goodbye second elder sone, goodbye younger sone, goodbye youngest sone — goodbye all dearr lovelyy sones'* but with no signature of *'parents'* or *'your fond but lukewarm mother and father'.* Instead they signed it *'dancers',* then there were four kisses, after which the sons never heard from their parents again. Except on TV. Increasingly this couple would be on TV, because they proved themselves, despite middle age, exceptional youthful ballroom-dancing champions. They were world-class, spectacular, blindingly focused and, owing perhaps to their charisma, their sparkles, and to the international kudos of stardom they were attaching to their country — though which country, 'over the border' or 'over the water', was tactfully never referred to — before long, and most successfully, they were reaching across that treacherous political divide. This meant they were one of those exceptions — as with the musicians here, the artists here, the stage and screen people and also the sportspeople, all those in the public eye who managed to rise above winning the complete approval of one community whilst bringing down upon themselves the disapprobation and death threats of the other community. This couple, as part of the chosen few, had everybody's approval. They were unanimously acclaimed and allowed. Not just on political, religious and anti-bigotry fronts too, were they allowed, but in normal dance terms too, they were applauded for bringing joy and enchantment into the hearts of all dance-loving people. Greatly were they esteemed by those cognisant of all things ballroom even if none of their sons were cognisant, or wanted to be, of anything ballroom. Maybe-boyfriend though, did point them out on the TV to me once. He did this casually whilst switching channels one evening and there they were: the International Couple. At this point they'd been running joint-first in the feverish Rio de Janeiro World Championship Tournament, with the announcer, before the International Dancing Board of Ballroomers, crying, 'Holy Christ! Historical moment! Oh, historical moment!', declaring everybody hold tight their hats for what was to be an unprecedented dance waltz-off. I wanted to see this waltz-off because after exclaiming, *'No shit! She's your . . . ! That's your . . . ! She's your . . . ! She's . . . ! That's . . . She's your ma! That's your ma!',* also, *'He's your da!'* though clearly, with those eyes, that face, that body, the mobility, the confidence, the sensuality and, of course, those costumes, I meant her really, there was no way I couldn't watch. Definitely I hadn't seen this coming but maybe-boyfriend said he didn't want to watch. So while I sat glued, open-mouthed, wide-eyed, picking my nails and exclaiming, 'He looks like her. Does he look like her? Is it that he has the same back as her? Is his father like her — I mean him — no, is he like his father?' maybe-boyfriend went out to tinker with some car.

As for the house, it became one of those 'men live here' establishments, with the brothers dossing down at random in it, living the way boys left to devices do. Often their friends, increasingly also girls for the night, or girlfriends for the week, or girlfriends for a while, would come and go, dossing also. Then times moved on and individually the three elder moved out. They drifted off to whatever life was to hold for them, then the house gravitated into being that of maybe-boyfriend. Then, because of cars and bits of cars, it gravitated further into a three-quarter working garage. Then he asked me to live with him which was when I intimated my three objections and he said, regarding one of them, 'I don't mean *here.* I mean we can rent a place in the red-light street.'

The red-light street was in a district that was just up the road from my area and just down the road from his area and it was called the red-light street not because red-light things went on in it but because it was where young couples went to live together who didn't want to get married or conventionally to settle down. It was not wanting to be wed at sixteen, babies from seventeen, to settle on the settee in front of the television to die like most parents by twenty. They wanted to try out — weren't sure — but something else. So, unmarried couples lived there. It was even rumoured two men lived there, I mean together. Then another two men went to live in another house there — also together. There weren't any women living together, though one woman was famously said to live in number twenty-three with two men. Mostly, it was unmarried males and unmarried females and although it was just one street, it had been on the news recently as threatening to spill over into the next street and that street itself was already famous because it had been housing mixed-religion married couples before that. Meanwhile, in that area, not just in the red-light street, normal people, meaning married couples, were moving out. Some weren't against the red-light aspect, they said. It was just they didn't want to hurt older relatives' feelings, such as those of their parents, their grandparents, their deceased forebears, their long-deceased fragile ancestors possibly set in ways easily to be affronted, especially by what the tenor of the media was calling 'depravity, decadence, demoralisation, dissemination of pessimism, outrages to propriety and illicit immoral affairs'. Next big question, said the news, was whether or not the unmarried couples now fornicating were of mixed religion also? So the normal couples moving out, anxious for the sensibilities of the ancient generation, made TV appearances as well. 'I'm doing it for me mammy,' said one young wife, 'for I don't think mammy would be happy with me living without integrity which I would be doing if I stayed in a street where people didn't take the marriage vows.' 'I don't want to judge,' said another, 'but holding no wedlock has to be judged and judged harshly, then condemned, for is this what we're coming to? Whoredom? Animal passions? Lack of chastity? Is this what we're fostering?' Again, there was more on depravity, decadence, demoralisation, dissemination of pes-

simism, outrages to propriety and illicit immoral affairs. 'Next,' said another couple,
loading up their removal van, 'there'll be
one-and-a-half red-light streets, then there'll
be two red-light streets, then the whole
district will be red lights with ménages-a-
trio popping up everywhere.' 'Doing it for
me mammy,' said another wife, though a
few said, 'Ach sure, what's wrong with it?
There's tribalism and there's bigotry and
for those you need history, but with these
sexual issues there's a faster turnover which
means simply you have to go with modern
times.' And on it went, mainly, 'We cannot
allow this' and 'People don't sleep with
people' and 'Marriage, after territorial
boundaries, is the foundation of the state'.
Especially it was, 'If I don't move out it will
kill me mammy'. That was television. Numerous possible future deaths of many
mothers were also reported extensively in
voxpop radio interviews and in the written
press.

So that street, in that area, which was not
a big area and which was really called
something or other in my native language
which I didn't speak and also called *'The
Groove of the Neck'* or *'The Crook of the
Neck'* or *'The Soft of the Neck'* in the translated language which I did speak, was just

down the road. I had never been in it although now maybe-boyfriend was proposing I go live in it with him. I said no because apart from the reason of ma and wee sisters, also of his hoarding which conceivably could continue and increase in the red-light residence just as easily as it was progressing in this current residence, there was that other reason of reservation, of us having perhaps as much intimacy and fragility of relationship as either of us could bear. And this was what happened. Always it happened. I would suggest closeness as a way of forwarding on our relationship and it would backfire and I'd forget I'd suggested closeness and he'd have to remind me when next I suggested closeness. Then the boot would be on the other foot and he'd suffer a misfiring of neurons and go and suggest closeness himself. Constantly we were having memory lapses, episodes of a kind of *jamais vu*. We wouldn't remember that we'd remembered, and would have to remind each other of our forgetfulness and of how closeness didn't work for us given the state of delicacy our maybe-relationship was in. And now it was his turn to forget and to say that he thought I should consider us living together, because we'd been nearly a year now into our 'maybe' capacity, so feasibly we could forward on proper coupledom by cohabiting. It wasn't as if either, he said, we've previously discussed closeness or moving in together — which, when he finished speaking, I'd have to remind him that we had. Meanwhile, during this era of asking me to live with him, he suggested we go for a drive the following Tuesday to see the sun go down. So then I thought, how come he has thoughts of seeing a sun go down when nobody I know — especially boys, also girls, women too, men too, certainly me — has ever had a thought of seeing a sun go down? This was new, then again, maybe-boyfriend always had new things about him, things I hadn't noticed in others, not just in boys before. Like chef, he liked cooking which was not usually done by boys and I'm not sure I liked him liking cooking. Also like chef, he didn't like football, or it was he did like it but didn't go on about liking it in the way required of boys and for that reason became known in his area as one of those males who wasn't a fruit but who didn't like football all the same. Secretly I had a worry that maybe-boyfriend might not be a proper man. This thought came in the darker moments, in my complex, unbidden moments, swiftly coming, swiftly going and which I wouldn't admit — especially to myself — to having had. If I did, I sensed further contraries would come in its wake because already I'd feel them gathering — to confront me, to throw off-kilter my certainties. Along with everybody, I dealt with these inner contradictions by turning from them whenever they appeared on the horizon. Maybe-boyfriend though, I noticed, brought them onto the horizon, especially the longer I was in that 'maybe, don't know, perhaps' dating situation with him. I liked his food even though I thought I oughtn't to like it and oughtn't to encourage him by liking it. And I liked being in bed with him because sleeping with maybe-boyfriend was as if always I'd slept with maybe-boyfriend, and I liked going anywhere with him, so I said yes, that I'd go with him on Tuesday, which was that coming Tuesday — that evening after my run with third brother-in-law in the parks & reservoirs — to see this sun go down. I wouldn't, of course, mention this to anybody because I wasn't confident that a sunset was acceptable as a topic to mention to anybody. Then again, rarely did I mention anything to anybody. Not mentioning was my way to keep safe.

Ma, however, had got wind. It wasn't of the sunset or of maybe-boyfriend she'd got wind, for he didn't come from my district and I wouldn't take him into my district, which meant we spent most of our time over in his district, or else downtown at the few inter-communal bars and clubs. Instead it was a rumour put into the air that had got her anxious. So the night before my run with third brother-in-law, also the night before my sunset with maybe-boyfriend, she came upstairs to see me. I heard her coming and, oh God, I thought, what now?

Since my sixteenth birthday two years earlier ma had tormented herself and me because I was not married. My two older sisters were married. Three of my brothers, including the one who had died and the one on the run, had got married. Probably too, my oldest brother gone errant, dropped off the face of the earth, and even though she'd no proof, was married. My other older sister — the unmentionable second sister — also married. So why wasn't I married? This non-wedlock was selfish, disturbing of the God-given order and unsettling for the younger girls, she said. 'Look at them!' she continued, and there they were, standing behind ma, bright-eyed, perky, grinning. From the look of them, not one of these sisters seemed unsettled to me. 'Sets a bad example,' said ma. 'If you don't get married, they'll think it's all right for them not to get married.' None of these sisters — age seven, eight and nine — was anywhere near the marrying teens yet. 'What would happen too,' went on ma, as often she would go on whenever we had this one-sided conversation, 'when your looks are gone and then nobody wants you?' I got fed up answering, as in 'I'm not telling you, ma. Never will I tell you, ma. Leave me alone, ma,' because the less I gave, the less she could get in. This was tiresome for her as well as for me but in her endeavours ma was not without back-up. In the district there existed a whole chivvy of mothers doing their damnedest to get their daughters wed. Their panic was real, visceral; certainly for them this was no cliché, no comedy, not to be dismissed, also not unusual. What would have been unusual would have been for a mother to have stepped forth from among them who was not of that scene. So it became a battle of wills between ma and me as to which of us would wear the other down first. Anytime she'd get whiff I might be dating (never through me), I couldn't walk in the door but it would be, 'Is he the right religion?' followed by 'Is he not already married?' It was vital, after the right religion, that he be

not already married. And because I continued to give nothing, this became proof he
wasn't the right religion, that he was married and, more than likely, not only a
paramilitary, but an enemy defender-of-the-
state paramilitary as well. She did horror
stories on herself, filling in blanks where I
refused to supply information. This meant
she wrote the entire script herself. She
began religious observances and visits to
the holy men with the intention, my
younger, gleeful sisters informed me, that I
give up these godless bigamous terrorists I
was falling in love with one after the other,
and that instead I fall in love suitably this
time. I let her do this, especially once I got
involved with maybe-boyfriend did I let her
do it. There was no way, ever, I was going
to give her him. She'd have done a process,
had him through the system, one assessment question after another assessment
question — hurrying things, hurrying
things, trying to complete on things, complete on things, end things (which meant
dating), begin things (which meant marriage), tie things up (which meant babies),
to make me, for the love of God, get a move
on like the rest.

So the religious observances and the visits
to the holy men — later also to the holy

women — continued, along with her three o'clock prayers, her six o'clock prayers, her nine o'clock prayers and her twelve o'clock prayers. There were also extra petitions at half past five every afternoon for the souls in purgatory who were now no longer able to pray for themselves. None of this o'clock praying interfered with her staple morning and evening praying, in particular her advanced working of intercessions under-taken for me to abandon these trysts she was sure I was having with heretical defend-ers at 'dot dot dot' places about town. Ma always called locations she disapproved of, or was sure she would disapprove of, 'dot dot dot' places which occasionally had my older sisters and myself speculating as to what, in her youth, she might have got up to in them once herself. As for her praying, her decreeing, all that became more ac-centuated, more quick-fire in supplication until one day owing to recklessness it got inverted. It had to. Given the fictitious premise she was basing them on — to rid me of men who had not ever, except in her own head, existed — it now looked as if she'd manifested the very thing neither of us wanted into place.

After my second meeting in the parks & reservoirs with the milkman, nosey first brother-in-law, who of course had sniffed it out, told his wife, my first sister, to tell our mother to come and have a talk with me. This was especially recommended after eldest sister's earlier chat with me hadn't gone as planned. So she came round to see ma, and this was the sister who didn't love her husband because still she was in grief over her ex-boyfriend. No longer was she in grief, however, because he'd cheated on her and taken up with a new woman. Now she was in grief because he was dead. He'd been killed in a carbomb at work because he'd been the wrong religion in the wrong place and that was another thing that happened. He was dead. And sister? My sister. She hadn't been able to get over him when he was living, so I didn't know how she'd do that now he was —

Here though, even in grief, eldest sister did as instructed. She informed our mother of the milkman situation, and ma had it confirmed in a contrary way by the pious women of the neighbourhood, all of whom by now had heard of it as well. These women were, like ma, people of the incant, the earnest beseech, the reasoned, even legalistic petition. So adept were they in their entreaties to the heavenly authority, so textured into the ordinary life were their treatments and demonstrations, that often this sorority could be heard muttering on their beads from one side of their mouths whilst carrying on everyday conversations from the other at the same time. These women then, along with ma, and with eldest sister and first brother-in-law and all the local general gossips, involved themselves in the situation of me and the milkman. Then one day, according to wee sisters, a pile of these neighbours came round to see ma in our house. Seemed my lover was a milkman, they said — though also they said he was a motor mechanic. He was in his early forties, they said — though also round about his twenties. He was married, they said — also not married. Definitely he was 'connected' — though 'unconnected' at the same time. An intelligence officer: 'Ach, you know, neighbour,' said the neighbours, 'the one in the background, the one who does that stalking, that tracking, all that shadowing and tailing and profiling, the one who gathers the information on the target then hands it to the trigger men who —' 'Baby Jesus!' cried ma. 'And you're saying my girl's involved with this man!' She grasped the arms of her chair, said wee sisters, as another thought ran through her. 'He's not *that* milkman, is he — the one of the van, that wee white van, that nondescript, shape-shifting —' 'Sorry, neighbour,' said the neighbours, 'but we thought it best you know.' They said then that at least my lover was a renouncer-of-the-state and not a defender-of-the-state, something to be grateful for, this, of course, a quiet allusion to my second sister who'd brought disgrace upon the family as well as upon the community by marrying-out to some state-forces person then going to live in some country over the water, maybe even *that* country over *that* water, with the renouncers in our district warning her never to return. Even after the death of this state-forces person — our second brother-in-law whom none of us except second sister had met and who had died, not because the renouncers had killed him but because of some ordinary non-political illness — still sister was not allowed to return which I think anyway she didn't want to do. 'At least this daughter can't be accused of traitorship,' reassured the neighbours. 'Though know't, neighbour,' they added, 'severals are saying that that milkman is no bit player but one ruthless character your girl's involved herself with.' 'Name of mercy,' said ma only this time she spoke quietly and wee sisters said she sounded flat, as if there was no life in her, not even shocked life, which at least would have been some energy. Instead she looked about as unhappy, they said, as when that business happened that banished second sister that time. 'Of course,' went on the neighbours, 'all that mayn't be true and it could be your daughter's not involved with that renouncer, or with any renouncer, but that instead she's in courtship with some twentysomething, nine-to-five, five-and-a-half-day-week, right-religion, motor-trade lad.' Ma continued unconvinced. The motor-trade aspect came across as spurious, as artificial, as a weak and fabricated attempt by her good friend Jason and those other kindly neighbours to cheer her up in the midst of this bombshell. Instead she opted for the targeteer, the one who bided his time, who kept on going, who persisted unassailably until he got the job done. Besides, the description given by these neighbours of this milkman fitted particularly — bar the wrong religion — the identikit of the person she herself had been praying against. So biased was ma therefore, in her foregone conclusion that I would take up with such a dangerous, deadly lover, that it never occurred to her, not once, that the man might be two men.

She sought me out and started in on the

conciliatory note. This was coaxing. This was 'why don't you give up this man who's too old for you anyway, who might impress you now but one day you'll see he's just another of them selfish "cake and eat it" fellas? Why not instead take up with one of them nice wee boys from the area, suited to and more consistent with your religion, your marital status and your age?' Ma's understanding of the nice wee boys was that they were the right religion, that they were devout, single, preferably not paramilitaries, overall more stable and durable than those — as she put it — 'fast, breathtaking, fantastically exhilarating, but all the same, daughter, early-to-death rebel men'. 'Nothing stops them,' she said, 'till death stops them. You'll regret it, daughter, finding yourself ensnared in the underbelly of all that alluring, mind-altering, unruly paramilitary nightlife. It's not all it seems. It's on the run. It's war. It's killing people. It's being killed. It's being put in charge. It's being beaten. It's being tortured. It's being on hunger strike. It's having yourself made over into an entirely different person. Look at your brothers. I'm telling you, it'll end badly. You'll hit the ground with a bump if he doesn't take you to death first with him. And what of your female destiny? The daily round? The common task? Having babies with the babies having a father and not some tombstone you take them to, to visit once a week in the graveyard? Look at yer woman round the corner. You could say she loved all her saturnine husbands, but where are they now? Where are most of those women's brooding, single-minded, potently implacable husbands? Again, six feet under in the freedom-fighters' plot of the usual place.' At this she turned to the duties of marriage, to the folly of confusing yearning for romance with real-life proper female aims and objectives. Marriage wasn't meant to be a bed of roses. It was a divine decree, a communal duty, a responsibility, it was acting your age, having right-religion babies and obligations and limitations and restrictions and hindrances. It was not failing to be proposed to then ending up, yellowed and desiccated, dying some timid but determined spinster on some long-forgotten, dusty, spidery shelf. Never would she budge from this position, though often as I grew older I'd wonder if this really was — in the undergrowth of her own recesses — truly what ma believed of women and of their destiny herself? And now she was back to the solution, to the nice wee boys, to those conducive to my being properly matched and proportioned. Here she ticked names off her fingers of sample ones from the area to give me a taster of the kind she approved of. Going by this list, I could have guaranteed, had ma been open to hearing, that none of them were in any way as matchable and proportionable as she described. Some weren't nice for a start. Also, an awful lot weren't devout and not a few were already married. A smaller number were living unmarried with their girlfriends in 'the red-light street' as the community called it and that 'dot dot dot' street as certainly ma, when she should come to hear of it, would call it. Others were renouncers or reputed to be renouncers, deeply committed either to furthering a personal agenda through a political agenda, or else genuinely devoted to the political-problems cause. So ma could pick them without knowing she was picking them, but I chose not to enlighten because I was still in my defensive, protective, 'giving nothing away' mode. This was a deliberate withholding on my part because never had it been in my remit not to withhold from my mother because never had it been in her remit to get my message and to take me at my word. It was only when she gave up suggesting 'that nice wee boy, now what's his name? — the one who developed that tic of referring to himself in the first person plural — ach, you know, Somebody McSomebody' as a candidate for me to marry and instead launched into 'Your sister says her husband says that he heard everybody else say that you —' that I felt my temper rising. Here we go. 'He's a hefty toad, ma,' I said. 'Bastard of the first batch. Don't go listening to him.'

Ma winced. 'I wish you wouldn't use that language, that blue french language. It wonders me how comes it you two use that language when none of your other sisters use it.' She meant me and third sister and it was true, we did use it, though third sister was more into the french of it than me. 'Gee-whizz, ma,' I said, and I said this without thinking, without attending to the fact — for it had been a fact — that I was angry and dismissive and wearied by my mother, frustrated at her living on another planet and insisting in her ignorance that I come live on it with her; also, that I considered her a stereotype, a caricature, something, of course, I would never become myself. So I said 'gee-whizz' and it was rude, absently rude. Had I considered though, probably I'd have thought she wouldn't catch onto it, wouldn't understand the scorn in it, that my dismissal of her would pass right over her head. But ma did catch on, did understand, and unexpectedly she dropped that comical role, the 'mamma anxious for wedding bells' role — a cliché gone away, fallen away — and her real self stepped forward. Now, full of bones and blood and muscle and strength and with a sudden self-definition which included anger, a whole lot of anger, she leaned over and took hold of me by the upper arm.

'Don't you be coming out with your proud words to me, your superior ways, your condescension, your wee belittling sarcasms. Is it that you think I haven't lived, daughter? Is it that you think I haven't intelligence, haven't learned anything in all the years I've been here? Well, I've learned things, I know things, and I'll tell you what one of them is. It's one thing to be off-colour in your talk, and another, worse thing to be full of yourself and mocking of other people. I'd rather you came out with your filthy, unfitting language for the rest of your life than for you to turn out one of them cowardly people who can't speak their minds but won't hold their peace and instead mumble behind hands and get their fights out in sneakery and in whispers. Those ones aren't as clever or as respectable, daughter, as in their own heads and in their dramatic love of themselves they think they are. Attend to your words and your tone. I'm disappointed. Thought I reared you to better manners than that.' She dropped my arm then, and made to walk away which was amazing, something that had never happened between us before. Usually I'd be the one who'd had enough, who'd become indignant, pronounce last words then, in exasperation, turn and walk from her. This time though, I stepped after and I put my hand out to stay her. 'Ma,' I said, though with no idea of what was to come next.

I didn't know shame. I mean as a word, because as a word, it hadn't yet entered the communal vocabulary. Certainly I knew the *feeling* of shame and I knew everybody around me knew that feeling as well. In no way was it a weak feeling, for it seemed more potent than anger, more potent than hatred, stronger even than that most disguised of emotions, fear. At that time there was no way to grapple with or transcend it. Another thing was that often it was a public feeling, needing numbers to swell its effectiveness, regardless of whether you were the one doing the shaming, the one witnessing the shaming, or the one having the shame done unto you. Given it was such a complex, involved, very advanced feeling, most people here did all kinds of permutations in order not to have it: killing people, doing verbal damage to people, doing mental damage to people and, not least, also not infrequently, doing those things to oneself.

This change in my mother sobered me. It propelled me out of the belief that she was some cardboard-cut-out person, out of mistaking her compulsive praying for a head full of silliness instead of maybe a head full of worry, out of dismissing her for being fifty with ten children out of her so that the rest of her life — as in any new way of living it — must now be at an end. In that moment I felt bad about the gee-whizz which meant I felt shame at having rubbished my mother. This was despite her own haranguing and prolonged mental battering of me. So I felt like crying when I never cried. Then I felt like cursing as a way to stay the crying. Then came the realisation that I could try to make amends. This could be the moment to say 'sorry' — without, of course, saying 'sorry' because 'sorry', like 'shame', nobody yet knew here how to say. We might feel sorry but, as with shame, we wouldn't know how to contend with the expression of it. Instead I decided to offer ma exactly what she was after, which was to tell all there was about the milkman and myself. So I did. I told her I wasn't having an affair with him, nor had I ever wished for an affair, that instead, it had been him, solely him, pursuing and importuning, as it seemed, to start an affair with me. I said he'd approached me twice, only twice, and I explained the circumstances of each meeting. I said also that he knew things about me — my work, my family, what I did of an evening after work, what I did at weekends, but not once, I said, had he laid a finger on me or even, apart from the first meeting, directly looked at me, adding also, that I'd never got into his vehicles even if people said I was getting into them all the time. I ended by admitting that I hadn't wanted to tell out any of this, not just to her, but to anyone. I said this was because of the twisting of words, the fabrication of words and the exaggeration of words that went on in this place. I'd have lost power, such as was my power, if I'd tried to explain and to win over all those gossiping about me. So I'd kept silent, I said. I'd asked no questions, answered no questions, gave no confirmation, no refutation. That way, I said, I'd hoped to maintain a border to keep my mind separate. That way, I said, I'd hoped to ground and protect myself.

During this ma looked at me without interruption but when I finished, and without hesitation, she called me a liar, saying this deceit was nothing but a further mockery of herself. She spoke of other meetings then, between me and the milkman, besides the two to which I admitted. The community was keeping her abreast, she said, which meant she knew I met him regularly for immoral trysts and assignations, knew too, of what we got up to in places too indecent even to give the 'dot dot dot' to. 'You're some sort of mob-woman,' she said. 'Out of the pale. Lost your intrinsic rights and wrongs. You make it hard, wee girl, to love you and if your poor father was alive, certainly he'd have something to say about this.' I doubted it. When da was alive, hardly ever did he speak to us and his last words to me as he lay dying — perhaps his last words ever — were alarming and focused on himself. 'I was raped many times as a boy,' he said. 'Did I ever tell you that?' At the time all I could think to reply was, 'No.' 'Yes,' he said. 'Many times. Many, many times he did me — me, a boy, and him, in his suit and hat, opening his buttons, pulling me back to him, in that back shed, that black shed, over and over and giving me pennies after.' Da closed his eyes and shuddered and wee sisters, who were with me at the hospital, came round the bed and tugged on my arm. 'What's raped?' they whispered. 'What's crumbie?' because now, with eyes still closed, da was muttering 'crombie'. 'Many awful times,' he said, opening his eyes once more. It seemed he could hear wee sisters, though I didn't think he could see them. He saw me though, even if unsure which daughter I was. That, of course, could have had nothing to do with dying, because da, when he'd lived, always had been in a state of distraction, spending overlong hours reading papers, watching the news, ears to radios, out in the street, taking in, then talking out, the latest political strife with likeminded neighbours. He was that type, the type who let nothing in except it had to be the political problems. If not the political problems — then any war, anywhere, any predator, any victim. He'd spend lots of time too, with these neighbours who were of the exact fixation and boxed-off aberration as him. As for the names of us offspring, never could he remember them, not without running through a chronological list in his head. While doing this, he'd include his sons' names even if searching for the name of a daughter. And vice versa. Sooner or later, by running through, he'd hit on the correct one at last. Even that though, became too much and so, after a bit, he dropped the mental catalogue, opting instead for 'son' or 'daughter' which was easier. And he was right. It was easier which was how the rest of us came to substitute 'brother' and 'sister' and so on ourselves.

'Backside,' was what he said next and wee sisters giggled. 'My legs,' he said. 'My thighs, but especially my backside. Always terrible, those sensations, nothing ridded me of them, those trembles, those shudders, those tiny persistent ripples. They just kept coming, kept repeating, kept being awful, my whole life through. But there had been a recklessness, wife,' he then said, 'an abandonment, a rejection of me by me that had begun years earlier — *I was going to die anyway, wouldn't live long anyway, any day now I'll be dead, all the time, violently murdered* — so he may as well have me 'cos he knew all along he was going to have me, couldn't stop him from having me. All shut down. Get it over with. Not going freshly into that place of terror, which was why, wife, it never felt right between me and you.' Wee sisters giggled again, this time at 'wife' though now there was a nervousness to their giggling. Then da said, this time with anger,

'That crombie, those suits, that crombie. Nobody wore crombies, brother,' and again wee sisters tugged at me. 'Did he,' da then asked, looking straight at me and seeming for a moment fully to comprehend me, *'Did he . . . rape you, brother . . . as well?'* 'Middle sister?' whispered wee sisters. 'Why's daddy saying —' but they didn't finish. Instead they gravitated closer and closer behind me. Da died of his illness that night after wee sisters and I were gone and ma and some of the others had turned up at the hospital to sit with him. I was left his scarf and his flat working-cap, also a lifelong distaste for the word 'crombie' which also I'd thought was 'crumbie' until I found it in the dictionary that evening on getting home.

And now ma was angry, threatening me with dead da because I'd lied when I hadn't lied, because I'd debased both of us, she said, with my falsehoods and hardness of heart when in truth it was that we had no faith in each other. 'You don't honour my instruction,' she said and I said, 'You don't honour me.' In response, and I suppose proving her right, I closed up again, took my teenage satisfaction in renouncing the attempt to seek out any leverage point that might have existed between us. Instead I thought, this is my life and I love you, or

99

maybe I don't love you, but this is who I am, what I stand for and these are the lines, mother. I didn't speak this, because I couldn't have done so without getting into a fight and always we were in fights, always making attack on each other. Instead I closed up, thinking, *gee-whizz, gee-whizz, gee-whizz, gee-whizz,* and I stopped caring too, from that moment, as to whether or not she blamed me. From now on she'd get nothing from me. But was that how it was to be always? Me, according to her, sharp of heart? And her, according to me, ending in nothing but arrowpoints herself?

And here I was the following day, with third brother-in-law, running in the parks & reservoirs. He was doing his mutterings and I was trying to dwell, not on the milkman as ma thought — as all of them thought — but on maybe-boyfriend, whom I was going to be seeing for a sunset that night. As for the milkman, there appeared no sign, which didn't mean *'Hurray! Got rid of! Wonderful!'* because, of course, he could be hovering. With hidden state security, hidden military intelligence, plainclothes people pretending not to be plainclothes people, plus all that general 'glimpsed one second, gone the next then back again' local demi-monde activity, the parks & reservoirs was definitely a hovering kind of place. But no. There appeared no sign and this was encouraging, meaning I could relax, could carry on in peace and quiet with my compulsive exercise addiction, aided and abetted by brother-in-law who beside me, was carrying on with his. Normally we didn't converse or chat or encourage exchange of words on our runs other than the functional 'Will we pick up pace here, sister-in-law?' or 'Will we add a bonus mile at the end, brother-in-law?' or other suchlike exercise expressions. This time though, familiar, reliable brother-in-law didn't prove as familiar and reliable as always he had before.

'May I intrude upon you for a few words of private conversation?' he asked, which struck me with trepidation for brother-in-law had never intruded upon me for such a thing before. Immediately I thought, this must be the milkman. He's going to launch into the milkman because he too, must have heard gossip even though it was unbelievable that third brother-in-law of all people — the last bastion against doing so — should let himself be swayed and directed by the gossip of this place. It turned out though, that he hadn't and he didn't. Instead he embarked on a careful disquisition that I guessed he'd been having for some time in his head. This was on the subject of my reading-while-walking. Books and walking. Me. And walking. And reading. That thing again. 'Are you talking to me?' I said. 'What can you mean? You've never spoken to me in your life.' 'It's that I think,' said third brother-in-law, 'that you should not do that, that it's not safe, not natural, not dutiful to self, that by doing so you're switching yourself off, you're abandoning yourself, that you might as well betake yourself for a stroll amongst the lions and the tigers, that you're putting yourself at the mercy of hard and cunning and unruly dark forces, that you might as well be walking with your hands in your pockets —' 'Wouldn't be able to hold the book then —' 'Not funny,' he said. 'It's that anybody could sneak up. They could run up,' he emphasised. 'Drive up. Good godfathers, sister-in-law! They could dander up, with *you* — defences down, no longer alert, no longer strenuously reconnoitring and surveying the environment and if you're reading aloud —' 'Ach! Not reading aloud! For goodness sake!' This was getting ridiculous. 'But if you're undertaking the unsafe procedure of reading-while-walking and cutting off consciousness and not paying attention and ignoring your surroundings . . .' which was priceless coming from someone who didn't know the political problems of eleven years were going on. That was something else I was using as a deterrent against the milkman. Another brother-in-law aberration besides that of the female was the rumour in the area that he was so firmly into his schedules of exercise and of fighting that he hadn't noticed the political problems of a decade's standing were happening. That was saying something and, in its oddness, I was sure could not help but keep the milkman away too.

I myself paid little attention to the problems, but I paid at least the minimum, something I could not have avoided because of osmosis. Brother-in-law, however, paid no attention either to osmosis, to the very noticeable social and political upheaval of the time and the place he was living in. Instead he went about blinkered, unaware, which was weird, very weird. I too, found it weird, which meant the milkman — that ideological seer of the dream, the bringer of the vision, someone dedicating his life to a cause that some outrageous person round the corner, deep in a hardly comparable personal fighting and exercise agenda, didn't know existed — would have considered such negligence as certainly unnerving, not to say indicative of third brother-in-law not being sane. This brings up the mental aberrations because in our area there existed two types of mental aberrations: the slight, communally accepted ones and the not-so-slight, beyond-the-pale ones. Those possessing the former fitted tolerably into society and this was pretty much everybody, including all the various drinkers, fighters and rioters who existed in this place. Drinking, fighting and rioting were run-of-the-mill, customary, necessary even, as hardly to be discerned as mental aberrations. Also hardly to be discerned as an aberration was all that repertoire of gossip, secrecy and communal policing, plus the rules of what was allowed and not allowed that featured heavily in this place. Regarding the slight aberrations, the convention was to rub along with, to turn a blind eye, because life was being attempted where you had to cut corners; impossible therefore, to give one hundred per cent. You could not give fifty per cent, you could not give fifteen per cent, you could give only five per cent, maybe just two per cent. And with those deemed beyond-the-pale, impossible it was to give any percentage at all. The beyonds had funny wee ways which the district had conceded were just that bit too funny. They no longer passed muster, were no longer conformable in the mystery of the human mind as fully to be accommodable and this too, was before the days of consciousness-raising groups, of personal-improvement workshops, of motivational programming, basically before these modern times when you can stand up and receive a round of applause for admitting there might be something wrong with your head. Instead it was best then, in those days, to keep the lowest of low profiles rather than admit your personal distinguishing habits had fallen below the benchmark for social regularity. If you didn't, you'd find yourself branded a psychological misfit and slotted out there with those other misfits on the rim. At that time there weren't many on the rim in our district. There was the man who didn't love anybody. There were the women with the issues. There was nuclear boy and tablets girl and tablets girl's sister. Then there was myself, and yes, took me a while to realise I too, was on that list. Brother-in-law wasn't on the list but that didn't mean he ought not to have been. Considering alone his avowals of devotion towards women, his mission of idolatry, his supreme glorification and deification and view that on earth in women was the life of things, the breadth of things, the cyclicality, essential nature, higher aspect, the best, most archetypal and utmost mystery of everything — keeping in mind too, this was the Nineteen-Seventies — there was no way, under normal circumstances, he would not have been placed in the category of our district's beyond-the-pales. The reason he wasn't was because of his popularity, but as for this knowing nothing of our political situation, and especially given his current criticism of me, I latched immediately onto that.

'Excuse me, brother-in-law,' I said, 'but about the political problems. Have you heard about the political problems?' 'What political problems?' he said. 'Are you referring to the sorrows, the losses, the troubles, the sadnesses?' 'What sorrows and sadnesses?' I said. 'What troubles? What losses? I'm sorry but this is unintelligent.' Then it was I learned two things. One was that that long-term rumour of third brother-in-law being in *la-la-land* as regards the political problems was incorrect because he *was* in touch with what was happening politically. Two was, the community, maybe both communities, maybe even the land 'over the water' and the land 'over the border', had moved things on to the tune of the political problems here being referred to now as the sorrows, the losses and those other things he had just said they were. 'Seems I know more about the political situation,' he then said, 'than you.' 'Not surprising either,' he went on, 'for as I've been saying, sister, you're not vigilant as evidenced in particular by this reading-while-walking. I saw you with my own eyes last Wednesday night-time committing social insanity by entering the area completely and dangerously blind to the lower forces and influences — your head down, the tiniest of reading-torches shining on your pages. Nobody does that. That's tantamount to —' *You know about the political problems?* I asked. 'Of course I know,' he said. 'Is it that you think I'm nuclear boy, so far gone in my America-Russo atomic bomb displacement condition that I can't tell my own brother's lying dead with no head beside me?' This was a reference to one of our district's beyond-the-pales. Nuclear boy happened to be Somebody McSomebody's younger brother — Somebody McSomebody being one of ma's eligibles for me to marry as well as the boy who was to get me with his gun in the toilets of the district's most popular drinking-club after the ambush and death of the milkman

— well, his brother, nuclear boy, was a fifteen-year-old with a serious armament problem. The arms race between America and Russia was a fixation about which nobody could get him to shut up. Constantly he fretted and was distraught, which would have been okay, thought everybody, as in, would have made some sense if he'd been fretting and distraught over stockpiling of weapons owing to the political problems in his own country. But no. He was referring to nuclear weapons being stockpiled in as far away as somewhere else. He meant America. And he meant Russia. And he worried and earbashed everybody, splurging uncontrollably about some imminent, catastrophic event. This disaster, he would say, would be because two immature, selfish nations were endangering all us other nations and he'd only ever talk America and Russia, never aware of anything going on in his face. Never worried, he didn't, when his favourite brother's head got blown off in the middle of the week, in the middle of the afternoon, in the middle of the street, right there in front of him. One moment this favourite sibling, the second eldest boy, the sixteen-year-old and the most calm and beloved of that family, was making his way over the street towards his nervous, panicked brother, to discourse with him, once again to try to soothe him in his wild nuclear distraction. Next, this teenager was on the ground with his head completely gone. Not ever, not even after the commotion died down, did anybody find it. And people looked for it. The man who didn't love anybody — another beyond-the-pale — and some other men, many men, even my da, had looked well into days and nights for it. Just after the explosion though, nuclear boy had paused long enough to pick himself up from where the blast had thrown him, then to get his bearings, then to remember where he'd been in his words about America and Russia, then to carry on from where he'd left off. Amidst the screams he went back to worrying, straight back to worrying. Not just for him to worry, he said. Not just him. We should all of us be worrying. Nobody could afford to ignore the risk that mad Russia and mad America were posing, with the rest of us thinking we could afford to ignore the risk. So nuclear boy was one of those outcasts, a beyond-the-pale, having put himself there with his strange Cold War obsession. This meant that if you saw him coming, quick as a flash, you ducked the other way. And here was third brother-in-law declaring that he himself wasn't nuclear boy, that he *was* politically and socially aware, that with his own routine of scrutinising and reconnoitring the environment he was the antithesis of nuclear boy. Besides, he said, just because you were aware of something didn't mean you had to broadcast it on the grapevine. 'And as for that grapevine,' he added, 'I must say, sister-in-law, I wouldn't have expected *you* to be perpetuating gossip, never mind telegraphing it through such a wide-ranging but distorting medium as that.' At this we ran in silence for a bit, with him thinking whatever it was brother-in-law did think and with me thinking, how come I'm the one turned into the gossip here? Also, he *does* know about the political problems. Also, he's criticising *me* when — but for the special dispensation granted him by the indulgent of the district — practically he himself is a notorious community beyond-the-pale. Brother-in-law then intruded upon me again, and again uncharacteristically by bringing up that book thing. 'Yes. Those books,' he said. 'And that walking,' and he started in from another angle, this time the angle of how, if I wasn't careful I'd be banished to the furthest reaches of darkness, ostracised and shown no mercy as a district beyond-the-pale. Already he warned that I was being talked about as the 'reading-while-walking' person. Rubbish, I thought. But this was him carried away, wild now in exaggeration and imagery. 'Okay,' I said. 'So if I were to stop walking-while-reading, and hands in pockets, and little night torches, and instead looked right and left and right again for dangerous, unscrupulous forces, does that mean I'll end up happy?' 'It's not about being happy,' he said, which was, and still is, the saddest remark I've ever heard.

But no mention of the milkman. Not a syllable. Brother-in-law, bless his soul, hadn't been listening to rumour which was in accordance with my respectful view of him as someone with no inclination for rumour. And of course I wouldn't mention the milkman either for — just as with me and maybe-boyfriend and my wariness of presuming, or of trying to explain only to be misunderstood, or of trying to explain only not to be taken seriously — I couldn't see in those days how I could speak of this dilemma I now found myself in. It was that I didn't speak to anybody of anything — partly because I wasn't used to telling anybody anything, partly because I didn't know how to tell or what to tell, partly too, because still it was unclear there was any-

111

thing of accuracy to tell. What had he done after all? Certainly it felt to me that this milkman *had* done something, that he was about to do something, that strategically he was working up to some action. I think too — otherwise why all this gossip? — others in the district must have been thinking the same as me. Thing was, he hadn't physically touched me. Nor that last time had he even looked at me. So where was my premise for speaking out on how, uninvited, he was pushing in? But that was what it was like here. Everything had to be physical, had to be intellectually reasonable in order to be comprehensible. I couldn't tell brother-in-law about the milkman, not because he'd rush to defend me, beating up the milkman, then getting himself shot which would then have the community turn against the milkman, leading to the paramilitary-renouncers in the area in their turn getting the community by the throat. Then the community would get the renouncers by the throat, refusing to hide them anymore, to house them, to feed them, to transport arms for them. No more either, would they warn of danger or be makeshift surgeons for them. The whole incident would cause division, would end that much-harkened pulling-together in order to overcome the enemy state. No. None of that. It was simply that brother-in-law would be incapable of believing that anything that wasn't physical between two people could, in fact, be going on. I also shared this belief, as did everybody else — about someone not doing something so how could they be doing it — which meant how could I open my mouth and threaten widespread disintegration of the current status quo? Especially this would be impossible in the context of the political problems, where huge things, physical, noisy things, were most certainly, on a daily basis, an hourly basis, on a television news-round-by-newsround basis, going on. As for the rumour of me and the milkman, why should it be down to me to dispel it, to refute gossip by people who fostered gossip and clearly wouldn't welcome either, denial of their gossip? And as for vigilance or non-vigilance? For switching off or not switching off? It was my opinion that with my reading-while-walking I was doing both at the same time. And why should I not? I knew that by reading while I walked I was losing touch in a crucial sense with communal up-to-dateness and that that, indeed, was risky. It was important to be in the know, to keep up with, especially when things here got added on to at such a rapid compound rate.

On the other hand, being up on, having awareness, clocking everything — both of rumour and of actuality — didn't prevent things from happening or allow for intervention on, or reversal of things that had already happened. Knowledge didn't guarantee power, safety or relief and often for some it meant the opposite of power, safety and relief — leaving no outlet for dispersal either, of all the heightened stimuli that had been built by being up on in the first place. Purposely not wanting to know therefore, was exactly what my reading-while-walking was about. It was a vigilance not to be vigilant, and my return to exercising with brother-in-law, that too, was part of my vigilance. As long as I continued to filter his unprecedented attack on my reading-while-walking, also filtering the more excessive of his exercise-talk which in my opinion, constituted his own mantle of protection, I could run with brother-in-law and not have to be here in the parks & reservoirs on my own. I'd be with a male person too, which would help because I'd sensed that the milkman operated best in cases of isolation. By running with brother-in-law therefore, I could carry on as if this milkman and our two earlier encounters had been insignificant, or even that they hadn't taken place at all.

So it had been books, just books, that 'walking and books' thing, and I decided to forgive brother-in-law for his out-of-character criticism, which was what I did, then a tree by the top reservoir took a picture of us as we ran by. This hidden camera clicked, just one click, a state-forces click, in the similar way to how that bush, positioned along this same reservoir, had done a week earlier. Oh dear, I thought. I hadn't considered that. What I meant was I hadn't considered that the state would now associate anyone I was associating with also with the milkman as they were associating me now with the milkman. Already within a week of that first click, I'd been clicked again four times. Once had been in town, once when walking into town, then twice coming out of town. I'd been photographed from a car, from a seemingly disused building, also from other bits of greenery; perhaps too, there'd been other clicks I hadn't picked up on at the time. On each occasion when I did hear them, the camera would snap as I passed and so, yes, it seemed I'd fallen into some grid, maybe the central grid, as part of the disease, the rebel-infection. And now, others in my company, such as poor, innocent brother-in-law, were to be implicated also as associates of an associate. Brother-in-law, however, just as had the milkman, completely ignored the click. 'Why are you ignoring that click?' I asked. 'I always ignore clicks,' he said. 'What do you expect me to do? Get outraged? Write letters? Keep a diary? Put in a complaint? Get one of my personal secretaries to contact the United Nations Amnesty International Ombudsman Human Rights peaceful demonstration people? Tell me, sister, who do I contact and what do I say, and while we're about it, what are you going to do about the click yourself?' Well, I was going to have amnesia of course. In fact, here I was, already having it. 'I don't know what you mean,' I said. 'I've forgotten,' his forthrightness having sent me immediately into *jamais vu.* That was my answer — something that should be familiar was not going to be familiar — though there was an uplifting in this camera business too. Brother-in-law hadn't expressed surprise at the click, or ignorance of the click. Indeed, he'd admitted to it, and not only to that click, but to other clicks upon him presumably not associated with me or the milkman. 'They're always doing that,' he said. 'People get photographed for the record,' which meant

I could stop worrying, stop feeling guilty about bringing state suspicion down upon brother-in-law's head. So I did stop worrying. I let it go and we continued our run, with brother-in-law now into his stride, which was not just a running stride, but also his new stride of why again I should stop reading-while-walking. I didn't listen. There was no way I'd stop reading-while-walking. I remained quiet though, because why, when it came to it, make a fuss when one's mind was already made up?

So on we ran, with him eventually dropping the reading-while-walking and slipping back to the usual minutiae of his exercise addiction. This time it was whether one should do a split-body routine or a full-body routine and if it were a split body, should it be a two-way split or a three-way split, all this being fine with me as I had my force-field up to filter the more draining of his persistence away. It wasn't that I dismissed brother-in-law though, because as with all women of the district, I too liked him very, very much. I was grateful to him also, not just because I could reinstate my runs after proving my plan successful in out-manoeuvring the milkman. It was also that I felt safe with him — in the knowledge and familiarity of him, in the relative relaxation of him, in that I could be in the company of someone who didn't, least not usually, harangue and meddle with who I was. He had no hidden agenda; indeed I was the one with the agenda. Also I'd forgotten how much I enjoyed — with our kindred understanding of running and the etiquette of running — being on these sessions with him. Eventually he petered out on that whole aspect of body-training and we returned to our norm of running in silence. Only once did he say, 'Will we go faster, sister-in-law? We don't want to end up walking, do we?' As for the milkman and my aim to oust him by reinstating runs with third brother-in-law, that had paid off exactly as planned.

THREE

Third time of the milkman was when he appeared not long after my adult evening French class. This class was downtown and it had surprising things. Often these would not be French things. Often too, there would be more of them than would be the French things. At this latest lesson, which took place on Wednesday evening, teacher was reading from a book. This was a French book, a proper French book — one that native speakers could read without considering it beneath them — and teacher said she was reading from it to get us used to what authentic French sounded like when strung together in full-on passages — in this case, a literary passage. Thing was though, the sky in this passage she was reading from wasn't blue. Eventually she got interrupted because someone in the class — spokesperson for the rest of us — naturally couldn't stand it. Something was wrong and he had a need, for the sake of all things generic, to point it out.

'I'm confused,' he said. 'Is that passage about the sky? If it is about the sky then why doesn't the writer just say so? Why is he complicating things with fancy footwork when all he need say is that the sky is blue?'

'Hear! Hear!' cried us or, if some of us, like me, didn't cry it, certainly we agreed in sentiment. *'Le ciel est bleu! Le ciel est bleu!'* shouted many of the others. 'That would have cleared matters. Why didn't he just put that?'

We were disturbed, and not a little, but teacher, she laughed which was something she did a lot. She did this because she had an unnerving amount of humour — another thing which ruffled us as well. Whenever she laughed, we weren't sure whether to laugh along with her, to be curious and engaged and to ask why she was laughing, or to be sulky and offended and seriously up in arms. This time, as usual, we opted for up in arms.

'What a waste of time and a confusion of subjects,' complained a woman. 'That writer ought not to be featuring in a French lesson even if he is French if he's not doing anything about teaching it. This is "learning a foreign language" class, not a class on burdening us with taking things apart which are in the same language to find out if they're a poem or something. If we wanted figures of speech and rhetorical flourishes, with one thing representing another thing when the represented thing could easily have been itself in the first place, then we'd have gone to English Literature with those weirdos down the hall.' 'Yeah!' cried us and also we cried, 'A spade's a spade!', also the popular *'Le ciel est bleu!'* and *'What's the point? There's no point!'* continued to come out of us. Everyone was nodding and slapping desks and murmuring and acclaiming. And now it was time, we thought, to give our spokespeople and ourselves a jolly good round of applause.

'So, class,' said teacher after this applause had died down, 'is it that you think the sky can only be blue?'

'The sky *is* blue,' came us. 'What colour else can it be?'

Of course we knew really that the sky could be more than blue, two more, but why should any of us admit to that? I myself have never admitted it. Not even the week before when I experienced my first sunset with maybe-boyfriend did I admit it. Even then, even though there were more colours than the acceptable three in the sky — blue (the day sky), black (the night sky) and white (clouds) — that evening still I kept my mouth shut. And now the others in this class — all older than me, some as old as thirty — also weren't admitting it. It was the convention not to admit it, not to accept detail for this type of detail would mean choice and choice would mean responsibility and what if we failed in our responsibility? Failed too, in the interrogation of the consequence of seeing more than we could cope with? Worse, what if it was nice, whatever it was, and we liked it, got used to it, were cheered up by it, came to rely upon it, only for it to go away, or be wrenched away, never to come back again? Better not to have had it in the first place was the prevailing feeling, and that was why blue was the colour for our sky to be. Teacher though, wasn't leaving it at that.

'So that's it, is it?' she said, and she was pretending amazement which confirmed further our suspicions about her; in short, suspicions that she was none other than a beyond-the-pale person herself. For yes, even though I was downtown, which meant outside my own area, which meant outside my own religion, which meant I was in a class containing people who really did have the names Nigel and Jason, that didn't

122

mean disorders, disharmonies and beyond-the-pales couldn't go on here as well. You got to know for instance, regardless of religion, who was of normal disharmony and who was a man-overboard person. Teacher certainly, appeared from the latter class. One thing that stood out was that French could never be sustained for long whenever she was the one teaching it. This evening as usual, English had taken over, which meant, also as usual, French was out the window. Next, she had us looking out this window. She had stridden over to it — a straight-backed woman on a majestic caparisoned horse — and had begun pointing through it with her pen.

'Okay, everyone,' she said. 'You need to look at the sky. You need, right now, to look at that sunset. *Magnificent!*' Here she stopped pointing and tapping on the glass in order to inhale this sky. After inhaling it, which was embarrassing, she exhaled it with a giant *'Aaaaahhhhh!'* coming out of her — more embarrassing. Then she went back to pointing and tapping. 'Tell me, class,' she said, 'what colours — do you hear that, *colours, plural* — do you see now?'

We looked because she made us, even though sunsets weren't part of our curriculum, but we looked and it seemed to us that the sky as usual was turning from light blue to dark blue which meant it was just blue. I knew though, since that recent alarming and alerting sunset I'd experienced with maybe-boyfriend, that that sky that night in the French class was neither those shades of blue. A person of any level of contrariness or entrenchment might have been pushed to have found any blue in the whole of our class's window. We were pushed. Also we were adamant.

'Blue!'

'Blue!'

'Perhaps a bit — no, blue,' came our all-out replies.

'My poor deprived class!' cried teacher and again she was bluffing, pretending sorrow about our lack of colour, our hampered horizons, our mental landscapes, when it was obvious she was a person too defined within herself to be long perturbed by anything at all. And how come she was this? How come she was doing this antagonising, this presenting of an anti-culture to our culture when she herself was of our culture, where the same rules of consciousness regarding the likes of colour — regardless too, of church affiliation — as applied to us ought equally to have applied to her? But she was laughing again. 'There is no blue in the whole of the window,' she said. 'Look again please. Try again please — and, class' — here she paused and, for a moment, did become serious — 'although there's no lack of colour out there really — *there's nothing out there really.* But for temporal purposes please note — the sky that seems to be out there can be any colour that there is.'

'Testicles!' cried some ladies and gentlemen and a *frisson* — the only French of the evening apart from *'le ciel est bleu'* and that literary guff the guy in the book had been posturing — went through us. It seemed to our minds that no, what she was saying could not ever be true. If what she was saying was true, that the sky — out there — not out there — whatever — could be any colour, that meant anything could be any colour, that anything could be anything, that anything could happen, at any time, in any place, in the whole of the world, and to anybody — probably had too, only we just hadn't noticed. So no. After generation upon generation, fathers upon forefathers, mothers upon foremothers, centuries and millennia of being one colour officially and three colours unofficially, a colourful sky, just like that, could not be allowed to be.

'Come,' she persisted. 'Why have you turned your backs?' For we had turned our backs; it had been instinctive and protective. But she made us turn round to face the sky once more. This time she proceeded to point through various panes at sections of sky that were not blue but instead lilac, purple, patches of pink — differing pinks — with one patch of green that had a yellow gold extending along it. *And green? How come green was up there?* Then, as the sunset was not most visible from this window, she marched us out of our classroom and along the corridor into the *littérateurs'* classroom. That evening their room was empty because they had gone to the theatre with pens, flashlights and little notebooks to watch and critique *Playboy of the Western World.* Here teacher bade us look at the sky from this brand new perspective, where the sun — enormous and of the most gigantic orange-red colour — in a sky too, with no blue in it — was going down behind buildings in a section of windowpane.

As for this sky, it was now a mix of pink and lemon with a glow of mauve behind it. It had changed colours during our short trip along the corridor and before our eyes was changing colours yet. An emerging gold above the mauve was moving towards a slip of silver, with a different mauve in a corner drifting in from the side. Then there was further pinking. Then more lilac. Then a turquoise that pressed clouds — not white — out of its way. Layers were mixing and blending, forming and transforming which was exactly what happened during that sunset a week earlier. 'Will we go and see the sun go down?' maybe-boyfriend, to my startled ears, had said. 'Why?' I accused. 'Because it's the sun,' he said. 'Okay,' I said, as if this wasn't unprecedented, as if people in my environment suggested sunsets to each other frequently. So I said yes, and after my run with third brother-in-law I went home, got showered, got changed, put on make-up and high heels and maybe-boyfriend picked me up where usually he picked me up, at the bottom of my district on our side of the interface road. This sad and lonely road ran between the religions and I would meet him there, not because he was the opposite religion, for he wasn't, but because it was easier to do that than to have him call for me at my door. Not long after this first sunset, however, he started to complain about our complex, perilous meeting arrangements, saying I didn't want him calling for me directly, or for us to do anything inside my area because I was ashamed to be seen with him which was unbelievable to my ears. I said there was

127

nowhere to go in my area which wasn't true and which he knew wasn't true because it was a known fact that eleven of our religion's best drinking-clubs existed in my district, including the most popular in the city for our particular creed. So he said I was being evasive which was true but not for the reason of being ashamed of him was I evasive. It was that I didn't want him calling to the door because of ma. It would have been questions. Then the marriage sermon. Then the baby sermon and, if not them, he'd get accused of being the milkman. Also there were those prayers she'd burst into at any moment, meaning there was just so much discomfiture I could take. So it wasn't shame of him, or to spare him, that we kept things convoluted and parlous by meeting at that dark and bitter sectarian flashpoint. It was to save me the awkwardness of having to explain her.

At that sunset with maybe-boyfriend which was before his bitter words over the pick-up point, he picked me up as usual on the road of separation and he did this in his latest put-together car. We took a drive out of town to some coastal place where he bought drinks and where we stood outside, along with strangers, all to await this event, this sun, which I didn't understand, go down. It wasn't just sunsets I didn't understand. I didn't understand stars or moons or breezes or dew or flowers or the weather or the avidity some people took — older people took — in what time they were going to bed at, and at what time the following day they were going to get up at, also what Celsius and Fahrenheit temperature it was outside, and what Celsius and Fahrenheit temperature it was inside, and the state of their bowels, their digestive tracts, their feet, their teeth, where one of them says loudly on the crowded bus, *'Do you know what? I'll have a nice slice of toast when I go home before my dinner,'* and where the companion replies equally loudly, *'I'll have a nice slice of toast in my house as a start before dinner too.'* If not that, then it's *'Did you have a nice slice of toast in your house yesterday?' 'Yes, but have you eaten yourself since?' 'Oh, I don't eat. Had scrambled eggs. Have this friend called Pam but stop me if I've already told you, but we used to go and buy kettles and ironing boards together . . .'* and it was entirely in order that I should not understand these things. Same too, with sunsets because it was not being labelled a beyond-the-pale young person and maybe-boyfriend, who was young himself — only two years older than me — shouldn't be understanding and appreciating either, what nobody our age would be odd enough to notice was there. Faced with his behaviour, and with this skyscape in front of me, and with the expectation I was supposed to observe it, witness it, attend in some way and have an appropriate reaction to it, I stood beside him and looked and nodded even though I didn't know what it was I was looking and nodding at. This was when I began to wonder, again, if maybe-boyfriend should be going to sunsets, if he should be owning coffee pots, if he should like football whilst giving the impression of not liking football, no matter I myself didn't like football but my not liking football, apart from that *Match of the Day* music, wasn't the point. Certainly he tinkered with cars and it was normal for boys to tinker with cars, to want to drive them, to dream of driving them if they couldn't afford to buy them to drive them and weren't sufficiently car-nutty to steal them to drive them. All the same, I did feel worried that maybe-boyfriend in some male way was refusing to fit in. Again this confused me for was I saying then, that I *was* ashamed of him, that mainstream boys, the ones who did fit in, the ones who wanted to beat up Julie Covington for singing 'Only Women Bleed' which they thought was a song about periods when it wasn't a song about periods even though everybody else, including me, also thought it was a song about periods; boys too, who, if they had an interest in you, would blame you for this interest in you — was I saying I preferred to be going on dates with the likes of them? Whenever I pondered this, which I didn't like to do for again it exposed to me my irreconcilables, those uncontrollable irrationalities, I felt uneasy. I knew I preferred maybe-boyfriend to any of my former maybe-boyfriends and that my favourite days of the week were the days I spent with maybe-boyfriend, that the only boy too, I'd wanted to sleep with so far and had slept with so far had been maybe-boyfriend. Also, given that since he'd brought up the idea of us living together and I'd refused, I found myself daydreaming of what it might be like to live with maybe-boyfriend — being in the same house as him, sharing the same bed as him, waking up every day right there beside him — could life together, if that were the case, really be that bad?

So I nodded at the sunset, at this horizon, which made no sense, all the while taken up with these contradictory sentiments, with maybe-boyfriend beside me, with all these odd people, also gazing upon the sunset, around me, and it was at that moment, just as I was thinking, *what the fuck are they* — that something out there — or something in me — then changed. It fell into place because now, instead of blue, blue and more blue — the official blue everyone understood and thought was up there — the truth hit my senses. It became clear as I gazed that there was no blue out there at all. For the first time I saw colours, just as a week later in this French class also was I seeing colours. On both occasions, these colours were blending and mixing, sliding and extending, new colours arriving, all colours combining, colours going on forever, except one which was missing, which was blue. Maybe-boyfriend had taken this in his stride, as had all those others standing about us. I said nothing, just as I said nothing a week later in this French class, but two sunsets in one week when before that there hadn't been any sunsets — that must mean something. Question was, was it a safe something or a threatening something? What was it, really, I was responding to here?

'Don't worry,' teacher then said. 'Your unease, even your temporary unhingement, dear students, in the face of this sunset is encouraging. It can only mean progress. It can only mean enlightenment. Please don't think you have betrayed or ruined yourselves.' She did more deep breathing then, hoping to encourage us by example into a more doughty and adventurous spirit. In the *littérateurs'* classroom, however, there was no sense of adventure, even less with the others than I think with me. At least I'd experienced the shock of the sky, the subversiveness of a sunset, and only a week previously, whereas from the look of them, and regardless of age, it seemed they were struggling with this encounter for the very first time. Of course the urge to panic was upon me also. I could feel it stirring in the air, as well as sense it coming in ripples, then in wave upon wave from the others. I think though, because I'd experienced this self-same panic during my earlier sunset, yet had discovered that by keeping still, by not letting it overwhelm me, gradually it had subsided, this time I was accepting of it and so, after a bit of tuning-in or tuning-out, and to get respite from what might have been, after all, a non-conforming, unfamiliar, restful consciousness, I glanced down to street level. This was when I saw a white van parked up the narrow entryway opposite. I froze, jolted out of the almost peaceful consciousness of just a moment before.

The bonnet of this van was peeping out of the entry, the entry running between the back of a row of drinking-bars on one side and the back of a line of businesses on the other. I managed to unfreeze enough to step away from the window in case he should be in there — with binoculars? telescope? camera? — looking up. And now I was thinking, *fool* — meaning me — for I'd considered myself successful, had taken cheer, self-congratulated in the belief I'd cracked the problem, that by reinstating my runs with third brother-in-law I'd succeeded in keeping this milkman away. So much for hypotheses. So much for inner boasting. Only a week gone by and already my circumvention of him had disintegrated. Why oh why had it not occurred to me that he'd switch tactics from pursuing me in the parks & reservoirs simply to resume interest in me from somewhere else?

Teacher started again. This time it was the fugacious (whatever that meant) black appearance of street trees owing to the crepuscular (whatever that meant) quality of the sky behind them, with the others — still in their own struggle — complaining that our town didn't have fugacity, crepuscules or

134

street trees, black or any colour, before being made to look again and conceding that okay, maybe we did have street trees but they must have been put in half an hour earlier as nobody here had noticed them before. During this, I was telling myself to wise up, to get a grip, that here I was, downtown, which meant that van could be anybody's van and how likely would it be anyway, that he'd so happen to park his vehicle right opposite the college where I so happened to have my night class? Very unlikely. Too coincidental. Therefore, couldn't be his. In proof of this, next time I leaned forward to peep, the van up that entryway was gone. With eagerness I sprang to recovery, forgetting the van, rejoining the class, the sky, the trees, whatever else they were now bickering about. At the same time I dismissed a strange bodily sensation that had run the lower back half of my body, during which the base of my spine had seemed to move. It *had* moved. Not a normal moving as in forward bends, backward bends, sideways and twistings. This had been a movement unnatural, an omen of warning, originating in the coccyx, with its vibration then setting off ripples — ugly, rapid, threatening ripples — travelling into my buttocks, gathering speed into my hamstrings from where, inside a moment, they sped to the dark recesses behind my knees and disappeared. This took one second, just one second, and my first thought — unbidden, unchecked — was that this was the underside of an orgasm, how one might imagine some creepy, back-of-body, partially convulsive shadow of an orgasm — *an anti-orgasm.* But then I dismissed this shiver, those currents, whatever they had been, and I returned to the window where some reactionary *'Fathers and forefathers!', 'Mothers and foremothers!', 'What's the harm in it — blue's utilitarian!'* were taking place. The majority of the class, however, remained subdued, also worried, for along with me, they knew that that sky that evening had been an initiation. And so quietness then came over us, which grew into complete silence. Teacher then sighed. Then we sighed. Then she led us back to our classroom, saying, 'Take further moments, dearest class, of calmness, of repose, of remembering what you have been gazing upon. Then we'll return to our literary passage and to those tropes in another language,' which, for the rest of the evening, was what we did.

I said goodbye on the college steps to

Siobhan, Willard, Russell, Nigel, Jason, Patrick, Kiera, Rupert of Earl and the rest because as usual they were heading to the bar to criticise the outrageousness and disharmony and the unfitness to be a teacher of our teacher, and of how we knew even less French now than in September when we joined. This time I didn't want to go because this was not the moment to be sitting down but one in which to think and always my thinking was at its best, its most flowering, whenever I was walking. So I set off and I didn't once consider taking *Castle Rackrent* out to read. I was too buzzy to read, thinking of teacher, of her manner of saying there were sunsets every day, that we weren't meant to be coffined and buried whilst all the time still living, that nothing of the dark was so enormous that never could we surmount it, that always there were new chapters, that we must let go the old, open ourselves to symbolism, to the most unexpected of interpretations, that we must too, uncover what we've kept hidden, what we think we might have lost. 'Implement a choice, dear class,' she said. 'Come out from those places. You never know,' she concluded, 'the moment of the fulcrum, the pivot, the turnaround, the instant when the meaning of it all will appear.' Well, weird.

But that was her philosophy and being philosophy, must not that mean God was in there somewhere? I wasn't sure how I felt about God being in there because, although she hadn't mentioned God, what would happen, given the delicate balance and the good manners existing in our class regarding religious sensitivities and the political problems when it came time and she did? As for this new sunset tradition, I'd had two in eight days which meant I needed only one more in order to do my homework. Teacher told us to describe three sunsets — 'in French if you like' — which betrayed, though we knew already, her priorities did not lie with that tongue. At her words there was further protest but milder protest, given that most of us were still dazed by the ensemble of that evening to work up our usual dissent and complaint.

So we packed up and left and they headed to the bar and I headed home towards my no-go area. After a bit of walking and thinking — about colour, about transformation, about upheavals of inner landscapes — I came out of my thoughts to give attention to my surroundings which was when I noticed I'd reached the ten-minute area on the outskirts of downtown. This ten-minute area wasn't officially called the ten-minute area. It was that it took ten minutes to walk through it. This would be hurrying, no dawdling, though no one in their right mind would think of dawdling here. Not that it was a politically hazardous place, that apart from the possibility of one of its dilapidated churches accidentally falling on you that something awful might happen to you in this spot because of the political problems. No. The political problems, for the duration of these minutes, seemed in comparison with this area to be naïve, clumsy, hardly of consequence. It was that the ten-minute area was, and always had been, some bleak, eerie, *Mary Celeste* little place.

It was shaped in a round, dominated by three giant churches spaced closely and evenly about its centre. These churches had long been out of action, disused, defeated, almost shells of buildings, though their black spires still towered up there in the sky. As a child I used to imagine those towers trying to touch tips, to converge, to make a witch's hat which everybody would then be forced to walk through. That had been the first noticeable thing for me all those years ago about this little place. Apart from the witch's hat, there were few other buildings and what there were also seemed deserted — supposed offices, a few residences — with nobody appearing to live in them or to work in them and people, should you happen to come across any, like you, would have their heads down as they too, went hurrying by. There were four shops in the circle but these were not classed as real shops despite their 'Open' signs, their unlocked doors, their clean fronts and the impression that life — not visible perhaps at that moment — was nevertheless going on behind them. Nobody was seen to go into these shops and no one was seen to come out of them; it was unclear even what kind of shops they were. There was a bus-stop too, outside one of the shops, the only bus-stop in the ten-minute area. It too, never had anybody; nobody waited to board from there and nobody ever alighted there. Then there was a letterbox which, apart from wee sisters posting something to themselves once during one of their many scientific investigatory moments to see if it would get delivered which it wasn't, nobody would dream of posting their post there. All this highlighted the ten-minute area as a ghostly place that simply you had to get through. After getting through, you moved on to your next landmark and I had seven landmarks that peripherally I'd tick off in my head as I read my book and walked along. The ten-minute area was my first landmark after leaving the boundary of downtown. Next came the cemetery which everybody, including the media, the paramilitaries, the state forces — even some postcards — termed 'the usual place'. After that was the police barracks followed by the house where always there was the smell of baking bread. After the bread house came the holy women's house where often they could be heard practising hymns, not once 'Ave Maria'. After the holy house came the parks & reservoirs through which, even if still light, at this time of night, never would I deviate and shortcut through. Instead I'd go the long way round and come to the street and the tiny house of third sister and third brother-in-law. This was the last of my personal landmarks because then came the few short residential roads which led to my street and my own front door. At present I was on the rim of entering the ten-minute area which of late had been disturbed within its own disturbance by a bomb going off in the centre of it. Because of this bomb, one of the three churches was no longer there.

At first the explosion had puzzled everybody. What was the point? There was no point. Why plant a bomb, said all parties, in a dead, creepy, grey place that everybody

141

knew was a dead, creepy, grey place and about which nobody would care anyway, if one day it was blown to kingdom come? The media suggested an accidental bomb, a premature bomb, perhaps a renouncer-of-the-state bomb in transit for the nearby police barracks; or maybe a defender-of-the-state bomb, intended for one of the opposite religion's segregated drinking establishments situated not far from the barracks but going the other way.

Whichever it had been, nobody had been killed by this bomb, just the unstable empty church which for decades had been unstable anyway, the reverberations of the blast completely bringing it down. So it had collapsed but the other two churches — still unstable, still on the brink — remained standing. The ghost shops too, were intact, their doors open, no windows broken, business as usual. The bus-stop also, still upright, still with nobody at it, so the place appeared not particularly more dead than it had been before the bomb had gone off. After official examination and forensic investigation and experts' reports, also after recriminations by one side against the other side, it transpired this bomb had been neither that of the renouncers nor that of the defenders. It had been an old bomb, a history bomb, an antiquity Greek and Roman bomb, a big, giant Nazi bomb. That was okay then, thought everybody. Not their side. Not our side. All slinging of accusation and of recrimination stopped.

'What is the provenance of the eeriness of the ten-minute area?' I asked ma once. 'You ask peculiar questions, daughter,' ma replied. 'Not as peculiar as those posed by wee sisters,' I said, 'and you answer them as if they were normal questions,' meaning their latest at breakfast. 'Mammy,' they'd said, 'mought it happen that if you were a female and excessively sporty and this thing called menstruation stopped inside you because you were excessively sporty' — wee sisters had recently discovered menstruation in a book, not yet through personal experience — 'then you stopped being excessively sporty and your menstruation returned, would that mean you'd have extra time of menstruation to make up for the gap of not having had it when you should have had it only you couldn't because your sportiness was blocking the production of your follicle-stimulating hormone, also blocking your luteinising hormone from instructing your oestrogen to stimulate the uterine lining in expectation of an egg to be fertilised with the subsequent insufficiency of hormones and oestrogen preventing the release of the egg to be fertilised or — should the egg be released but not fertilised — to the degeneration of the corpus luteum and the shedding of the endometrium or, mammy, would your menstruation stop at the time it was biologically programmed to stop regardless of the months or years of excessive sportiness when your menses didn't come?' Ma conceded that yes, she did do this, that she treated wee sisters' questions as if they were normal questions, but that wee sisters were wee sisters — even their teachers said so — meaning that always they were to be untoward and strange in their querying and acquiring of knowledge, whereas, she said, being of a different cerebration from the wee ones, she had hoped I would have grown out of all of that by now. Then she said she didn't know, but that always that ten-minute area had been a strange, eerie, grey place, that even in her mother's day, in her grandmother's day, in antebellum days — had there been any — still it had been an eerie, grey place, a place attempting perhaps to transcend some dark, evil happening without managing to transcend it and instead succumbing to it, giving in to it, coming to want it, to wallow in it, even, in fact, deteriorating so far in character as to feel a great need for it, dragging down too, she said, neighbouring places along with it when who knows? — she shrugged — there mayn't have been anything evil that happened in it in the first place. 'Some locations are just stuck,' said ma. 'And deluded. Like some people. Like your da' — which would be the point when I'd regret having opened my mouth. Anything — be it in any way dark, any way into the shadow, anything to do with what she called 'the psychologicals' — always it brought her back to the subject of, and especially to the denigration of, her husband, my da. 'Back then,' she'd say, meaning the olden days, meaning her days, their days, 'even then,' she said, 'I never understood your father. When all was said and done, daughter, what had *he* got to be psychological about?'

She meant depressions, for da had had them: big, massive, scudding, whopping, black-cloud, infectious, crow, raven, jackdaw, coffin-upon-coffin, catacomb-upon-catacomb, skeletons-upon-skulls-upon-bones crawling along the ground to the grave type of depressions. Ma herself didn't get depressions, didn't either, tolerate depressions and, as with lots of people here who didn't get them and didn't tolerate them, she wanted to shake those who did until they caught themselves on. Of course at that time they weren't called depressions. They were 'moods'. People got 'moods'. They were 'moody'. Some people who got these moods stayed in bed, she said, with long faces on them, emanating atmospheres of monotonal extended sameness, of tragedy, of affliction, influencing everybody too, with their monotones and long faces and continuous extended samenesses whether or not they ever opened their mouths. You only had to look at them, she said. In fact, you only had to walk in the door and you could sense coming from upstairs, from his room, their room, the exudation of his moody, addicted atmosphere. And — should the moody be of the type who did manage to get out of bed — that hardly precluded them, she said, from blanketing the atmosphere as well. Again with long faces and unvaried pitch they'd be at it, slouching down the street, dragging themselves over the terrain, round and about and down the town in their epidemic grim fashion, infecting everybody and — given they'd got out of bed — they'd be doing this on a much wider, enveloping scale. 'What these people with the moods and heavy matter should realise,' said ma — and not just once would she say this but almost anytime da was mentioned in a conversation — 'is that life's hard for everybody. It's not just for them it's hard so why should they get preferential treatment? You've got to take the rough with the smooth, get on with life, pull yourself together, be respected. There are some people, daughter,' she said, 'people with much more reason for psychologicals, with more cause for suffering than those who help themselves to suffering — but you don't see them giving in to darkness, giving in to repinement. Instead with courage they continue on their path, refusing, these legitimate people, to succumb.'

So ma would be back to her onwards-and-upwards talk, to her hierarchy of suffering: those who were allowed it; those who were allowed it but fell down badly by outstaying their quota in it; those who, like da, were upstart illegitimates, stealing the right to suffer that belonged to somebody else. 'Your da,' she said. 'Your da. Do you know that even his sister said he'd lie abed during the sirens with places around him on fire and not go to the shelters with the other people? Only young too — sixteen, maybe seventeen — with me twelve years old at the time and having more sense than he had. Crazy. Wanting those bombs to fall on him. Crazy,' which at first time of hearing — for this was not first time — also before my own depressions started — I used to think was crazy too. And now she was talking of the big war, that world one, the second one, the one — ask any teenager — with nothing to do with up-to-date humanity and modern-society living; the one no one my age could attend to which wasn't surprising, given most of us could hardly attend to the current, more local one, we were in. 'After the war,' said ma, 'even after we married, for years until his death, and especially when the sorrows started, all you'd get would be him burying his head in them dark things.' She meant his newspapers, his tomes, his logs, his collecting and collating of everything to do with the political problems; meeting up too, with likeminded friends exactly as brooding, obsessive and overhung with cliffs, crags, ravens, crows and skeletons as him. They would share their docking and filing, their categorising, their updating of all the tragedies of the political problems, to the extent too, that it seemed as if it were their job to do it when it wasn't their job to do it and of course da, after a bit, couldn't keep it up. Even we, his children, could see that all that hyper-engrossment, all that exactitude, the fixation, had to crash at some point. And it would, with him collapsing with it, plunging headlong from ledgering, from scrapbooking, from all his prescriptive newspaper-cutting, only to sink down deep again into despondency when all he'd be fit for then would be his bed, the hospital, his comics, his sports pages, or those Holocaust programmes on the TV. Natural disaster programmes too, such as David Attenborough talking about insects eating other insects and ferocious wildlife pouncing upon gentle wildlife. Never would he watch programmes about heather or how to keep butterflies in happy, carefree countenance. Those types of programmes never drew him, never interested him, wouldn't ever, as ma put it, 'be allowed to cheer him up'. Of course the whole household knew that the Holocaust and the world wars and animals eating other animals, all those anaesthetics which also included our political problems when he could get back to them didn't cheer him up either. It was clear though, they served some purpose, some sense of *'See! Look at that. What's the point? There's no point,'* thus confirming for him, solacing him even, in his despair, that as things stood, as always they'd stood, there couldn't be triumphs and overcomings because overcomings were fancies and triumphs were daydreams, effort and renewed effort a vain waste of time. 'I knew your da was in a good way,' said ma, 'when he'd sing, and I knew he was in a bad way when he'd lie abed all day, be up all night, not sleeping, not opening curtains, instead filling in chinks, blocking out the nightlight and all the natural daylight. His melancholy, daughter. Not natural. If it were natural, would he not have felt good on it? Would he not have looked well on it? But what reason, what reason, tell me, had he for keeping himself always in that dark, brooding place?'

So with da and his type, unlike ma and her type, it wasn't a case of *'I must be cheerful because of the Holocaust'* or *'I've a boil on my nose but yer man down the street's missing a nose so I must be cheerful he's missing a nose whereas I'm not missing a nose and he must be cheerful because of the Holocaust.'* With da it was never *'Must get down on knees and give thanks that others in the world are suffering far worse than me'.* I couldn't see how he couldn't be right too, because everybody knew life didn't work like that. If life worked like that then all of us — except the person agreed upon to have the most misfortune in the world — would be happy, yet most people I knew weren't happy. Neither in this workaday world, in this little human-being world, did we spend time counting blessings and eschewing the relative in favour of the eternal. That relative, that temporal plane — where sensitivities vary, where no one has the same personal history even if they have the same communal history, where something which is a trigger for one person passes off unnoticed by another person — definitely was the plane where the raw living of life and the imperfect mental response to that living of life took place. Even ma and her type — for all their intolerance of depressives and of especially getting down on knees in the face of tragedies to offer thanks that there for the grace of God would have gone them only some other poor buggers had been selected by God to suffer such dreadful fates instead of them — even they didn't rest easy. As for the few, those very few who did seem to rest easy, or who at least continued to give off a constant goodwill and a trust in people and in life even in the face of not exactly resting easy, well, both ma and her type, and da and his type, pretty much everybody I knew, including me, had difficulty coming to terms with that type too.

My attention was first brought to the issue of the shiny people, those rare, baffling, radiant type of people, by that film, *Rear*

Window. I saw it when I was twelve and it unnerved me because of what I believed initially to be its point. A little dog gets killed, strangled, neck broken, which is not the message of the film but for me was the message of the film because its owner — bereft, in shock — wails out her window over all the apartment building, *'Which one of you did it? . . . couldn't imagine . . . so low you'd kill a little helpless friendly . . . only thing in this whole neighbourhood who liked anybody. Did you kill him because he liked you, just because he liked you?'* and it was that *'killing him because he liked you'* that caused shivers to go down my spine. I knew immediately, *oh God! It's true! That is why they killed it! They killed it because it liked them!* Turned out that wasn't why the dog was killed but before I discovered the real reason, absolutely it made sense to me, in the world I was in, that it had happened that way. They killed it because it liked them, because they couldn't cope with being liked, couldn't cope with innocence, frankness, openness, with a defencelessness and an affection and purity so pure, so affectionate, that the dog and its qualities had to be done away with. Couldn't bear it. Had to kill it. Probably they themselves would have viewed this as self-defence. And that was the trouble with the shiny people. Take a whole group of individuals who weren't shiny, maybe a whole community, a whole nation, or maybe just a statelet immersed long-term on the physical and energetic planes in the dark mental energies; conditioned too, through years of personal and communal suffering, personal and communal history, to be overladen with heaviness and grief and fear and anger — well, these people could not, not at the drop of a hat, be open to any bright shining button of a person stepping into their environment and shining upon them just like that. As for the environment, that too, would object, backing up the pessimism of its people, which was what happened where I lived where the whole place always seemed to be in the dark. It was as if the electric lights were turned off, always turned off, even though dusk was over so they should have been turned on yet nobody was turning them on and nobody noticed either, they weren't on. All this too, seemed normality which meant then, that part of normality here was this constant, unacknowledged struggle to see. I knew even as a child — maybe because I was a child — that this wasn't really physical; knew the impression of a pall, of some distorted quality to the light had to do with the political problems, with the hurts that had come, the troubles that had built, with the loss of hope and absence of trust and with a mental incapacitation over which nobody seemed willing or able to prevail. The very physical environment then, in collusion with, or as a result of, the human darkness discharging within it, didn't itself encourage light. Instead the place was sunk in one long, melancholic story to the extent that the truly shining person coming into this darkness ran the risk of not outliving it, of having their own shininess subsumed into it and, in some cases — if the person was viewed as intolerably extra-bright and extra-shiny — it might even reach the point of that individual having to lose his or her physical life. As for those living in the dark, long attuned to the safeness of the dark, this wasn't wee buns for them either. *What if we accept these points of light, their translucence, their brightness; what if we let ourselves enjoy this, stop fearing it, get used to it; what if we come to believe in it, to expect it, to be impressed upon by it; what if we take hope and forgo our ancient heritage and instead, and infused, begin to entrain with it, with ourselves then to radiate it; what if we do that, get educated up to that, and then, just like that, the light goes off or is snatched away?* This was why you didn't get many shining people in environments overwhelmingly consisting of fear and of sorrow. In this environment which was my environment, there existed but a few. There was French teacher from downtown. Then perhaps there might have been, were it not for the state of his hoarding, maybe-boyfriend. The only person though, in my own neighbourhood who was unanimously agreed upon to be one of the rare shining was the sister of our district poisoner, tablets girl. This sister was my age, which meant younger than tablets girl, and it wasn't that everybody wanted to dislike her. Indeed part of the problem was we didn't dislike her. It was that it was hard to deal with the threat she posed by going about completely holding her own. She was translucent, untouched by our darkness, walking in her light in our darkness. Strangely though, she herself was very ordinary about this. Instead of taking hope from whom she was and from what she represented — especially as she came from our area yet had managed to get beyond the prevailing temperament and thought-race of this area; instead of thinking, *why, if this one person can do it, can walk abroad with all this sunlight playing about her and within her, then perhaps we* . . . ? But no. Easier to remain unchallenged at our diminished acculturated level; also to designate tablets girl's sister as similar to her sister, that is, a full-on, ostracised, district beyond-the-pale.

So shiny was bad, and 'too sad' was bad, and 'too joyous' was bad, which meant you had to go around not being anything; also not thinking, least not at top level, which was why everybody kept their private thoughts safe and sound in those recesses underneath. As for da and ma, da went too much *'the long face'* way, and ma too forcibly the *'onwards and upwards'* way, with da periodically breaking down and having to go to hospital, and with ma subsequently forgetting *'onwards and upwards'* and getting angry at him for yet again abandoning her with us in this place. For years I didn't know, along with the younger in my family, that da was going into hospital, also that it was a mental hospital. We thought, because we were told, that whenever he disappeared he was off to long hours of work, long days of work, lengthy weeks of work in some faraway town or country or, if not that, that he was seeing some specialist doctor far away because of the pains he was getting in his back. But it was mental hospitals, and it was mental breakdowns, which meant cover-up, which meant shame, which meant even more shame in his case because he was a man. Males and mental hospitals went together far less than females and mental hospitals went together. In a man's case, this equalled a gender falling-down in pursuance of his duties, totalling a failure above all to keep face. Again, at first, I didn't understand. Didn't know either, that ma, under emotional pressure, under peer pressure, shame pressure, was presenting her take on da's illness to the neighbours, who of course had their own take on it themselves. *'Faraway work in faraway lands, our backsides,'* they'd say, and ma knew this, which was why she blamed da — even after he became no longer living — even more. Often it seemed she didn't love him but instead she hated him. 'Sad story!' she'd flounce. 'What sad story? No pain really. All in his head really. Nothing out there really.' And she'd pretend, though wouldn't be able, to shrug da off. I hated it when ma did this, when she'd speak ill like this, especially to us to whom she should not run down our father. But she'd continue because once started, she'd fixate on his fixating to the point where, primed and triggered and far, far too angry, she'd have to run the course because she couldn't stop. I used to puzzle over the extent of this anger, of all of ma's blaming and haranguing and complaining. It was only much later that I came to realise that this was a case of her not forgiving him for many things — maybe for all things — and not just for not cheering up.

That was what she did. She brought this unforgiveness into every tenuous connection, into such too, as the ten-minute area. Like da, according to ma, it also entertained no hope to brighten up. 'Too stuck,' she said, 'too lingering, too brooding. There's no rhyme or reason for it, daughter. It's imaginary — that's its provenance, meaning it has no provenance.' 'I see,' I said, which of course, regarding the mystery and signature of the ten-minute area, I did not. And now here I was, walking through it, initially mindful of sky and of our teacher, of her words on light and dark and our automatic response of *'Dark! We'll have the dark please!'* As for the Nazi bomb, most of the wreckage had by this point been cleared. The ground was still bumpy, not yet flattened, with the site where the church had stood probably *not* to be turned into a carpark in the way other bombed places here usually ended as carparks. The historical and inexplicable desolation of this ten-minute area would put paid to any possible desire on the part of anybody to come and park their car here.

There were a few smaller bits of broken masonry still, and they were to be stepped over, skirted around, which was what I was doing as I made my way through and on towards my next landmark. Glancing up towards it, towards the graveyard, I noticed for the first time trees within it, which brought me back to the sky having earlier been green. But if green can be up there, I wondered, or sometimes up there, does not that mean the ground, also at times, can be blue? This had me glancing to the ground and this time I saw that there was something on it. Lying to the side amidst the uncleared rubble was a decapitated, still furry, matted-furry, little cat's head. The face was turned to the ground, the ground here consisting of bombed-up concrete. My first impression was that of a child's ball, some toy, a play-moneybag pretending to be a real moneybag, with animal-like ears and fur and whiskers. But it was a cat, the head of a cat, one that had been alive up until that explosion. Something had died then, I realised, in that bomb from long ago after all.

Cats are not adoring like dogs. They don't

care. They can never be relied upon to shore up a human ego. They go their way, do their thing, are not subservient and will never apologise. No one has ever come across a cat apologising and if a cat did, it would patently be obvious it was not being sincere. As for dead cats — as in the deliberate killing of cats, killing them as a matter of course — I have come across that many times. The days of my childhood was when I would come across it, during the time cats were vermin, subversive, witch-like, the left hand, bad luck, feminine — though no one ever came out and levelled the feminine except during drunkenness with the drunkenness — should violence then ensue towards some hapless female — later being blamed for the cause. Men and boys killed the cats, or at least in default of killing them, kicked them or catapulted them with stones on passing. It was one of those things that happened, so you didn't mention the occasions when you happened to come across a dead cat. As for myself, I did not kill cats, did not want to be around either, the killing of them. So conditioned was I, however, by those times, by a learned revulsion, that I feared to come across one that was living even more than seeing one that was dead. I would have dreaded the contact, would have screamed myself silly to have touched one. Lots of cats then, years ago, dead. Dogs, on the other hand, were in abundance and absolutely they were okay. Dogs were sturdy, loyal, feudal, good for man's account of himself and with a slavish need to be obedient to someone. Acceptable therefore. To be proud of. To be viewed as vicious, as protective and everybody had one but that didn't save them either, because one night nearly all of them, bar two of them, got killed as well. They got killed once, the dead dogs, all at once, and this great canicide, as opposed to the casual, everyday felicide, also took place in my childhood, took place too, in a macabre, spectacular fashion when the soldiery from 'over the water' slit the district's dogs' throats in the middle of one night. They left the dead bodies in a giant heap, strategically placed at the top of one of the entries, those same entries where usually the milkcrates of ragged-up petrol bombs would be stacked for the next district riot that would take place at some point during that same day. Everybody knew it had been the soldiers, that it had been a statement by them to teach us, the natives, a lesson, to announce they could deal with our dogs, could overcome our dogs barking and snarling and warning renouncers of their presence. Our dogs though, had never been just about that.

It had been for the benefit of all of us that they should bark and snarl and be alarm dogs, not just for the benefit of the renouncers. By doing so, our dogs alerted everyone, particularly all boys and men — young men, older men, renouncers, non-renouncers — for males got it worse — to the presence of those soldiers, who'd arrive in saturated numbers in their armoured cars and vehicles from which they'd leap out and patrol with heightened suspicion all our streets around. Everyone appreciated the early warning system the dogs offered owing to the few moments' leeway it afforded, because in that manner easier it was, usually, to get oneself out of their way. It wasn't agreeable to go out your door otherwise, and to be stopped on the street and, outnumbered and at gunpoint, ordered to answer questions, to spread against a wall, to be searched against that wall — beside the entries, the tops of those entries — to stay put in that exact search position for as long as those soldiers thought appropriate; not agreeable either, to be smirked at by these grown men with their guns, should you — the wife, the sister, the mother, the daughter — come out your door to bear witness to what was being done to your son, your brother, your husband or your father. Especially was it not agreeable when it was made clear that your son or your brother or your husband or your father would stay put against that wall for as long as you remained there, being witness to what was going on. So do you continue? Do you stand strong? Do you bear witness, even if, in the process, you cause more suffering and prolonged humiliation for your son or your brother or your husband or your father? Or do you go away, back inside, abandoning your son or your brother or your husband or your father to these people? If not that, then it couldn't possibly be agreeable to any woman coming out her door to have the drip-drip effect of sexual comments made to her, goaded by those lewdsters of the very bad remark. *'Your boot,'* they'd say. *'Your box,'* they'd say. *'Your suitability for doxiness.'* Then, *'What we'd do to your face if . . .'* or something like that, and again with their guns and barely contained, often uncontained, emotions, spilling out over the brim. Naturally — or maybe not naturally but understandably — it wouldn't be untoward for the girl or the woman on the receiving end of this language to think, *if a renouncer-sniper from some upstairs window takes your head off now with a rifle-shot, soldier, not only would your passing not chagrin me, I think it would be a pleasant, mentally relieving, charming, karmic thing.* So this was hatred. It was great hatred, the great Seventies hatred. One must set aside too, the misleading and cumbersome inadequacy of the political problems, and all rationalisations and choice conclusions about the political problems, in order appropriately to gauge the weight of this hatred. As someone, a very ordinary person from 'over the road', once said on TV, succinctly too, because he wanted to kill every person of my religion in my area — which meant everybody in my area — in retaliation for some renouncer-of-the-state from my area walking over the road and bombing to death many people of his religion in his area, *'It's amazing the feelings that are in you.'* And he was right. It is amazing, no matter it may not be yourself who pulls the trigger in the end.

And that was why the dogs were necessary. They were important, a balancing act, an interface, a safety buffer against instant, face-to-face, mortal clashes of loathsome and self-loathsome emotions, the very type that erupt in seconds between individuals, between clans, between nations, between sexes, doing irreversible damage all around. To stay it, to evade it, to push away those bad memories, all that pain and history and deterioration of character, you hear the barking, the onset of that savage, tribal barking, and you know then to wait indoors — quarter of an hour thereabouts — to let that soldiery go its way. In that manner you don't come into contact, you don't have to feel the powerlessness, the injustice, or worst of all, how you — a normal, ordinary, very nice human being — could want to kill or take relief at a killing. And, if you're already out there on the street which is the battlefield which is the street when you hear that sudden barking, well, simply you listen and determine by its direction which way those soldiers are heading and, should they be heading your way, easily then, to nip down a sideway into another, less-exposing street. But they killed the dogs, taking out the middlemen, and so, until such times as new dogs were to be born and bred and schooled in partisanship in our area, it appeared we were back to that close-up, face-to-face, early ancient hatred. First though, on the morning after the night of the dog-slaying, and confronting the reality of that enormity of corpses, came the equally face-to-face local response.

Mostly it was silence. Or at first silence, with one dog — initially considered the last surviving dog in the district — looking on along with the rest of us, whimpering periodically, its tail drawn deeply in between its legs. As for myself, it seemed to me, at nine years old, that there were so many of these dogs that the district could never have contained the overrun of them, that the soldiers must have bussed in extra, but once the locals started to identify and to claim them, they claimed all of them, every single one. Also to my child eyes, and to those of third brother who was standing beside me, it seemed the heads of all these dogs, amidst this huge stack of dogs, were missing. We thought they'd been beheaded. 'Mammy! The heads! They took the heads! Where are the heads?' we cried. 'Where's Lassie, mammy? Where's daddy? Have the brothers found Lassie? Where's daddy? Where's Lassie?' And we tugged at her coat, then third brother began to cry. His crying set me off, then the both of us set off all the other children. Then the last surviving dog began to howl as well. There were many of us that day, many children, and we huddled and clung to our adults. So at first there was the silence, then there was our crying, then, at the sound of our crying, the adults galvanised themselves into action and set their shock aside. They began to deal with the massacre, with the males — young men, older men, renouncers, non-renouncers — beginning to wade through the slimy, pelty mass. They disentangled the heavy sogginess and the swampiness to differentiate one body from another body, passing each through and along the chain to whoever had come to claim it, was waiting for it, to bring it home on go-carts, in prams, in wheelbarrows, in supermarket trolleys or, more often, bundled up as something that used to be alive in their arms. As for da, I remember third brother's urgency and my own in asking for him, in pleading for him to be there, to be a man among men, doing normal men things, as he did manage to do years later when searching with the others for Somebody McSomebody's brother's head. Perhaps the day of the dogs though, had been a bad day, one of his bed days, hospital days, a Holocaust or an ancient, yellowed, boxing-magazine day. Whichever it had been, he wasn't there. But the brothers were there and, along with the others, they were digging and it seemed right through to the earth. They were in the middle of the earth, gone below, and still they were digging. I added shovels to them and in my head they were digging with these shovels, the ground now sodden, with the brothers and the men up to their waists. Clots, clumps, streaks, getting redder, browner, darker, stickier — getting black — as they dug down deep to get those dogs out. I remember the sight of the brothers, of all our dogs, of us, the surrounding people. I remember not a thing though, of any death smell. At one point third brother cried, 'The dogs are moving! MAMMY! THE DOGS ARE MOVING!' and I looked and they were moving, tiny heavings up and down. Our mother too, I remember — her stoniness, her lack of response to our tugging, to our 'LASSIE, MAMMY!', 'WHERE'S DADDY, MAMMY?', 'THE DOGS ARE MOVING, MAMMY!' Eventually, someone, second sister, explained. She said the heads were still there, that they were bent back, meaning, I realised later, that the throats were cut so deeply towards the bone that it looked to our eyes as if the heads were missing. This explanation seemed easier on the mind, I think too, on third brother's mind, that the heads should still be there than that they should be missing, than that the soldiers had taken them to make fun of them, to kick them, to prolong the dishonouring of them; or maybe it was relief at being given any explanation at all. We carried on crying, however, as did other children, especially when a particular dog was brought out or as panic heightened in anticipation of a particular dog. There were waves of hope too, that maybe they weren't dead because yes, they were moving. 'They are not moving,' said the adults, then finally, we became too much in our hopeful despair that some older siblings were instructed to take us younger ones home.

First and second sister brought third brother and me home, and at this time we were the youngest in the family. We two continued to look back, to cast back, taking long last backward glances, our minds full of Lassie as we went from that entry where still the brothers and the other males were. These were our dogs, and they were street dogs, meaning every day you put your dog out onto the street to have adventures just as you put your children out to have adventures. At night-time the dogs and children would return except that night the children returned but the dogs did not. So brother and I were led home, away from that entry, with our older sisters' arms about us. Still we glanced back until nearing the house when new hope sprang within us again. Although the other dogs had died, bar one, and although she'd stayed out all night just as the dead dogs had stayed out all night, maybe Lassie had returned and was even now in the house. So we picked up speed and rushed in the door and there was Lassie. She was lying by the hearth and she lifted her head and growled at us — opening doors on her perhaps? Letting in draughts and disturbing her perhaps? Lassie was no pedigree, as none of these dogs had been pedigree. She had no qualifications, no certificates, wasn't playful, wasn't vocational, not one to fetch help for those in danger or to save children from drowning. Lassie had no time for children, for the young of the family, but for us it was the happiest day to see her and to hear her, to know she had a throat still to growl and be petulant with. We didn't fall on her of course, because Lassie wouldn't have liked that. But it was a very bad morning until she reappeared. After that, I forgot. I forgot the dogs, their death, the district grief, the shock, the undoubted triumph of the soldiers. That evening after dinner, still nine years old, I set out on my latest adventures, passing that same entry which was now stacked as usual with petrol bombs for the next district riot. There was no hint of dead dogs although I did get a whiff of that powerful cleaner, Jeyes Fluid. *That* I would remember, given that up until that moment always I'd loved that particular household smell.

So the soldiers killed the dogs, and the locals killed the cats, and now cats were also being killed by the Luftwaffe. I glanced at the little head lying in the detritus and I felt jolted as I hadn't remembered ever feeling jolted, not understanding why either, in this instance I was having this strong response. I dealt with it by averting my eyes, by walking firmly on, yet it stayed with me. It carried on accompanying me until I found myself stopping and turning round. I retraced my steps and was again beside the head and this time I looked closely and saw that it was wet, a bit black, blood-black, soggier at the neck, or where the neck had used to be. I got down on my hunkers and with a bit of rubble, edged the head around. Its face now fully upwards, I saw it was recognisable still as a cat, bigger eyes perhaps, or bigger sockets because one of the eyes was missing. The empty socket was huge and the head itself had something going on inside. Insect activity was what I thought, and as proof I saw clumps, bulges — at the nose, the ears, the mouth, and the remaining eye had a bulge also. There were a few

171

sluggish maggots visible, though as yet, and apart from something sweetish and yeast-like, there wasn't much of a smell. As for the rest of the body, I glanced around but I couldn't see it. The head by itself though, was enough for now. Then it was too much. I stood and walked away again because that French class had been nice. I'd enjoyed it, as always I enjoyed it — the eccentricity of teacher, her talk of that *'still, small voice'*, of *'living in the moment'*, of *'abandoning what you think should happen for what then might happen'*. There was too, her *'Change one thing, class, just one thing, and I assure you, everything else will change also'* — and to say that to *us,* to people who were not only not into metaphors, but not into admitting to what patently was there. But it had felt valuable. She felt valuable, and I didn't want to lose that feeling. It seemed though, that with this head in the dirt — and before that, the van, the ten-minute area, the war-time bomb which had brought up dead da and his depressions with ma attacking him for his depressions — already all that *'What's the point? There's no use in having any point?'* had started to reappear. *'Attempts and repeated attempts,'* teacher had said. *'That's the way to do it.'* But what if she was wrong

172

about attempts and repeated attempts, about moving on to next chapters? What if the next chapter was the same as this chapter, as had been the last chapter? What if all chapters stayed the same or even, as time went on, got worse? Again, during my thoughts, I had physically brought myself back to the cat, retracing my steps as if having no choice in the matter. *Don't be daft,* I said. *What are you going to do — stand forever and just stare at it?* I'll pick it up, I answered. I'll take it to some green. Now, this surprised me. It astonished me. Then I astonished me with hedges, bushes, the root of a tree. I could cover it, not leave it in this open awful place. *But why?* I argued. *In less than one minute you could be out of here. You could have reached the graveyard, your second landmark. Then it'll be the police barracks, then the soothing smell of cinnamon from that house with the bakery, then —* Of course! I interrupted. The usual place!

Already I had my handkerchiefs out, and these were real hankies, fabric, not paper, and not that long ago they used only to be male ones, those big white linen ones, because pretty as the female ones were, they weren't much for blowing your nose. I grew to appreciate them, however, after being presented with a boxed set by wee sisters one Christmastime. Since then, I'd carry a female one for cultural, aesthetic purposes and a male one for practical purposes and that evening I intended putting both to practical and symbolic use. First, I opened out onto the ground the small, dainty, female one, then with the big, plain, male one, gently I nudged the head over onto it. As I did so, I could feel the cat's front fangs pricking through the fabric and the skin on its head begin to slide. Some hair loosened and here I panicked, thinking the skull was going to slip from its covering. But then, mission accomplished, and with the head in the middle of the female, I wrapped the fancy embroidered cotton all around. After that I placed the female hankie containing the head onto the now spread-out big male hankie, wrapping that one around as well. *Proof of madness,* I continued. *You're actually going to walk up the road with a head, knowing full well that no matter how deserted a place seems, at least one person somewhere is watching? This means more gossip, more fabrication, more elaboration on the deterioration of your character.* In that moment though, I didn't care. Besides, I couldn't stop myself. It would be only a moment, I estimated, because quickly I'd find the right spot — a place of privacy, of quietness, by the far wall perhaps, where the ancient plots were, where the ground was tangled and clumpy with unmown grass that the gravetenders never bothered their arses with. By now I had tied the ends of the big hankie together and was all for fulfilling on my intention when I stood up and almost collided with the milkman. So silent had he been, and so engrossed had I been, that I hadn't sensed his presence. Now he was inches from me, and I from him, with only those hankies, with their dark, dead contents, acting as buffer in between.

First thing that happened was again I got those spine shivers, those scrabblings, the scuttlings, all that shiddery-shudderiness inside me, from the bottom of my backbone right into my legs. Instinctively everything in me then stopped. Just stopped. All my mechanism. I did not move and he did not move. Standing there, neither of us moved, nor spoke, then he spoke, saying, 'At your Greek and Roman class, were you?' and this was the only thing, ever, in his profiling of me that the milkman got wrong. Not that I hadn't considered Greek and Roman, as in Greek and Roman Classical Studies instead of French for my night class. I'd been attracted by those ancient peoples — their uncontained emotions, their unprincipled characters, their myths, rituals, all that macabre, outlandish, paranoiac scheming and purging. Then there were their capricious gods and the curses the common people supplicated from these gods to have put on all their enemies, these enemies turning out to be the very people next door. It was all very alice in wonderland, as were those immodest Caesars marrying apple trees and making consuls out of their horses. Something there interesting, something psychological, something not normal that a normal person with only acceptable aberrations could get their head around. This was why I got as far as perusing the prospectus to see if I could enrol in this night class, but Greek and Roman was on Tuesday nights and maybe-boyfriend was my Tuesday nights, so French being Wednesday became my choice instead. That meant the milkman got it wrong and I didn't correct him for getting it wrong because it gave me hope that in the middle of his knowing everything he didn't know everything. Not real hope though, as I was to realise when I got home and did a deconstruction on this later on. He'd read my thoughts about the class, yes, and they'd been top-level thoughts, thoughts from the topsoil, meaning unimportant, not secret, not vulnerable enough to be encrypted. Any of those Toms, Dicks and Harrys therefore, had they been inclined, easily, very easily, could have walked in. All the same, he'd read them when he hadn't even been near me during the time I'd been thinking them. This struck me as eerie, indicative too, of a thorough research carried out by a man who gleaned, docketed and filed each and every bit of information, even if on this occasion he mistook the outcome in the end.

As on the last two occasions of our meeting, that is, of his orchestrating of our meeting, this time too, mostly he asked questions, though without appearing anxious for any response. This was because his questions weren't real questions. Not sincere requests for information or for confirmation of his surmises. These were statements of assertion, rhetorical power comments, hints, warnings, to let me know he was in the business of knowing already, with those tag-on *'weren't you?', 'didn't you?', 'isn't that right?', 'is not that so?'* appended for pretence of query at the end. So he made his remark about the Greek and Roman and as he was doing so, I thought of that van, that white van, and of how it must have been his all along up that entry. Was he following me then? Had he been sitting in that van all the time I'd been in my French lesson, watching me, watching the others, noting our anxiety as we underwent our sunset? And again he was talking as if he knew me, as if previously in some appropriate manner we'd been introduced to each other. This time too, as in the parks & reservoirs, he was looking aslant and not directly at me; more of a gaze to the side of me. Then it was another question, this one about maybe-boyfriend, someone he hadn't made reference to until this point.

He did so in the manner of it being time, that it was time, was it not, that we should have our little discussion about this so-called, kind of, boyfriend? He said, 'That guy you see sometimes, the young guy,' and he said 'young guy' as if maybe-boyfriend was too young, as if he wasn't two years older than myself. 'You dance with the young guy at the clubs outside your area and inside his area, don't you? At those few clubs in town too, and the others up around the university? You go drinking with the young guy, yeah?' Here he listed specific bars, exact places, days, times, then said he'd noticed I didn't always catch the weekday bus now into town. He didn't mean the morning bus I used to get that he'd spoken of last time, but already the new one that recently, in attempts to evade him, I'd gone out of my way to catch. That was because, he said, on certain mornings I'd get a lift to work from the young guy after spending the night in the young guy's house. So he knew maybe-boyfriend's house, his district, also his name, who his mates were, where he worked, even that he used to work in that car factory that had to close that time with the entire workforce made redundant. He knew too, that I slept with maybe-boyfriend and here I became annoyed for feeling myself caught because of the connotations that could be, and that I knew were being, implied by those words. 'Not a date though, is he?' he said. 'Not a proper dating, nothing steady, nothing established, something you're treading water with, isn't he?' during which I was wrong-footed because if I'd been expecting anything from this milkman at this, our third meeting, it would have been reproof at my continuing to go running when, according to him, I should not only be pacing myself by walking-during-running but also, shouldn't anymore be walking because — had he not said last time? — I did too much walking, therefore a disappointment to him that here I was, still doing both. Not only

179

that, I was doing the running with third brother-in-law in the parks & reservoirs. But he didn't mention third brother-in-law, nor my continued use of legs, nor the parks & reservoirs. Completely therefore, was I thrown by this new line of talk.

He said — just a tiny mention — that the young guy still worked with cars, didn't he? So now it was the exact whereabouts of maybe-boyfriend's current place of work. He said too, about the Blower Bentley. Then it was that supercharger. Then that flag from 'over the water' which was when the rapidities at the back of my legs took on an unpleasant rhythmic hold. He had down all maybe-boyfriend's routine, all his movements, just as he had down my routine and my movements. Then he said the young guy liked sunsets and he said this as if it were an incongruity that anyone — particularly anyone male — should even notice sunsets, as if in all his years of researching, of shadowing and of setting people up to be murdered, never had he come across anybody odd enough — *actually odd enough* — to take time to drive to a sunset which — excepting the research and the shadowing and the setting people up to be murdered — was exactly where I, regarding maybe-boyfriend and sunsets, was coming from myself. Then he said, 'Each to their own,' and this was said quietly, perhaps more to himself, in the manner of it affording some light, diverting entertainment. Then he returned to the supercharger, or rather, to that rumour now circulating in maybe-boyfriend's area regarding him and the supercharger, and of his supposed leanings — traitorous leanings — at having such a quintessential 'over the water' item that had that red, white and blue thing on it in his house.

In response I found myself doing something out of character. 'He didn't take that flag bit,' I said. 'There was no flag bit. That's being put about by the gossips of his area.' Then I contradicted myself by adding, 'Some guy from "over the road" at my boyfriend's place of work got the bit with the flag on' — and here three things were new. One was, I was lying, making up completely about someone from the other religion at maybe-boyfriend's work getting the bit with the flag on. In truth, I didn't know if there were people from the opposite religion at the mechanics where maybe-boyfriend worked. Second thing was, I had turned 'maybe-boyfriend' into 'my boyfriend', the first time ever for me to do so. This had been out of protectiveness to stop this milkman from discerning any chink of a 'maybe' by which he could slip in between me and maybe-boyfriend and third thing was, all this sudden talking I was doing, this gabbling, splurging — and as I say, lies, in my attempt to defend and to shield maybe-boyfriend from this sinister, omniscient milkman — was in marked contrast to my hardly ever opening my mouth to defend or shield myself. I didn't understand what was happening, what I was doing, but I sensed the similarity between this and shouting out the window that time at eldest sister when she came round, unjustly, to berate me because her husband had sent her, unjustly, to berate me. I felt then, as now, the losing of my step. I was falling over, slipping in, when my usual procedure was to keep away from gossip, from loose tongues, from that feeding of the five thousand. The very momentum of that invidious group mind was enough to sway and trick a person in. Hardly I knew what I was about, why I was speaking, why explaining and excusing on behalf of maybe-boyfriend, and this, the first time since our initial meeting — when I'd been reading *Ivanhoe* and he'd pulled up in his car beside me — that I'd attempted any words to this man at all. I carried on though, with my authentic-sounding story, reiterating about the guy from 'over the road', saying it ever so casually in order to make it sound real. It occurred to me then, that perhaps I shouldn't have invented the guy from 'over the road', that instead I should have stuck to the truth of there having been no bit with the flag on. But then, everybody 'this side of the road', 'our side of the road', 'our religion', knew that taking a part of anything that came from even a suspected patriotic, 'over the water' item might suggest — exactly as maybe-boyfriend's jealous neighbour had suggested — that flag or no flag, maybe-boyfriend should instinctively have recoiled from partaking in a raffle to win any part of such a car at all. Then there was that whole matter of a raffle, of winning something, of suddenly appearing in the area to have come into a generously sufficient and increasing supply of money, both in pocket and in material possessions that couldn't in normal terms be accounted for. Usually when that happened rumour was informership was involved. 'Tell them you've come into some money,' would say the state handlers to their informers. 'Tell the local boys, the renouncers, that you won this money — this paltry whatever it is we're giving you in exchange for information — say you won it in a raffle or in a game of housey-housey and we'll see to it that genuinely you do win it in a raffle or in a game of housey-housey.' And the informers, unbelievably, would say just that. 'Won it in a raffle,' they'd say, and they'd combine their words with extravagant shrugs meant to convey that of course they themselves were not informers and that nobody was to think them informers. It was that they couldn't seem to learn in spite of the number of informer corpses stacking up in local entries that they were fooling nobody, least of all the renouncers. 'Won it in a raffle,' still they would say. 'It's in the papers even!' they'd continue, meaning the nationally printed word of their having won it was evidence that really and truly they weren't informers. Again though, they meant the 'wrong' papers, the papers from 'over there'. Such a declaration in such a publication was more likely to condemn and seal a fate in my community and in maybe-boyfriend's community than excuse and save fates in our communities. But despite those newspapers being considered suspect as colluders with the state, the informers would stick to their story as primed by their briefs. Of course, maybe-boyfriend really had won it in a raffle, in a spontaneous game of chance at his workplace. What kind of petty informer anyway, would demand — and get — a supercharger from a Blower Bentley in exchange for what would probably amount to low-grade information on our local renouncers? But complex. Very complex. And twice in this meeting now I'd experienced how easy it was to fall into traps. One can rumour, continue in rumour, get stuck and be unable to get out of rumour, which basically was why I carried on. I had started in on the lie, that of maybe-boyfriend winning a *neutral* bit of a *neutral* car when possibly there'd been nothing neutral about it. And now, having pitted myself against a sharp, cold intelligence such as how I imagined was that of the milkman, hardly could I backtrack and present a simpler story — the true story — for if I did, that would only compound matters for maybe-boyfriend as well as reveal to this milkman I'd been lying all along.

This is mad, you're mad, I told myself. *What are you gonna say next and what if this flag business ends up at kangaroo court level? Will you propound that the guy from 'over the road' — Ivor, shall we say? — who must be assumed, more because of his religion than because of his fictitiousness, not to want to appear in person in an enemy-renouncer commandery, might be willing all*

185

the same, in support of his workmate, to write a little note? Is Ivor in this notelette going to vouch that it was he who possessed the bit with the flag on, perhaps enclosing a Polaroid of himself beside this bit with the flag on, with other indications in the background of his 'over the road' status — more flags perhaps? That should do the trick. This predictive if sarcastic part of myself again brought back the rashness of maybe-boyfriend and of how badly he must be suffering car fever and compulsive hoarding-to-the-rafters that he should transgress the imperatives of our political, social and religious codes. With boys it's not the same as with girls. That business of 'what's allowed' and 'what's not allowed' was more rigid with them, more difficult and most of the male side of that I wasn't terribly up on. Things such as beer, lager, even certain spirits; sport too, I wasn't up on, because I hated sport, and I hated beer, and I hated hard spirits and the same with lager, so I never paid attention to the urgent aspect of the indigenous male's political and religious choice of these things. Not really cars either did I know, which ones were acceptably 'over the water' and which were a no-no. As for the Blower Bentley, even I had come to feel that that vehicle definitely suggested some kind of nation-defining emblem — but could it not be possible, I wondered — as maybe-boyfriend's gentle, diplomatic neighbour earlier had wondered — for it to qualify as one of those permissible crossover exceptions? The angry rumour currently circulating in maybe-boyfriend's area seemed to suggest not. No neutral bits therefore. All traitorous bits therefore. And what if Ivor was bigoted and refused to write the note?

'A carbomb blows up and out.'

This was the milkman and I jumped at his words. He said, 'It had been "a device", hadn't it? What quaintly they call "a device", attached to the inside of the exhaust before it was dropped off for a routine service? I must say, I'm surprised your sister's ex, given his profession, didn't discover something so obviously to be found by a motor mechanic as that.' At this I thought, no, that's wrong, he's got that wrong. Sister's dead ex, the one who cheated on her then got killed in his car when sectarian workmates of the opposite religion planted a bomb underneath it in the factory carpark, had been a plumber not a motor mechanic. Maybe-boyfriend was the motor mechanic. Then I thought, but why's he talking about sister and her ex? It seemed to me that although the milkman had got Greek and

Roman wrong, it couldn't be possible that such as he would be ignorant as not to know something that wasn't even a secret. And, of course, he hadn't been ignorant. Hadn't mixed up plumbers and motor mechanics. It was that my own powers of inference hadn't yet twigged to the suggestive way in which he liked to deliver his words. But he talked on, dropping hints, giving me time, a generous opportunity. Seamlessly he slipped back and forth, from sister's dead ex and the defender bomb that had killed him to, 'He's working now on a battered car at home, isn't he?', meaning maybe-boyfriend. Then it was back to the dead husband, who never did become the husband, but the real one nonetheless of his grieving widowed ex-girlfriend's heart. He shook his head then, feeling sorry for them, for sister and her dead lover. 'Wrong place, wrong time, wrong religion,' he said, also saying that he hoped first sister would recover and not grieve perpetually for the loss of the motor mechanic: 'Fine woman, still a fine woman. Very good-looking' — all the time too, making no reference to the man she did marry, to her actual husband, to first brother-in-law. By now I was confused. Is it sister then? I was thinking. Have I got this wrong and all the time it's been first sister and not me he's after? But why mention her ex-boyfriend? And why that bomb that killed him? And why maybe-boyfriend? Meanwhile, during all this puzzlement, those unpleasant waves, biological ripple upon nasty ripple, kept up assailment on my legs and backbone.

Owing to this milkman's intimations, I found then my fears starting to shift from the outraged of his own area wishing harm on maybe-boyfriend — for neglecting his history, for forgetting his community, for bringing home outrageous emblems not wanted in his area and stacking them sky-high along with his motorcar parts in his hoarded-up cupboards in his hoarded-up house. Shifted too, my fears did, from that of a more personal revenge by envious workmates of any religion wanting the worst for maybe-boyfriend because he'd won a world-famous prized car part that they themselves had wanted to win. Now, at the milkman's words, I became worried that maybe-boyfriend was in a danger more imminent than that. Certainly he worked with cars, lots of cars, probably too, to the extent of being blasé, of leaping into them, of casually turning keys in ignitions. As for the religions at his work, I had never asked maybe-boyfriend about that. It might be he worked in a mixed environment and if so, it could be a decent mixed environment or one of the more likely bitter, tense, murderous mixed environments. I didn't know. And he too, didn't know, hadn't asked the same about me. I did work with some girls from the opposite religion, though never would I have felt the need to discover whether or not they were the opposite religion except that these things tended to come out by themselves. Sometimes this would be gradually, as with time passing when people naturally got to know each other; more often though, it would happen quickly, as for example, upon hearing each other's father's, grandfather's, uncle's and brother's names. For me and maybe-boyfriend, never did that conversation arise, though naturally we didn't hold soft spots for the other country's army, or for the police here, or for the governing state here, or for the governing state 'over there', or for the paramilitary defenders-of-the-state 'over the road', or for anybody of any religion going at it with intent to find out another's persuasion. Of course, as regards living here, a person could not help but have a view. Impossible it would be — in those days, those extreme, awful crowd days, and on those streets too, which were the battlefield which were the streets — to live here and not have a view about it. I myself spent most of my time with my back turned in the nineteenth century, even the eighteenth century, sometimes the seventeenth and sixteenth centuries, yet even then, I couldn't stop having a view. Third brother-in-law too, for all his exercise obsession and of whom everybody in my district could have sworn didn't have a view, turned out to have a sharp view. There was no getting away from views and of course, the problem was these views between the areas, between one side and the other, were not just not the same. It was that each was intolerant of the other to the extent that highly volatile, built-up contentions periodically would result from them; the reason why too, if you didn't want to get into that explosive upsurge despite your view which you couldn't help having, you had to have manners and exercise politeness to overcome, or at any rate balance out, the violence, the hatred and the blaming — for how to live otherwise? This was not schizophrenia. This was living otherwise. This was underneath the trauma and the darkness a normality trying to happen. Observing the niceties therefore, not the antipathies, was crucial to co-existence and an example of that would be our French class, a mixed class, where it was okay to run down France, say, or more to the point, French metaphorical writers, but where absolutely it was not okay, not for one second, in respect of the proprieties, to demand someone declare themselves or make reference to their view or to your view at all. As for the renouncers — as in maybe-boyfriend's and my view of the renouncers — we didn't talk of them either. For my part, this was because two things dominated my mind then. One was maybe-boyfriend, and two was our 'not quite on, not quite off' relationship. Now, also, there was the milkman — so three things, not two things. Then, if the complexity of the renouncers was to gain entrance, forcing me to have a comprehensive — meaning, conflicting — opinion about them, that would mean four things. Then the political problems, because I couldn't have the renouncers in my head without the reason for the renouncers — so that would be five things. *Five things.* This is what happens when doors swing open on inner contraries. Impossible then, with all these irreconcilables, to account, not just politically-correctly, but even sensibly for oneself. Hence, the dichotomy, the cauteris-ing, the *jamais vu,* the blanking-out, the reading-while-walking — even my consideration of whether to forgo the current codex altogether for the safety of the scroll and papyrus of earlier centuries. Otherwise, if unmediated forces and feelings burst to my consciousness, I wouldn't know what to do. I could see the necessity for them, for the renouncers, for how it was they came about, how it seemed they had to come about, given all the legalised and defended imbalances. Then there was that lack of listening, a stubbornness unyielding, an entrenchment indicative of those turbulent times themselves. So the cracking of the faultlines was inevitable; so too, were the renouncers inevitable. As for the killings, they were the usual, meaning they were not to be belaboured, not because they were nothing but because they were enormous, also so numerous that rapidly there became no time for them. Every so often, however, an event would occur so beyond-the-pale that everyone — 'this side of the road', 'that side of the road', 'over the water' and 'over the border' — couldn't help but be stopped in their tracks. A renouncer-atrocity would send you reeling with, *'God o God o God. How can I have a view that helped on this action?'* which would be the case until you'd forget, which would happen when the other side went and did one of their awful things.

Again this was reeling and spinning. It was revenge and counter-revenge. It was joining peace movements, showing commitment to cross-community discussions, to those all-inclusive marches, to true, good citizenship — until the point it was suspected that these peace movements and goodwill and true, good citizenship were being infiltrated by one faction or the other faction. So then you'd leave the movements, drop hope, abandon potential solutions and drift back to the view that always was familiar, dependable, inevitable. In those days then, impossible it was not to be closed-up because closed-upness was everywhere: closings in our community, closings in their community, the state here closed, the government 'over there' closed, the newspapers and radio and television closed because no information could be forthcoming that wouldn't be perceived by at least one party to be a distortion of the truth. When it got down to it, although people spoke of ordinariness, there wasn't really ordinariness because moderation itself had spun out of control. No matter the reservations held then — as to methods and morals and about the various groupings that came into operation or which from the outset already had been in operation; no matter too, that for us, in our community, on 'our side of the road', the government here was the enemy, and the police here was the enemy, and the government 'over there' was the enemy, and the soldiers from 'over there' were the enemy, and the defender-paramilitaries from 'over the road' were the enemy and, by extension — thanks to suspicion and history and paranoia — the hospital, the electricity board, the gas board, the water board, the school board, telephone people and anybody wearing a uniform or garments easily to be mistaken for a uniform also were the enemy, and where we were viewed in our turn by our enemies as the enemy — in those dark days, which were the extreme of days, if we hadn't had the renouncers as our underground buffer between us and this overwhelming and combined enemy, who else, in all the world, would we have had?

Of course you did not say this. Which was why, eighteen years old, I didn't talk about the renouncers, was unwilling to reflect upon them, pulled down shutters against the topic of them. It was that I wanted to stay as sane in my mind as I thought then I was. This too, was why maybe-boyfriend, at least when with me, also didn't talk about the renouncers, also perhaps why he was into cars in the way some people were mad on their music. This didn't mean we weren't aware, just that we didn't know how not to be partisan. So there was a loop of regard, at least for the old-school renouncers, those with the principled reasons for resistance and for fighting before most ended up dead or interned, bringing in a preponderance, as ma put it, 'of the hoodlum, the worldling, the careerist and the personal agenda'. So yes, keep the lid on, buy old books, read old books, seriously consider those scrolls and clay tablets. That was me then, age eighteen. It was also maybe-boyfriend. And we didn't speak on this, didn't dwell on it, but of course, along with others we imbibed the day-by-day, drip-by-drip, on-the-street effect of it. And now, helped along by this milkman, it came the case that my own fearful fantasies and catastrophic thinking were predicting maybe-boyfriend's violent death. It wasn't really prediction, of course, because in his own phraseology this milkman had pretty much spelled it out for me: death by carbomb, though carbomb may not have been the actual method intended, but only an example utilised for image and effect. It wasn't either, that his colleagues from 'the other side' at work, if there were any, were going to kill maybe-boyfriend out of sectarianism. No. It was that, just as the milkman running in the parks & reservoirs had been about me and not about running in the parks & reservoirs, maybe-boyfriend was to be killed under the catch-all of the political problems even if, in reality, the milkman was going to kill him out of disguised sexual jealousy over me. Such appeared to be underlined by this milkman in the subsoil of our conversation. And so, in the rush of these thoughts — which were confused, panicked thoughts, not my usual nineteenth-century, safe-and-sound literary thoughts — I failed to know how to respond. I knew how not to respond, which was to confront, to question, to push for clarification. Absolutely, that wouldn't do at all. I knew he knew that finally I'd grasped what it was he was saying to me; also what it was I was socially conditioned into pretending he hadn't said to me — which wasn't just social conditioning, but a nerves thing as well. At public, grassroots level I wasn't even supposed to know this man was a renouncer, which anyway was true because I did not. I accepted he was simply because amongst all the unmentionables here that managed all the same to get mentioned whilst retaining a patina of not being mentioned, there existed a widespread 'taking for granted' which in this case — the case

of whether or not this milkman was a renouncer — the unmentionable on the grapevine was, 'Don't be silly, of course he is.' I
was supposed to accept this, just in the way
I was supposed to accept that certain others
in the area also were renouncers. Given,
however, there was that other recent unmentionable — that of myself being in an affair
with the milkman when I knew for certain,
if nobody else did, that I wasn't in an affair
with the milkman — might it be in a similar
vein that this man wasn't a paramilitary
after all? He may have been some chancer,
some fantasist, one of those Walter Mitty
people who, whilst not being in anything
themselves, attempt, or even manage, to
have built up around themselves mythic
reputations — in this case as some top renouncer intelligence gatherer — all based
entirely on others' misperceptions of him.
Could it be that this milkman had started
off as one of the armchair supporters, the
type who, in their ardour and fanaticism for
the renouncers, sometimes went batty and
started to believe, then to hint, then boast,
that they themselves also were renouncers?
That did happen. Periodically it happened.
It happened to Somebody McSomebody,
that boy who was to threaten me after the
milkman's death when he cornered me in

the toilets of the district's most popular drinking-club. Certainly, he'd been in the throes of considering that he was some top-drawer renouncer-of-the-state himself.

Somebody McSomebody probably would not agree with this assessment of himself but I consider it fair and accurate. When we were both seventeen, and after he approached me for the first time in order to make a move on me which was when I rejected him because I wasn't attracted to him, it struck me that McSomebody was of the grudge-bearing, stalker type. 'We will follow you,' he said and continued to say as soon as it dawned on him that he was being rebuffed by me and not accepted by me as he had presumed to be accepted. And although I'd tried to be respectful in my rebuffing it didn't work because, 'We will be next you, always next you. You started this. You made us look at you. You made us think . . . You suggested . . . You don't know what we're capable of and when you least expect it, when you think we're not there, when you think we've gone, you'll pay back for, oh, you'll pay back for . . . You'll . . . You'll . . .' See? Stalker-type behaviour, referring to himself now too, in the first person plural whereas not long before he'd been a normal first person singular like everybody else. The other thing about Mc-Somebody was that he was a teller of untruths. I don't mean he lied as in vulnerable, nervous, panicked lies such as the type recently I'd invented on the spot and poured out to the milkman regarding maybe-boyfriend and Ivor and the supercharger and that flag from 'over the water'. I mean Somebody McSomebody was so far gone in his makings-up that I think he thought every word true himself. These lies started in the James Bond mode, though of course, no one here, on 'my side of the road', on 'this side of the water', acknowledged James Bond. That was another no-no, though not as no-no as watching the news about our political problems as relayed by what was considered their manipulative network, nor as no-no as reading the wrong type of newspaper — again one from 'over the water' — and certainly not as no-no as giving the time of day late at night to that anthem being played on the TV. It was that James Bond was another of the disallowed because, like the supercharger, it was another quintessential, nation-defining, 'over the water' patriotism and, if you were from 'our side of the water' as well as 'our side of the road' and you did watch James Bond, you didn't make a point of saying so; also you kept the volume very, very low. If someone caught you at it, quickly you'd splutter, 'Rubbish! Huh! Not realistic! As if those things could happen!', meaning how implausible it was that James Bond, in full dinner jacket, could be in a coffin one moment at the crematorium, pretending he was dead, then next breaking out of the coffin, defeating villains for his country, going to all the parties and having sex with the most beautiful women in the world. 'Unlikely,' you'd say. 'It's that they think they're Americans but they're not Americans! Huh! Huh!' That way you excuse yourself for what might come across as a treasonous lack of support for the eight-hundred-year struggle, as well as aligning yourself with the likes of Oliver Cromwell, Elizabeth the First, the invasion of 1172, and Henry the Eighth. So that was James Bond in the general sense, that day-to-day disallowed historical and political sense. Telling lies though, in the James Bond mode was at a slightly different angle from this. It involved making use of that patriotic, great-guy image, the good guy, the heroic guy, the invincible, sexy, maverick male defeater of all bad guys for the glory of his country, only in this case, in our culture, on 'our side of the road', who was who and what was what had to be swapped around.

In our district the renouncers-of-the-state were assumed the good guys, the heroes, the men of honour, the dauntless, legendary warriors, outnumbered, risking their lives, standing up for our rights, guerrilla-fashion, against all the odds. They were viewed in this way by most if not all in the district, at least initially, before the idealistic type ended up dead, with growing reservations setting in over the new type, those tending towards the gangster style of renouncer instead. Along with this sea change in personnel came the moral dilemma for the 'our side of the road' non-renouncer and not very politicised person. This dilemma consisted of, once again, those inner contraries, the moral ambiguities, the difficulty of entering fully into the truth. Here were the Johns and Marys of this world, trying to live civilian lives as ordinarily as the political problems here would allow them, but becoming uneasy, no longer certain of the moral correctness of the means by which our custodians of honour were fighting for the cause. This was not just because of the deaths and the mounting deaths, but also the injuries, the forgotten damage, all that personal and private suffering stemming from successful renouncer operations. And as the renouncers' power and assumption of power increased, so too, did the uneasiness of the Johns and Marys increase, regardless too, that the other side — 'over there' — 'across the road' — 'across the water' — would be hard at it, doing their own versions of destruction as well. There was also that day-to-day business of dirty laundry in public, and of the district renouncers laying down their law, their prescripts, their ordinances plus punishments for any perceived infringements of them. There were beatings, brandings, tar and featherings, disappearances, black-eyed, multi-bruised people walking about with missing digits who most certainly had those digits only the day before. There were too, the impromptu courts held in the district's hutments, also in other disused buildings and houses specially friendly to the renouncers. There were the myriad methods our renouncers had for levying funds for their cause. Above all, there was the organisation's paranoia, their examination, interrogation and almost always dispatch of informants and of suspected informants, but until this discomfort with the inner contraries took hold of the Johns and Marys, the renouncers had constituted iconic noble fighters in pretty much the whole of the community's eyes. To the groupies of these paramilitaries however — and this would be certain girls and women unable to grasp with mind and emotion any concept of a moral conflict — men who were in the renouncers signalled not just wonderful specimens of unblemished toughness, sexiness and maleness, but through attaining to relationship with them, these females could push for their own social and careerist ends. This was why that female demographic always was to be found in the vicinity of renouncers: frequenting renouncer haunts, inhabiting renouncer circles, pushing into renouncer cavities and, if ever they were seen draped over any unknown male inside or outside of the area, you could bet both your grannies that this man receiving the lavish adoration could be none other than a renouncer-of-the-state himself. To the groupies too, it wasn't so much these men should be fighters for the cause as that they should be the particular individuals wielding substantial power and influence in the areas. They didn't have to be paramilitaries, didn't even have to be illegal, could have been anyone. It so happened though, that in the set-up of the time, in each of those totalitarian-run enclaves, it was the male paramilitaries who, more than anyone, ruled over the areas with final say. Although not, of course, inter-communally accepted — such as were those crossover rock stars, the film stars, the sports stars and now those two ballroom-dancing champions — nevertheless the paramilitaries, in their respective areas, in relative terms of local celebrity, were on a par with the more famously accepted across the divide. As far as the groupies were concerned then, these *were* the James Bonds, though not Bond in that other country's service. This was Bond in his irresistible, irrepressible, superhuman, bucking-the-trend demeanour, especially the higher up the renouncer-ladder of rank any individual prepared to die for his cause happened to be. As for this cause — all that 'our side of the road' and 'our side of the water' and 'their flag isn't our flag' and so on — well, again, in terms of the personal, of the primal, of drives and motivation, that didn't matter to these groupies. Wasn't always either, about life's lovely things. Not always nice clothes, nice jewellery, nice shopping, nice dinners, nice parties or lump sums in cash in secret strongboxes, all to spell brilliant times, good lives and happy lifestyles. Often, at least in the old days, the days of the dedicated, intractable, ruthless old-time renouncer, there wasn't money to spare for personal aggrandisement because all monies garnered — illegally, very illegally and most spectacularly illegally — really had to be spent on the cause. In terms of personal materialistic gain therefore, there wasn't any, and the old-style renouncer hadn't seemed interested in any. As far as the groupie woman was concerned then, what represented true attainment for her was the prized position of becoming *the* woman of *the* man. He had to be leader, Number One, making her in turn Number One Attachment. If position of Number One Attachment happened to be taken — owing perhaps, to some charismatic groupie possibly getting in before her — then lady-in-waiting to Number One Attachment — itself promising attendant, if less puissant connections — wouldn't be out of the running after all. Should he happen to be married, this Man of Men, this Warrior of Warriors, and providing that the wife wasn't influential — not, for example, some female renouncer prepared to kill any woman moving in on her husband — then that would be all right as well. So the groupies were happy to be the other woman, to be mistress, because that guaranteed status and a wedge of the kudos and the glory. Those 'fast, breathtaking, fantastically exhilarating rebel-men' as my mother again put it when she came to accuse me of being a paramilitary groupie, were the very men then, through whom these ambitious women hoped to fulfil on their own cause.

Which was why she was still coming to see me. My mother. To upbraid me. To harangue me. To command me to cease being — even though I wasn't — one of those women. Word had gotten round — and after only two encounters between me and the milkman — that I was edging myself towards, had placed myself next to the groupie territory, that I was knocking on the door to be admitted to the chamber of the powerhouse, drugged to the eyeballs too, it was said, with ambitions, aspirations and dreams. Ma continued to warn me, to reiterate that I was to wake up, to realise these men were not movie stars, that this was no make-believe, no template of a grand passion such as foolishly I pursued in those old-time storybooks I read and walked about with. Instead this was a case, she said, of a naïve ill-working of my creative raw material to fashion a lover out of untamed maleness. 'But what the books don't say, daughter,' she said, 'is that you're not seeing him for who he is but for whom you want and imagine him to be.' Although she added that she herself wasn't old-fashioned, that she wasn't ignorant, that she hadn't entirely forgotten her youth so could nod her cap certainly at the allurement of vertiginous, heady and extraordinary excitement. In reality though, not only was I trying to seize love, she said, in a dreadful unladylike, pawing, stalking fashion, but also that I was in danger of slipping into that far from minor female world of accessory-to-murder itself. 'When it comes to it,' she said, 'those dark adventurers — the pioneers, the saviours, the outlaws, the devils — whatever anyone chooses to append to them — are sociopaths, maybe even psychopaths. And even if they aren't,' she added, 'the fact their warlike individualism and single-minded mentalities qualify them superbly for what they get up to in their movement, such mindsets and individualism hardly render them fit in this world for anything else.' Not nine-to-five jobs, she said. Not personal relationships. Not fulfilling on family and on family obligations. Not even an average lifespan. 'So not for mixing with, daughter. And anyway, a proper girl, a normal girl, a girl with morals intact and a sensibility attuned to what's civilised and respectful, would get the hell out of there, wouldn't even have got in there.' Another thing she said was that I hadn't even *properly* got myself in. This meant we were back to matrimony, to the marriage vows. It seemed that even here, while trying to ward me off those supernatural, dangerous revolutionaries, still she couldn't stop herself from seeing the wedlock side of things. She meant I wasn't *decently* in, that I wasn't the wife, that if I really felt I had to cleave to a renouncer, could I not officially have gotten myself married to him? That way I'd be accepted. 'Though goodness knows,' she said, 'being the wife can't be easy in itself. All those prison visits. The tombstone visits. The being spied upon by the enemy police, by the soldiers, by fellow renouncer-wives and renouncer-comrades of the husband. Indeed the whole community would be at it,' she said. 'Making sure of her fidelity. Making sure no liberties were being taken, that she wasn't insulting her husband with her conduct but instead properly behaving herself. So no,' she said. 'Not an easy life. Instead it must be an exhausting, damaging, very lonely life. But at least she's in there, daughter. Married. Registered. With reputation intact and with herself and her children to be looked after when he ends up dead or in internment.' In contrast, according to ma, by choosing the path of the tagalong woman I'd ruined her upbringing of me as a respectable female some man some day might want to have. I had degraded myself, she said, along with any remaining prospects to the point where I would become 'soiled goods enough' even to drop down the groupie pecking-order. 'Then you've had it. Then you've ruined yourself, all your chances, all your opportunities — and for what?' She shook her head. 'They don't legitimate those field-women, daughter,' she warned.

She ended this homily with her usual, 'Mark my words, you think you're having this cake and eating it, believing this is what brings you alive, that ordinary life is boring, that the rest of us are boring, but the truth will cut across your life, wee girl, whether you want it to or not. There's nothing wrong with being ordinary, with marrying an ordinary man, with carrying out life's ordinary duties. But I see you're hypnotised by the flashiness, blinded by the ornament, by money, by subcultures, by being taken in, by your very own youth, your immaturity. But it'll end badly,' she said. 'You'll come a shell, moulded by him, controlled by him, emptied, leached of all your strength and your animating spirit. You'll be lost, will lose yourself, will slide down into evil. And as for all that vague something of what he did, of what he does, all that — *Now what was it? What was that vague something, all that something of vagueness that in his paramilitary lifestyle he gets up to?* — you won't remember. Deliberately you'll misremember and it's strange I didn't see this till now, but the more I encounter you as an adult, the more like your father in his moods and psychologicals, in his belief in nothing, you also, daughter, in your attraction for the shadows, seem to be.'

So that was that. That was me told. And no longer was I a vile old spinster refusing to get married, but now most definitely an unconnected, unbonded loose woman, but her words, insulting and disdaining, came not from her daughter's ill-working of creative raw material, but from her own ill-working of creative raw material; relaying to me too, the latest rumour of me and the milkman whilst managing to perpetuate it on at the same time. As with the milkman — as with all of them — here again was someone who knew the answers so wasn't asking questions, wasn't interested either, in how I might respond. Not that anymore I would respond or be anxious to explain to her that still I was not the milkman's. With that *'liar!'* insult still stinging me from last time, and doubtless my silence still rankling her from last time, simply she'd throw the words out and I'd refuse to admit their impact. They were though, having an impact, as were the differences I'd also started to perceive in the district's attitude towards myself. Not just from the gossips of the area either, attending to, then furthering on their stories and their updating of their stories. It was that the local paramilitary groupies were also now paying attention. It was they who next decided to call.

It happened one evening when six approached me in the toilets of the district's most popular drinking-club. They surrounded me and regarded my face in the glass. One asked if I'd like a piece of her chewing gum. Another offered me to try out her lipstick. Yet another passed over her Estée Lauder. And they were friendly, or pretending to be friendly and I accepted this friendship or overture of pretend-friendship for no other reason than to buy time because I was afraid.

'I'd always have a tough guy,' said the oldest-looking, the one who'd handed over the perfume. She was at the sink beside me, talking to my reflection, before transferring her gaze over to herself. She looked at her cleavage. Seemed pleased. Adjusted it. Readjusted it. Seemed more pleased. 'A dangerous man,' she said. 'Masculine. Very. Has to be. Love that sort of thing.' As she invited my reflection to agree another interrupted. 'But that searching for the extreme, the one-way ticket, no change of mind, no walk-away an option, I mean all that life and death and heroism,' she said. 'Don't forget that.' 'It's always a dice game,' said a third. 'Has to be, because no matter the rehearsal, the going-over of points, everybody knows he could have an off day, with that off day spelling his last day, but still . . .' — here she left her sentence hanging, then — 'The average man,' said another, 'cannot do that. Not even the average renouncer.' 'Yes, and you're always a little afraid, aren't you?' came someone from the back. 'A little anxious, that you're living your last hours with him, that if a mission goes wrong — it's *boom!* it's *bang!* it's *too bad!* — he falls, he dies or he faces life imprisonment. It's like you have to get into training for it, have to stay motivated for it' which was when I learned what motivation, in paramilitary groupie terms, meant. 'Let him know how much he means to you,' they said. 'Look good. Look classy. Always dresses. No trousers. High heels, mind — and jewellery. Never let him down. Never go to the bar yourself. Never get on the dancefloor with another fella or find yourself alone with a guy on the edge of flirtation. Never consider another relationship, not even a maybe-relationship. Honour him. Do him proud. Don't be loud. Don't spill beans and don't ask questions. Appreciate,' they said and on they went, instructing, because I came to realise this was what it was, instructing. With these women, in these toilets, I was being handed the hangers-on welcome pack.

Before I could formulate an answer, or know in the moment how to formulate an answer, they were back to the risk, to the appeal, to why it was all worth it. 'That buzz,' they said. 'The deference, the entourage. All that confident, fantastic, elemental male presence. It's a force of nature. It's that they take control, they keep control, they have everybody wrapped around their fingers.' Listening to these women, I learned that not only was the average man incapable of being a renouncer, but apparently the average woman wasn't up either, to being the woman of a renouncer. 'Wouldn't be able to stand it,' they said. 'Would long for that lifestyle but be too repressed for it — far, far too fearful of it. The common woman,' they said, 'nice, ordinary, boring — she can't have that.' 'She loves dully,' they went on. 'Takes no gamble, is terrified of risk, fills her life with timid tasks and mundane men, not men of high calibre, of the high-wire, commanding the tumultuous, the unpredictable. These women live the secure, safe bubble, the nine-to-five, decent bubble. But who wants sleepy bubbles when you can have the excitant of the power, the stimulus of control, even of the cruelty. All that gradual, cunning, imperceptible advancement. Don't you just love,' they said, 'the sudden erotic alarm?'

So ma was wrong, terribly wrong, because listening to these women, these strange, self-satisfied women, it was clear to me that everything she'd warned of their turning of the blind eye, of their vagueness, of their blocking from consciousness of all the dark deeds committed by their lovers, seemed instead to be the very requirements that were attracting these women on. Not a case of being unable to face reality. More a case, I'd say, of getting out the magnifying glass and having a good gawp at it. And for that much-touted woman — she who misreads the bad boys, who mistakes the bad boy for the good boy and strives to tame and transform some socially misunderstood man who hadn't really meant all that mayhem — it was obvious these women weren't that

215

woman. Here were females who did love the sound of breaking glass.

They said my name then, my first name, thereby crossing over and shunning the interface. And there I was, in the middle of them — one of them — even though so far I hadn't said a word. That wasn't how it would look, of course, to anyone coming into these toilets and encountering us. And girls were coming in and they were encountering us — glancing towards us, then quickly glancing away. That was what I used to do, who I used to be, whenever I'd come across these groupies, or any groupies, in this club, in other clubs, in these selfsame toilets or anywhere in the areas. I'd look, look away, turn away, because this type, they seemed to me quite mad. It was that I considered them alien, that they were creatures of another planet operating in currents not at all comprehensible. Not only were they not me, but firmly I had decided they were very far below me. That wasn't only my opinion because, had they not been sexual attachments to the district's great hero paramilitaries, long ago they would have been ostracised as more of our district's beyond-the-pales. Omens of danger. Holders of strange passions, especially sexually drugged-to-the-eyeball passions. I was in no doubt their lifestyle could be nothing but anathema to me. At eighteen, however, I was never going to admit that, regarding sex, there was an awful lot I didn't understand about it. These women — through their appearance, their words, the very way they moved their bodies — also liking to be watched moving and conducting those bodies — were threatening to present sex to me as something unstructured, something uncontrollable, but could I not be older than eighteen before the realisation of the confusion of the massive subtext of sex and the contraries of sex should come upon me and uncertain me? Could I not remain at *'been there, done that, having it with maybe-boyfriend so know all there is to know about it'*, no matter that, given my so far tidy and limited sexual experience with maybe-boyfriend, I knew next to nothing about it? Surely at eighteen, I ought to have been allowed to think for a little longer that I did.

So I wasn't ready for that, to admit I might be on some threshold, about to glimpse that again — just as with the political problems here and my maybe-relationship with maybe-boyfriend — I was coming up against the ambivalences in life. As these women spoke on — of their behaviours, their carnality, of pain being arousing so that they trained themselves not to resist, so that always they were going around in pleasure, so that always pain all the time was pleasure; also of being in toils, in trance, unable to act voluntarily; racing hearts, they said, skin ripples, permanent states of arousal — it got to the point where my master control couldn't cope any longer and just as with third brother-in-law whenever he would get into an overload of exercise talk, I stanched all openings to block them off. Eventually they dropped this enthral-ment talk and moved on to 'You have lovely hair' which startled me and which wasn't true because I didn't. Absolutely I didn't. But they said it again, adding this time that my hair was just like Virginia Mayo's or even like Kim Novak's. The patent falseness of this did not put them off. Now it was, 'You look like Joan Bennett in that film *Woman in the Window,'* and no, again, I didn't. But they carried on, paying me compliments, including me as one of them, attempting to get in with me. This told me that in their eyes I must now be his. If not yet his, then their inside information, their barometer, even just their sentient understanding of these matters must have indicated to them that before long I was going to be his. They were surrounding me and instructing me, not as rivals but as confidantes, suivantes, wanting to know where in the hierarchy they might stand with me. Hence that constant assurance that I was every inch the lick and spittle of whichever *film noir* star they were estimating I would most prefer to be.

And now it was my cheekbones. They were just like Ida Lupino's. Me and Gloria Grahame were something. And Veronica Lake and me. And Jane Greer and me. And Lizabeth Scott and me. And Ann Todd and me and Gene Tierney and Jean Simmons and Alida Valli and they were like wee girls, dressing up as movie stars, as *femmes fatales,* with myself now invited to play along. 'We should sit together,' they said. 'You come and sit with us. Anytime you like, leave those drinking-friends you're with and come and sit with us.' Then they left but not before, 'Here — but not till you're indoors.' It was a pill. A shiny black one. Plump. Tiny, with a tinier white dot right in the middle of it. They extended this to me and my hand opened and received it, as if expecting it. More than anything, it was as if I'd fallen into the very person, according to everybody, I was now supposed to be.

It seemed though, that before that evening of the groupie bonding session in the toilets of the district's most popular drinking-club,

also before realising which powerful renouncer had set his stalker-sights upon me,
Somebody McSomebody — my amateur
stalker — must have heard I was aspiring to
paramilitary groupiedom and so thought to
chance his arm with his new romance-
advancement plan. This new plan was part
of his second attempt to come at me after
that first time when he'd been rejected by
me. This time he was going all-out in his
wooing in the hope that when he revealed
his true self to me — given too, I was ambitious of falling in love, not with any auld renouncer but with the utmost, super-eminent
of renouncers — that I would think, Christ!
One of those guys! Yes please, I'll have that.
Up until this point, Somebody McSomebody had been known about the area as a
fervent supporter of the renouncers and
certainly he came from an entrenched renouncer family. After being the rabid type
for a while, however, he fell into that other
category, the one of thinking himself a renouncer which meant, he implied when he
made this second move on me, that I'd
made a mistake in rejecting him first time.
He said that although he'd come out with a
lot of stalk-talk on that occasion in response
to my rejection of him, he hadn't meant all
that 'just you wait, filthy cat, you're going to

die'. He said he hoped I hadn't taken it in the wrong vein but instead had known really, had accepted his words really, as expressive of his natural desire for my company. And now, after some thought, he had decided, he said, that the time had come to trust me with the most secret information of his life. This was when he said he was a renouncer-of-the-state, a true patriot, one of those heroes humbly willing to lay down his life, to sacrifice everything for the movement, for the cause, for the country. He was convinced, I could see, that this time round his words would produce quite the opposite effect upon me — as in favourable, as in advantageous — especially as I'd had two brothers in the renouncers myself. Contrary to the grapevine, however, and to all those gossipy unmentionables of supposedly knowing who was a renouncer in the area and who wasn't a renouncer, I hadn't known two of my brothers were re-nouncers, not until the funeral of one of them when the coffin got draped in that flag 'from over the border', with the cortege then making its way, not to the commoners' plot of the usual place, but to the renounc-ers' plot of the usual place, where three of them in uniform appeared speedily out of nowhere and fired a volley of shots over his grave. That came as a surprise, I mean to me, and a further surprise was later, when I enquired of others about this aspect of the brothers. This was when I discovered that my mother and all my siblings, including wee sisters, had known that second and fourth brother had been renouncers, though none showed sympathy or patience at my being left out of this knowledge; not surprising, they said, owing to my deliberate obfuscation of reading while walking about. As for McSomebody springing his secret upon me, it was embarrassing. Plain as day too, that he wasn't a renouncer and that in his gone-mad fever he was taking in nobody but himself. But he carried on. One minute he was an actual paramilitary. Next, he was top adviser having the respectful ears of the utmost of paramilitaries, the point being I should be impressed by his sexy hero-standing and leap into his arms before it was too late. He said, or rather boasted, assuming too, that I was on-message with him, that he had found it imperative to hold the nerve, to keep faith no matter what might happen when you were out on operations. 'We can have an off day,' he said, 'with that off day spelling our last day. The average man, you know, even the average renouncer,' he shrugged, 'can't, when it comes to it, always manage that. We get a little enervated, a little nervous' — and here he said my name, my first name, forename — 'because just beforehand,' he went on, 'we have this feeling that we're living our last hours and that there are three options — we'll live, we'll die, we'll be injured, we'll fail, the state will catch us,' which was five options. I decided not to cut in to correct, for that would encourage him on. 'When we're playing with our life,' he said, 'we don't take anything for granted,' and here he said my name, my forename, once again. 'For three or four hours,' he said, 'we're acutely aware that we're going to be on edge until it's over. If, at the end, when it is over, when we've accomplished our mission, well then,' he said, 'that's when we realise how beautiful life is.' There was more to this modest boast, along the lines of 'psychological drive', 'nerves of steel', 'superhuman endurance', 'the unique sacrifice of a normal domestic lifestyle'. Shorn of its context though, and indeed, even in its context, it was another of those earbashings, such as I'd been undergoing of late with various people in this place. 'For us, as you know,' he said, continuing to refer to himself, as again he was, in the first person plural, 'as with our family — though also we think as with your family — the army life is as important as eating, breathing and sleeping. But you can't question us' — here he put up his hand actually to stop me from questioning him, all the while looking at me pointedly, stressing the bond that linked us together, as if indeed, we were in this together, as if he'd just put himself in my favour by telling me where he stood in the paramilitary-renouncer world. 'Cept he hadn't. Hadn't impressed me, hadn't put himself in favour, wasn't either, a renouncer. Even if he was, even if all he'd said had managed romantically and sentimentally to have bowled me over, still he was Somebody McSomebody, telling lies as usual in the James Bond mode.

Now it was true he did have renouncer links. His father and his eldest sister and his eldest brother — until their deaths — all had been renouncers. But you can't claim credit, least not forever in a staunchly anti-state, paramilitary stronghold, for what your da did, for what your big sister did, for what your big brother did, if you weren't forwarding on the cause with actions yourself. You might get leeway for a while, a bit of attention, some respect filtering down because of your blood connections. In particular, visitors to the area, history-seekers, that type, might be impressed and even esteem you because how would they know better? The locals though, did know better, and the thing with these feverishly demented supporters who end up thinking they're paramilitaries when they're not paramilitaries is that they distance themselves from everybody with their self-advancing showing-off. That was the true position of McSomebody and it didn't occur to him — for you could buy a balaclava anywhere — how completely he was transparent. It was said he'd been doing his peddling of superhero freedom-fighting to such a noisy extent now that the renouncers themselves were thinking of having a word. He came to me again then, regardless of my earlier rebuff, and he started in on this new chat-up. He said he could see how someone like me would understand, given my own renouncer-blood credentials, that any day now he might — as in the case of my fourth brother — have to go on the run. It was very annoying. At first I was again polite, wondering what amount of time could be passed before saying, 'I have to go now.' It's that they have this idea, these people, that you're stupid, that you're incapable of discerning that they think you stupid. Also, they don't see you as a person but instead as some cipher, some valueless nobody whose sole objective is to reflect back onto them the glory of themselves. Their compliments and solicitousness too, are creepy. They're inappropriate, squirmy, calculated, rapacious, particularly as not long afterwards — or not long before as in my case — you know it's going to be insults, threats of violence, threats of death and variations on stalk-talk. It's that in their own lack of intelligence they think they see you coming when it's you who sees them coming, the question then being whether to be kind or to swat them with viciousness out of your way. But I was polite for there had been further deaths in McSomebody's family, the last two happening only months before. These latest deaths now took that family almost to the number one spot as the one with the most violent deaths to have occurred in it in our area, except my longest friend from primary school came from a family in which everybody in it was now dead from the problems bar her. Poor McSomebody though. It was clear that his relatives' deaths had affected him, that they had unhinged him, that they must account, at least in part, for his losing grip so spectacularly like that. First his father, then his oldest sister, then his oldest brother, all killed over the last ten years in various renouncer

226

activity. Then there'd been that favourite of the family, the second oldest male, who'd died that time while crossing the road. Two months on from the favourite's death, there came a day when the fourth boy, still in his nuclear-arms distraction, also died. Pills, drink, a plastic bag over his head and leaving a note which astounded everybody: *'It is because of Russia and because of America that I am doing this.'* After that, and out of that original family of two parents and twelve siblings, there was only Somebody McSomebody, his now psychologically debilitated mother, his six sisters and the three-year-old boy left. Not my fault though. Not my fault either, that I didn't find him attractive. You cannot go out with someone just because you feel sorry for them because they've had a long run of death in their family; and particularly you cannot do it if, from the outset, from the first moment ever of setting eyes on them, even before any interaction were to take place with them, something about them made you feel sick. Initially I'd feel guilty about the sick bit, but then I stopped feeling guilty when he started in on his death threats after that first rejection of him. Then I became further resolved in not feeling guilty after my second rejection when he spoke of 'our kindredship' because of 'our renouncership', making mention too of 'our relationship' when we didn't have a relationship, which was when I realised he was treating those two rebuffs as if they'd been acceptances, as if indeed, they had constituted our first dates. As for all this stalk-talk he did, and his surety of our relationship, and the futurity of our coupledom, never could I have imagined that the menacing, deluded, obsessive, deranged types of this world could instantly recover from being menacing, deluded, obsessive and deranged and instead backpedal like no tomorrow into sycophancy and obscurity. That was what happened to McSomebody when news reached him of the interest about to be furthered in me by the milkman, by an individual even McSomebody could grasp was of a far more menacing and stalking capability than him.

Now, after the cessation of McSomebody's romance hostilities, here I was, standing beside this milkman, my thoughts easily to become terrified, not helped either by the dead cat's head I was holding in my hands. All through our exchange I made no reference to this head, nor did I look at it. He too, appeared not to look at it. I knew though, that he was well aware of what it was. Probably had gotten the detail of my picking it up, of walking back, walking forth, all that dithering about beforehand. I was sure too, he'd have clocked my rolling it in the hankies, lifting it, perhaps also mind-reading my intention to carry it up to the usual place. Just as I was saying nothing about it though, he also was saying nothing, as if it were inconsequential to be standing where nobody ever stood at a quarter to ten of a summer's night beside a teenage girl holding a decapitated head, while chatting to her about taking the life of the boyfriend she was maybe-involved with. No wonder then, given the effect his appearance and words were having upon me, that for a tiny space of time I had forgotten the head was there. Just for a moment, however, because then it reminded me. As the milkman opened his mouth, once again to say something that I knew was going to unnerve me, my hands, which had been tightly cupping the handkerchiefs, now began in a fitful way to fidget the fabric about. One of my fingers came upon a long front tooth and in my confusion I turned this to the long front tooth coming through the fabric upon my finger. And it was at that moment that my spine again moved. It did so in that similar unnatural fashion it had moved in the classroom earlier. After that came the leg shudders, those hamstring currents, all those neural, rippling dreads and permeations around my thighs and backside. Then my mind free-associated back to maggots — to those clumps about the nose, the ear, the eye and now he was talking again. This time he'd moved off the subject of murdering maybe-boyfriend, which had not been spelled out as murder anyway in that everything had been suggested. Much older than me, more assured than me and with no waste of energy despite that languid-seeming indifference, this man was back to offering me lifts in his cars.

Again, as at our second meeting in the parks & reservoirs, he said he wasn't happy, that he was concerned, that walking about in this place — downtown, anywhere outside the area — never could be good for me, that it wouldn't be safe for me. He added he hoped I'd remember it was of no bother to him to lay on transport for me — his own or, when busy, that of someone else. He'd speak to others, he said, about assisting me during those occasions when he himself wouldn't be available to. And here he spoke again about my work. Not to worry, he said. He'd get me safely to it, then, end of day,

I'd be collected from it. I'd be spared the bother of bus-jackings, of those public vehicles getting caught up in every riot and crossfire, plus I'd be spared all other irritations of daily public transport as well. Again, this was suggestion, with his continuing in that friendly, obliging vein, the one of doing me favours, of helping me out by taking my walking away, taking my running away, taking away maybe-boyfriend. There was no overt sense here that he could be transgressing so that again perhaps I was mistaken and he wasn't transgressing. As he spoke on, however, and no matter my confusion, I knew I must not — as a crucial bottom line — ever get into his cars. It seemed everything had microscoped down to that last one threshold, as if to do so, to cross over, to get into one, would signal some 'end of' as well as some 'commencement of'. Meanwhile, I continued to stand there, in this territory of things pretended and not clearly stated, also in this area where individuals shouldn't just hurry, but should make a point really, of never entering in the first place. But here I was, in it. And there he was, in it, and by this time I'd got so worked up that I'd reached that state of agitated emotion which easily brought on fractures of the psyche — where suddenly I

might say 'No!' or 'Fuck off!' or where I
might scream or drop the head or even —
who knows? — fire it at him. What did happen though, was that other men appeared.

They didn't appear exactly, for it turned
out they'd been waiting in this area already.
This surprised me because the reputation
of this place — for dark arts, for witchcraft
stories, sorcery stories, bogeymen rumours,
human-sacrifice rumours, scary tales about
upside-down crucifixes; regardless too, of
whether or not the state security forces with
their black ops and their dupery of a general
public were thought, least in these present
troubles, to be at the bottom of it — meant
most people might hurry through the ten-
minute area because they had to get from A
to B but other than that, would tend to stay
away. The fact I myself was in it, talking to
a sinister man while holding the head of a
cat that had been bombed to death by Nazis
was proof, if anything, that the ten-minute
area was not for normal things. But there
they were and there were four of them. It
seemed too, they were coming out of concealment or at least from half-concealment.
The first stepped out from a shop recess,
the shop being closed now because it was
evening and not because it was eerie and
should never have been opened. He came

from within the shadows and for a brief moment glanced towards us, then he looked away. After that he stood there ignoring us, though again why should he stand there? Two others then emerged from the decayed grounds of each of the derelict churches a little bit up from us and they too, briefly looked our way. Then they stood about — all three standing, expectant, waiting. They were also equi-distant from each other, with the milkman and I down at the other end. At first I had the fearful notion that these were plainclothes men about to ambush and shoot the milkman, which meant most likely they'd shoot me as an associate of this milkman. However, I sensed then that, as well as some current of mental triangulation going on between those three, there was a further connection reaching from them to us. It was that they were together, those three and the milkman. At that point a fourth and final man walked right by me and I jumped for I hadn't seen or heard him come up. He passed inches from me, without glancing or acknowledging either me or the milkman. This was when I gave another jump, for on turning away from him and back to the milkman, I realised that he had gone as well.

He had left me, and I didn't know why

that should have shocked me, given that not one thing about this man's presence had so far reassured me. It was that the instants and the suddens of him had each time caught me unawares. Automatically I looked again behind, townwards, in the direction that the fourth man was taking, to see if I could glance the milkman accompanying him. He couldn't have gone the other way, for I'd have caught sight of him heading towards those others. At that moment those men then chose also to walk by me and, although they did this individually, I continued to feel the coordination and sense of a shared plan. They were together. All four together. And all five — of this I was sure — were going to converge before long at the same point.

You're a mad person.
Once more this was me talking to myself after the milkman had left me. He and the others, doing that pretence of not being together, had gone off separately in the direction of downtown. I was now alone and had started to walk the opposite way out of this ten-minute area, my thoughts on tacit no-running threats, tacit no-walking threats and especially that tacit carbomb murder threat. Plus there was that cat's head I was

holding in my hands. With the time just off ten o'clock, and with only the tiniest of daylight remaining, there was no way, now, I was going to take it to the usual place. Things were different in the dark, but even if the last of the light should suffice to see me in there, get me down the back and in amongst those ancient stones and grasses; if it should suffice further to enable me to locate a place of repose for the head as initially I had intended, I felt that now, in spite of his having already met me and delivered unto me his latest commands and wishes, still that milkman could make another appearance from behind some Tombstone of Dracula to carry on the next part of his plan. I knew by now, regarding me, that he had a plan, some workable agenda. Therefore I couldn't be going to the graveyard. Still though, I did want to take the head some place. Deep foliage was what was wanted. Some patch of green, and, of course, such existed in the parks & reservoirs. As with this ten-minute area though, the parks & reservoirs, especially at night, were particularly not to be entered. Why transport a head anyway, from one dark place only to leave it in another dark place? And even if I managed to steel myself to go into the parks & reservoirs, to bury it

in some bush or hide it in some undergrowth, those state spies in the bush or in
the undergrowth — especially given their
sense of conviction of my association now
with the milkman — would dig it up immediately to see what it was. So not *that*
green. But there were other greens. The
weedy surrounds of the two remaining
churches were green, but yet again, they
were depressing. Besides, they were still in
this ten-minute area. There were gardens,
other people's, because we didn't have a
garden, so how about I choose an overgrown
one on my way home and sneak in and leave
it there? By now, this development of plan
had become overly involved and fretful,
meaning I wanted to give up which was not
at all the attitude. The attitude, however,
had been dissipating bit by bit even before
the appearance of the milkman. From the
moment I'd left teacher and my classmates
in town and had started to walk out of the
centre and up towards my own area, I'd felt
that constriction, that insidious *'There's no
point, what's the use, what's the point?'* coming over me or building up from within me
and it was while in that state of dithering
and of discouragement, also of berating
myself with, *'You're a mad girl, drawing
enfeeblement to yourself by your madness by*

the minute,' even as I was thinking too, to set the head down, just set it down, any-where, on the next bit of concrete and leave it, I realised I was already out of the ten-minute area and had walked up as far as the usual place. So I was at the ancient, rusted cemetery gates, and this was when I heard a car behind me. Instantly I had another attack of shudders. *Oh no. Him! Walk on. Keep walking. Don't look round or engage.*

I passed the graveyard entrance just as the vehicle drew alongside me. A voice called out. 'Hello! Hello there! Are you all right?' I stopped for it wasn't the milkman. It was someone else. It was real milkman, for there was a real milkman, one who lived in our area, who did take milk orders, who did have a proper milk lorry and who really did deliver the district's milk. He was also the man who didn't love anybody, one of our district's official beyond-the-pales. He lived around the corner from us and had been judged beyond-the-pale because one day he came back from that country 'over the water' where his brother had been dying and realised something was wrong in his house. He lived alone and had gone out his back to get a shovelful of coal and saw someone had been digging. So he dug too, to find out why. After a bit, and very dirty, he came out his door, carrying two armfuls of rifles. These rifles were wrapped in plastic and he carried them into the middle of the street and dumped them on the road. As he did so, he shouted, 'Bury them in your own backyards, why don't you!', then he returned to his house and came out with more. This continued because after the rifles came handguns, dismantled guns, heaps of ammunition and further stockpiles wrapped in cloths and more plastic. Everything got thrown, with him beside himself in temper, continuing to shout until he saw a pile of children who had been playing — up to the point he'd altered their landscape — on the spot where the guns now were. At first the children had jumped to the side and from there had been watching proceedings. When he caught sight of them, the man who didn't love anybody stopped shouting. Then he resumed shouting, this time at them. 'Get out of it!' he yelled. *'I said out of it!'* and he was so explosive that the children, now targets, did get out of it. A handful though, remained frozen to the spot and began to cry. The man who didn't love anybody then shouted to his neighbours who had come out their doors to see what the commotion was. He told them to come and get these children, demanding to know too, if any of these good neighbours had been aware of what, during his absence, the renouncers-of-the-state had been up to in his house. So he fought with everybody, this man who didn't love anybody, this real milkman. He even fought with children. But to draw the distinction: he became known as a beyond-the-pale because he'd dumped arms when everybody knew if you found arms in your house after they'd got in and buried them, you were supposed to lump it and put up with it; and he became known as the man who didn't love anybody because once, without compunction, without even saying sorry, he had made children cry.

So he wasn't popular with the renouncers for digging up their arsenal; not popular with them either, when he voiced dissent over their local rules and regulations; not popular again when he objected to their courts of nuisance and to the rough justice meted out by them whenever we inhabitants didn't obey their rules and regulations; and whenever he made a fuss over the disappearance of suspected informers, once again, and by the renouncers, he was disliked. Another point about him was that he never got credit from the residents of the area whenever credit was due to him. This would be during times he helped people, which often he did, in spite of his unloving reputation suggesting he did not. This inability of the community to acknowledge his good deeds was because his reputation for general all-round unfriendliness had become so fixed in the district consciousness that it would have taken an enormous explosion of conscious effort to shift that particular bit of hearsay on to the truth. As there was little inclination for re-adjusting even the tiniest of misperceptions here, such conscious mental effort to reach awareness on the part of the community on behalf of real milkman was never going to happen anytime soon. But he did help people. He helped nuclear boy's ma, who was also the mother of that renouncer-in-fantasy, Somebody McSomebody. On the evening of that day when nuclear boy had suicided, real milkman had gone looking for her, as others in the area had also gone looking for her. She'd gone missing on hearing the news of this latest family death. It was rumoured that just as with the son, she too, had gone off to suicide, but real milkman found her, roaming the streets of another district, distracted, dishevelled, not knowing anybody or even who she was. In spite of bringing her home, and in spite of seeking further help for her from the pious women who were also our medicos of the district, the designation still stood that real milkman was none other than the most horrid of people you could know. I myself didn't consider him horrid or very cross, or even much beyond-the-pale, that is, considering the other beyond-the-pales in our area. There was tablets girl, then her disconcerting shiny sister, then poor nuclear boy when he'd been alive, then the heavy-handed, preachy issue women. They all seemed far more on the rim than ever had been this man. Probably I viewed things that way because real milkman and my mother had been friends ever since their schooldays, which meant he paid visits to our house on a regular basis in order to see and to catch up with her. He assisted her too, with free milk and extra-fortified dairy, bakery and tinned provision products. And he helped out also with our house's DIY. He did the plumbing, the painting, the carpentry, even insisting on taking over the electrics from wee sisters. So, no matter his misanthropic ways, or his reputation for such ways, he did possess the characteristic of having a stern concern for people. And now, this man, real milkman, the man beyond-the-pale who was the man who didn't love anybody, had turned up that evening by the graveyard to help me.

First thing that happened was I got those shudders, although they died instantly upon realising this was not the milkman but the other one instead. He was in his lorry and it was a proper milk lorry, also the only vehicle I had ever seen him in. I turned to face him as the handbrake went on. He opened his door and jumped out and came over towards me. Next thing he was beside me and this hadn't been the first time he'd addressed me but it was the first time he'd said more than the polite, customary few words. Normally these words were 'hello', 'goodbye', or 'tell your mother I was asking'. Definitely, except for ma, real milkman and I didn't move in the same circles and even then, apart from living in the same house as her, I didn't exactly move in ma's circles, but with them two being friends, it stood to reason I'd run across him at close quarters now and then. This would be on the street, or outside our door, or inside our parlour, where ma would have made special barley bread or one of her other sweetbreads to share with tea with him. Sometimes too, I'd see her in his lorry, being dropped off home from the chapel or bingo or from doing her messages, jumping out of his lorry and laughing as if she were sixteen. So these were the occasions when me and him would meet and we'd greet each other and exchange general nods or 'hellos' and now he was asking again if I was all right. He asked if something had happened, if there was anything he could do for me. I nodded, though I'd no idea which question I was nodding in answer to. In truth I had difficulty rationalising what it was I was feeling or even how socially to respond to any question. It seemed I'd just encountered four renouncers — because probably those concealed men had been renouncers — going off to do some deed most likely to make top billing on the news later on. Then there'd been the milkman — probably not Walter Mitty but instead, as everybody said, another renouncer. And now here was real milkman, friend of my mother and one of the designated, outlandish beyond-the-pales. We were standing on the kribbie next to his lorry which was next to the graveyard, and I noticed he looked at the bundle of balled-up handkerchiefs I was holding between us. Then he stopped looking and returned his attention to my face.

I said, because it came out, 'I need to go somewhere and leave this or bury it, it's a cat's head.' 'Right,' he said as if I'd said, 'It's an apple,' and for that I liked him. I didn't explain how I'd come to have this head, or its link with the second world war or with the ten-minute area. He said, 'I'll take it off you. Will I take it off you?' And I handed it to him, quite easily, no hesitation, just like that. After I did I said, 'Don't throw it away but. Will you not just take it and throw it away but? Don't wait till I'm gone then dash it in some bin or throw it to the ground somewhere. If you don't want to do it, to take care of it properly, I mean, then I'll do it, but please don't pretend.' These were many words to come out of me, also true words for there was no excusing of myself here, no asking for permission or for approval. Later I was surprised at my forthrightness in speaking out to a male, to one of my elders, to someone too, with the fiercest reputation for being cross. I knew though, that my emotions had reached criti-cal point over what had happened between me and the milkman, also over holding this head for too long. There was something in this man's manner that seemed to make talking easy. And in this manner too, he was carrying on. 'I won't pretend and I won't throw it away,' he said. 'I want to give it some green,' I said. 'The right place is where I want to take it.' 'I know,' he said. 'Tell you what. I have green. Out my back there's a patch of green, so how about I put it there, dig a spot and bury it? Does that sound all right with you?' I nodded then I said, 'Thanks.' After that, he stepped to his lorry, reached in at floor level and drew out a green cloth bag and inside were billiards. He emptied these balls out into the deep hold between the lorry-seats, then slipped the head, which was yet in the hankies, into the bag and drew the string at the top. He came back round to me and said, 'Don't you worry. You leave it with me. Get in but, for it's late and I'll take you home now.' It seemed, and again I liked this, that this exchange was taking place in that *'How can we get this done?'* manner, that same manner of maybe-boyfriend, also of teacher, not the prevalent *'What's the point, nothing is of use, it's not gonna make any difference is it?'* and this surprised me. Real milkman, solemn, austere, yet here he was, giving me his time, bringing me hope, listening to me, taking me seriously. He had grasped all, he knew what I meant so that there were none of those enervating and exhausting questions. Yes, a surprise, but he was a surprise and I surprised myself at being able to hand over this burden, then to get in his lorry without worry and to know he could be trusted to be honest and to get the job done.

He put the head in the lorry and that was when the camera clicked — one of *their* cameras, the sound travelling from the first floor of a supposedly empty building just across the road from us and again, as with the milkman that time in the parks & reservoirs, I said nothing about it. Real milkman, however, said, 'Bloody —' then he checked himself. 'Can't go anywhere but they're at it,' he added. 'Well, they can make of this what they will.' This attitude again surprised me, and also unexpectedly up-lifted me. If he could acknowledge one of the unmentionables, also acknowledge he was unable to do anything to alter this unmentionable, maybe that meant it might be possible for anybody — for me — even in powerlessness, to adopt such an attitude of acknowledgement, of acceptance and detachment too.

We were driving along, with the bag contain-ing the hankies containing the head placed on top of the billiard balls in that roomy compartment bit of the lorry between us. This was when I heard of the latest death in our area which had taken place that day. It had occurred again in the family of Some-body McSomebody when wee tot, their youngest, fell from their upstairs back bedroom window. Real milkman said that at first it seemed he'd jumped, which was what had been assumed on the grapevine, that the toddler had leapt to his death but that the death hadn't been deliberate. It was because he'd thought himself Superman, the neighbourhood said. Or Batman. Or Spider-Man. Or one of those other heroes. He was always going about with that red pillowslip pinned to the back of him, shouting, *'Biff!', 'Bash', 'Whamo!', 'Bamo!', 'Lights out!', 'Aarrgh!'*. It hadn't been proved though, said real milkman, that that was how his death in reality had come about. It was being rumoured that way, he said, because that was the thing people invented here because you couldn't just die here, couldn't have an ordinary death here, not anymore, not of natural causes, not by accident such as falling out a window, especially not after all the other violent deaths taking place in this district now. It had to be political, he said. Had to be about the border, meaning comprehensible. Failing that, it had to be out-of-the-ordinary, dramatic, something startling, such as thinking oneself a superhero and accidentally jumping to one's death. People expect that now, he said. So a three-year-old mite, not understanding gravity, or that he was just a wee boy left on his own in the back upstairs room — with his mother also upstairs in the front room but who wasn't coming out since retreating there in grief, lying on her bed, her mind wandering — made a fatal mistake but not one which proved enough of a reason for someone to die now in the area. Life here, said real milkman, simply has to be lived and died in extremes. It turned out the child had been found in the backyard in the late morning by one of his sisters. There hadn't been any pillowslip pinned to the back of him either. That day it had been unpinned to be put in the wash.

I listened to real milkman tell me this, telling also that ma wasn't at home, that he'd left her recently at the house of Somebody McSomebody, that the other neighbours — the pious women, with their brews and first aid and other top-secret concoctions — were also round at McSomebody's, all trying to comfort that dead child's poor ma. Real milkman himself had just come from the morgue and he too, he said, was now heading back to the McSomebodys'. He spoke more on the tragedy then, spoke too, of tragedy in general, its waste, the lack of foresight, of prevention, of all the ramifications stemming from poverty and these stubborn, entrenched political problems. He went on, mentioning neglect and disadvantage and disfavour and the loss of good opportunities and for a while seemed to go away in his thoughts. When he came back, and I didn't know if this was by way of association, but he had moved on in his talk to wee sisters, and to me, and to ma.

'Your younger sisters,' he said. 'Such bright little girls, such wonderful curiosity and guts and passion and engagement. A natural sense too, they have, of entitlement which as you know in this place is rare. More often it's the case that keenness and initiative get stifled here, turned to discouragement, twisted too, into darker channels. But it's that in their nonage they are little girls somewhat wild and uncontained. At times they're ghoulish,' he went on, 'and I'm sure too, they must be a mighty handful for your mother.' He said that probably they would become more so as the years progressed and they expanded in their thirst for knowledge and for intellectual adventure. He had another think then said, 'It's that I believe she might not understand, your dear mother, maybe doesn't notice their uniqueness, what might be called their genius. And I don't know why either, their teachers aren't picking up on it. Are their teachers picking up on it? Have they spoken to your mother about it?' I thought for a moment then said, 'I don't know.' Then he asked about their school reports and I said, 'I don't know,' and in fact, it was 'I don't know' to every question about wee sisters thereafter that he put to me. But truly I didn't know and how could I be expected to know when these were just wee sisters? They went to school. They read their books. They had discussions and forums and compendia and symposia and comparing and contrasting and exchanges of ideas and what they referred to too, as extra-curricular activities and I didn't know all they had them on. I had vague notions that their teachers were involved in accounts of this intelligence and talent and precocity. They sent letters and reports to ma. I myself never looked at this correspondence because again, why would I involve myself in school talk to do with wee sisters? I am eighteen, their sibling, not their mother, not their father, not their guardian, so to involve myself in all that would be akin to going on about sunsets and temperatures and false teeth and aches and pains and 'What are you having for dinner?' and all those things old people did tend to go on about. Why would I? I think some teachers though, did come to speak to ma. They called her into the school too, because now that I was remembering, it was for special meetings on how to further wee sisters' something or other that they invited her. 'Educationese' I recalled had been mentioned. Or 'educationalese'. Something like that. They came out to the house too, those teachers, also other educationalese type of people, and they had more discussions and I'm not sure ma herself understood all it was these experts were saying to her, though I did know she'd been meaning to have that letter that subsequently arrived from that child-genius academy interpreted for her by wee sisters only she hadn't managed to get round to showing it to them yet. As for regular school-term reports, I'm not sure ma read them, or gave account to them, or even wee sisters themselves gave account to them. School reports and certificates here, they didn't mean much. 'Not to criticise your mother,' real milkman was saying, 'for she's one fine woman, still a fine woman, a lovely woman, and I know she's had a hard time what with your father dying and your second brother dying and your second sister — well, you know what happened with your sister. Then there's your other brother, the fourth one who — but you know what happened with him as well. I think I might ask her about this because there's great potential here and rightly it should be channelled and firmly directed before another terrible disaster occurs, another waste, another of these tragedies. Such misdirection of energy and enterprise is to be avoided. They need guidance, need to be discerned and attended to. Could take a wrong turn otherwise,' and I said, 'Yeah,' because I was trying to be conversational but then something came into my mind as to what he might mean by 'a wrong turn'. He had said about potentiality and naïveté getting twisted, about lack of experience being put to mistaken ends, to dangerous ends, which of course I took to mean — for what else was there? — bad outcomes stemming from the political problems. And although wee sisters hadn't shown any inordinate interest in our political problems — not any more, that is, than their interest in phonological places of articulation, or Early Kingdom Egyptology, or the finer points of technical singing, or the state of the universe before it was reduced to order, or the Apotheosis of Heracles, or indeed any of their other many indices and appendices and marginalia and small notes at backs of books and all the rest of it — there was a time a while back when me and the older sisters came in the door and found wee sisters reading the papers from 'over there'. It was the broadsheet newspapers they were reading and they had a few tabloids from 'over there' also. We couldn't imagine where they'd got them but they had them and at that moment had them spread out in broad view all over the floor. Until that point wee sisters had never looked at these papers, or watched the political news on television, least not watched in any avid way. Instead they'd been going through their Joan of Arc phase. While in it, they let it be known that they were not fond of that country from 'over the water', not though, because of the usual legacy of history, and of the power of history that had been built up and passed down and reshaped and elaborated upon over what had taken place involving that country and this country — but because of their very natural support of the French. However, it was also because of the betrayal of Joan that they then turned temporarily against the French, with the dauphin, never a favourite to start with, so unpopular with wee sisters to the point that, had anyone in my area been inclined to put in a word for him, they'd have been wise not to have done so within earshot of the girls. So that was how disliked too, the French had become, so that any age-old antipathy between the country 'over the water' and this country hardly got a look in. But my older sisters and I came in that day and we found them, no longer deep in Joan but now at those papers. *'Wee sisters!'* we cried. *'Where'd you get these? What on earth is going on?'* 'Hush, older sisters,' they said. 'We're busy. We're trying to understand their viewpoint.' After that they returned to poring over their broadsheets and tabloids while we, their elder sisters, disbelievingly looked on. Then we looked at each other — me, third sister, second sister and first sister. *Trying to understand their viewpoint!* What obscurity would wee sisters utter next? As for their remark, it was of the type that instantly could taint any person in our area. Did 'INFORMANTS BEWARE' mean nothing to those three at all? In our wisdom we tried to point this out, saying that by associating themselves with disallowed paraphernalia they were laying themselves open to accusations of traitorship. But they didn't heed us, hardly chose to attend us, had forgotten us, so deep were they in those papers from 'over there'. It was clear to us, their elders, that they'd no care for any motive a passing neighbour, chancing to look in our window, might decide to put upon this matter. Third sister leapt to the window and drew the curtains, which annoyed wee sisters, so one of them sprang up and switched the overhead light on. Another clicked on ma's two favourite old-time glass lamps and the third got out their three little flashlights. But where'd they get those papers? Had anybody from our area caught sight of them procuring those papers? And so it was on that day that we elder speculated as to whether ages six, seven and eight might not be considered too young by the paramilitaries to punish in the usual manner those thought to be informers, or whether wee sisters might be rebuked only, then ordered by the renouncers to leave off those periodicals and to return instead to *Bamber the Pig* like little children everywhere else. So was this what real milkman was referring to when he spoke of naïveté, of misdirected keenness, of an ongoing sense of adventure being subverted? I didn't dare ask. Instead, and because he'd grown silent again, I offered that bit about their teachers getting involved and the talk that was made about exceptional learning establishments and in saying this I felt some relief that after his helping me with the cat, I could contribute something of reassurance to him as well. But he wasn't reassured. He expressed again his worry about wee sisters and about ma having to cope unaided which was when it struck me that he mightn't have been ruminating out loud but instead could have been dropping hints for me to pick up on. Was he imputing that the guidance and direction of wee sisters should be down to me, their sister, as well as down to ma? Had I, along with ma, to become involved, to be responsible, to take a hand in their orientation and upbringing? At this I felt dismay. If I had to co-manage wee sisters, definitely I wouldn't be able to move in with maybe-boyfriend. Again this surprised me that even now, ever since he'd asked me and I'd said no, still I was playing out the scenario of how it would be if I were to move in with maybe-boyfriend. Hopes I hadn't known I'd entertained were being threatened because of my having to become an apprentice-mother along with my mother. Real milkman, meanwhile, had moved to a new subject. That was the one of the milkman and me. He didn't say outrightly, 'Are you having an affair with that man who is two hundred years old?' Instead he intimated that he was aware there might be an encroachment upon me by some person of paramilitary intent, also one of might and influence in the area. He asked that if that were so, would I feel strong enough to be able to stand up and speak out? As he spoke, I felt myself tighten, whereas until that point with real milkman I'd felt increasingly relaxed or at least not so very anxious. The shudders had stopped. The unnatural movements had stopped. But all returned, as did my confusion, which was when I noticed he was confused as well. He began to apologise for blundering into territory that was not his business. Then he brought up the issue women of our area, mentioning that indeed, they seemed to know an awful lot about gender history and sexual politics. 'I regret to say,' he said, 'that I myself don't understand mickle-much of these up-and-coming women's topics. Given though, they have all this expertise, and because it's well into their chosen territory, might you, if you feel unsafe speaking out on the matter generally in the area, go and have a wee word with them instead?'

Go and have a wee word? Was he crazy as well as blind and deaf and dumb to what was said about those women in this area? I'd be committing social suicide even to catch eyes with one of them in the street. So no thanks. Not keen to have a word, not now, not ever. These women, constituting the nascent feminist group in our area — and exactly because of constituting it — were firmly placed in the category of those way, way beyond-the-pale. The word 'feminist' was beyond-the-pale. The word 'woman' barely escaped beyond-the-pale. Put both together, or try unsuccessfully to soften things with another word, a general word, one in disguise such as 'issues' and basically you've had it. Awful things were said about these women with the issues in our district, not just behind their backs but to their faces as well.

It started with a notice put in the window of a house by the housewife who lived in that house and who seemed traditional and normal until she put up this notice. She had a husband and children, with nobody violently killed in her family either, to have accounted, it was said, for her subsequent out-of-character behaviour, but she put this notice up and it was far from the usual type of proclamation to be seen in windows of certain houses in our area at this time. The usual ones said things like 'KEEP OUT OF THIS PROPERTY ON PAIN OF DEATH — THIS, THE ONLY INTIMATION' then signed 'DISTRICT RENOUNCERS' as a warning to any of us wayward inhabitants, including children, who might have a notion to break into some vulnerable person's residence — to have a play there, to have a teenage person's dossing-down drinking session there, to explore and poke about there, even to squat there — without giving any thought to the usually far-gone and wretched alcoholic who already lived there and whose house it was. They were making it clear, our renouncers, that if we persisted in our unjust, inconsiderate and merciless behaviour towards the more fragile of our district, then ramifications would follow that certainly we would all regret. In contrast, this housewife's notice said 'ATTENTION ALL WOMEN OF THE DISTRICT: GREAT GOOD NEWS!!!' then followed information about some international women's group that had been inaugurated recently into the world. It was seeking to set up sister branches in all the world's countries, with no place — no city, no town, no village, no hamlet, no district, no hovel, no isolated residence — to be excluded from the remit, with no woman — again, any colour, any creed, any sexual preference, any disability, mental illness or even general dislikeability, indeed, of any type of diversity — to be excluded from the venture, and amazingly a sister branch of this international women's group sprang up in our very downtown. Its first monthly meeting received shocking reports in the media both before and after it happened, reports based mainly on this meeting having had the audacity to come into existence in the first place. The criticism was bad, very bad, much along the lines of 'depravity, decadence, demoralisation, dissemination of pessimism, outrages to propriety' as had been levelled at that red-light street when first it became inaugurated. However, the media backlash did nothing to prevent at least some women from some of the areas moseying along downtown to see what all this sisterhood branch of international women's issues was about. These female participants hailed not just from the two warring religions here, but also from a smattering of the lesser known, lesser attended to, indeed completely ignored, other religions. One woman from our district went along and did so too, off her own bat. She didn't seek permission, didn't seek approval, didn't ask anyone's opinion or request they go with her for moral support and protection. Instead she put on her shawl, took her purse, her key, and went out her door just like that. It turned out this woman was the housewife who subsequently stuck up the

notice. 'And she stuck it up,' said neighbours, 'barely a fraction of time after she
got back from that meeting downtown.'
Meanwhile, in liaison with the downtown
sister branch, which was itself in liaison with
the overall international women's movement
of the world headquarters, this woman was
now seeking to set up a sub-sorority branch
in our district, just as some other women
from other districts were now attempting in
theirs. That was what she did. In her notice
in the window, and in a daring modern
fashion, she invited all women from the area
to put their children out for their evening
adventures as usual then, unencumbered, to
make their way of a Wednesday evening to
her house to hear talk. They would be
amazed, promised the poster, by points of
female significance such as had arisen during that downtown branch meeting; also,
should they themselves feel inclined to air
views on anything which could be classed
as an overall women's issue, such would be
fed back monthly to the next downtown
meeting, then fed quarterly to the next
overall international meeting. Confusingly,
there was no mention in this notice of our
border issue or our political problems here
at all. Men and women in the district were
astonished. 'What can she be about? What-

ever can she mean to put such a thing in her window?' And they gossiped about her, and her notice, leaving off only to move back to normal topics, such as who might be an informer, who was having the latest adulterous sex, and which country might win Miss World when next it had its airing on the TV. So this notice was talked to death, then it was dismissed, with most in the area of the opinion that nothing could come of it other than the woman would be felt sorry for or, if she persisted, wondered at as another candidate for beyond-the-pale. At worst, the renouncers-of-the-state would take her away as the latest person acting suspiciously in our area, which would be, more or less, true. Instead, and in the first week since the notice went up, two local women appeared at the door of this house-wife, which made three for the inaugural Wednesday Women's Issues Meeting. The following week there was added another four. No more women turned up after that, but altogether there were now seven of these individuals and they met every Wednesday evening, being joined fortnightly by a knowledgeable coordinator from the down-town group. This coordinator would give pep talks, speak of expansion, introduce historical and contemporary comment on

262

women's issues, all to help bring, she said, women from everywhere out of the dark and into the fold. Once a month too, this group would travel downtown to the branch meeting of the combined sub-groups from all districts 'this side of the water' and 'this side of the border' which had managed to get themselves inaugurated. Naturally, by this time, in our area, the usual paranoid stories started up.

One story circulating about our group of sub-branch women centred around the place of their meetings because after the first three Wednesdays the first housewife's husband didn't want them carrying on in this feminist fashion in the actual house he and his wife lived in because, nice as he was, conciliatory as he'd like to be, he was sorry but there was his own reputation to look out for. This didn't deter the women for they set about making the first woman's backyard shed nice and cosy for their meetings instead. Before this though, they had approached the chapel to see if one of the tin hutments on the wasteground could be made available for them. The chapel owned the hutments and often it permitted various bodies — chiefly, the renouncers — to have use of them for their business, such as defence-of-the-area meetings, furtherance-of-the-cause meetings, kangaroo-court meetings but it refused to let the women borrow one or hire one because there'd been a transformation in opinion regarding these women by this time. No longer were they viewed as harmless, as childlike, as objects of raillery, as playing about at holding adult-issue meetings because here they were, now seeking a proper venue in which to pursue these meetings. A new belief sprang into existence as to why exactly they'd want to do that. 'If they get a hutment,' said the area, 'they could be up to anything in it. They could be plotting subversive acts in it. They could be having homosexual intercourse in it. They could be performing and undergoing abortions in it,' the result being, of course, that the chapel said no. It stated that in accordance with . . . , in contravention of . . . , on the grounds that . . . , to grant the women's request would be as scandalous and unprincipled of the chapel as already it was for the women to be making it. So they disallowed use of the hutments owing to disgrace and unspeakableness which didn't stop the women, for right away they set about painting and decorating the shed. They put up shelves, curtains, brought in oil lamps, a primus stove, colourful teacups, a tea caddy, a biscuit tin, warm fluffy rugs and flowers and cushions. Around the walls they put posters of exemplary worldwide issue women obtained from the downtown sister branch which had obtained them from the international women's headquarters. But before that, our seven women got the husband of the first woman to go into the shed to deal with the spiders and the insects for them, which the husband, under condition they kept silent about his involvement in this matter, agreed in the dead of night to do.

The second story put about about these aborting homosexual insurrectionists was that the eighth one, the woman who wasn't from our district but the wise, knowledgeable facilitator from the downtown sister branch who'd come to visit our women fortnightly — to buck them up, to encourage with zeal and who brought with her each time mounds of pamphlets on the abundance of women's issues — was from the other side's religion and also from the country 'over there'. Normally this would have been fine, completely all right given that, first of all, she was female, which meant of lesser significance as a potential threat to district paramilitary activity than would have been some visiting male person to the area. Two, she'd been invited into the area by seven local women which ordinarily would have been ample reference and recommendation for her. However, owing to these particular women being themselves hardly normal, any invitation they might extend would carry nowhere near the same weight as that of anyone else. This meant the eighth woman could no longer be allowed to enter, least not until vigorously vetted. After all, warned the grapevine, might she not be an issue woman really, a women's libber really, but instead some slippery *agente provocatrice* for the state? After a bit of exaggeration and the usual escalation of rumour, a spy, of course, became what she was. In the eyes of the community, and especially in the eyes of the paramilitaries, this eighth woman was an enemy out to entrap into informership our seven naïve and dotty women. So one Wednesday night-time the renouncers burst into the shed to take her away. They barged in — in Halloween masks, balaclavas, with guns, with a few secure enough in power and stature to eschew any type of facial covering — but all they found when they got inside were our seven women in their shawls and slippers, having tea and buns and discussing in chintz earnestness the ramifications of the massacre of the women and children by the yeomanry at the nineteenth-century Battle of Peterloo. On the walls around the shed, and overshadowing, also momentarily stunning the renouncers, loomed enormous, larger-than-life pin-ups of inspirational, prototypal past and present wonderwomen: the Pankhursts, Millicent Fawcett, Emily Davison, Ida Bell Wells, Florence Nightingale, Eleanor Roosevelt, Harriet Tubman, Mariana Pineda, Marie Curie, Lucy Stone, Dolly Parton — those sorts of women — but there was no eighth woman, because the other seven, attending carefully to the grapevine in our district, had warned their sister of this imminent danger and instructed her in no small terms not to come. All the same, the renouncers, recovering from the brain-shock of the false impression produced by additional, enormous women from down the centuries being present in that moment with our seven women, ransacked the tiny shed, which took a second, looking for the eighth woman. Then they warned the issue women not to have her back on pain of her being killed as a spy-agent with they, themselves, severely punished for aiding and abetting the state. Owing, however, to a burgeoning outlook that encompassed an attitude of confidence and entitlement, something snapped within the issue women and unexpectedly they declared they would not. What they meant was, they would not be dictated to, that in spite of the eighth woman probably never to return because the renouncers ruined everything, should she choose to do so, not only would they not reject her, they'd stand foursquare behind her and the renouncers themselves could go hang. Things were said then on both sides, with further threats from the renouncers and declamations on the ills of patriarchy and of pedagogy from the issue women. Finally, 'Over our dead bodies,' said the seven in a somewhat fatalistic 'digging their own graves' fashion, which of course, played straight into the renouncers' hands. Unlike the traditional women from our district who, on occasion, would instinctively unite and rise up to put an end to some gone-mad political or district problem, these seven women — bold as they'd been in their inspired moment of standing up to the renouncers — didn't and couldn't constitute the same robust critical mass. So they said, 'Over our dead bodies' with the renouncers replying, 'Okay then. Over your dead bodies' and if it hadn't been for the traditional women, including ma, getting to hear, then involving themselves in this matter, our particular sister branch of the international women's movement — owing to the sudden and violent demise of all of its members — would there and then have come to an end. As it was, the district's normal women did get to hear and, uniting once more, they threw themselves into action. This too, was in spite of reservations they held, not just of having to deal with what was, in its own amassment, a tenacious killing-machine of renouncers, but because of the third story doing the rounds about these tiresome issue women, one which impacted adversely and exasperatingly upon the traditional women themselves.

Women always broke the curfews. That would be the traditional women because until recently, there hadn't been any new-fangled branch of sisterhood women. This breaking of the curfews too, would be because the traditional women's patience would have been stretched far enough. It would have been over-tried, overtested and the subsequent snapping of it would be directed towards any group of men, any religion, any side of the water, setting up rules and regulations, overreaching them-selves with their rules and regulations, expecting everyone else too — meaning women — to go along with the preposterousness of the silliness they had concocted as rationale in their heads. Basically, it was the toybox mentality, the toy trains in the attic, the toy soldiers on the toy battlefield and, in the case of the state and the military, the particular toy of choice that they'd get out of the box every so often was curfews where the rules were, if you broke one without a permit after eighteen hundred hours and sometimes after just sixteen hundred hours, without fear or favour, without respect for station, on sight you would be shot. So it was bad enough having to deal with your own particular brand of paramilitaries with all their touchy rules and pedantic expectations. But when also you had to factor in the other side with their equally ridiculous runners and riders, it was out of the question really, that the traditional woman's forbearance would not, in these circumstances, snap. So it would snap — because life was going on — children to be fed, nappies to be changed, housework to be done, shopping to be got in, political problems, best as could be managed, skirted around or in some other way accommodated. So patience would snap then, united, and in spite of the police and military poring over and adjusting beloved touches to tactics and game-plans before setting out with rifles and loudhailers to make sure nobody was breaking the curfew, these women would break the curfew by taking off their aprons, putting on their coats, shawls, scarves and with the bush telegraph already up and running, they'd go out their doors in their hundreds and deliberately, and permitless, and after eighteen hundred hours or just sixteen hundred hours, encumber the pavements, the streets, every patch of disallowed curfew territory, amply spreading themselves all around. Not just themselves either. With them would be their children, their screaming babies, their housepets of assorted dogs, rabbits, hamsters and turtles. Also they'd be wheeling their prams and carrying their pennants, their banners, their placards and shouting, 'CURFEW'S OVER! EVERYBODY IS TO COME OUT! CURFEW'S OVER!', thereby inviting all in the area who weren't already out, to come out, so that everybody could enter into state defiance and every time so far when the traditional women had done this, when they'd reclaimed sanity, the police and the military would find the latest curfew, right before their eyes, had stopped. To shoot up a district of women, children, prams and goldfish otherwise, to run them through with swords much as one might like

271

to, would not look good, would look grave, sexist, unbalanced, not only in the glare of the critical side of the home media, but also in the eyes of the international media. So, curfew over, the military and the state would go back to the playbox to find out what else might be in there, with the traditional women — after further obligatory banner-waving, picketing, pressure protests and interviews — returning home in haste, emptying the streets in seconds, all to get in to get the evening tea on.

So that was the usual procedure for the breaking of the curfews. Regarding the latest to be broken, however, events unfurled in not quite the same way. This was because our seven issue women decided this time to involve themselves in it. As usual, and so many days into the curfew, the normal women had had enough. They went out their doors, amassing in contrariness to 'RETURN TO YOUR HOMES. THIS IS NOT A GAME. THIS IS THE LAST INTIMATION. OBEY THE SIXTEEN HUNDRED HOUR CURFEW. IF YOU ARE NOT OFF THE STREET IN . . .' This time, however, our issue women were among the normal women, with the latter at first thinking nothing of it. Everyone, after all, should be welcomed in standing up to the state. To the exasperation of the traditional women, however, and just as they themselves had once more defeated the curfew and were about to rush home to deal with the potatoes, the women with the issues usurped the purpose of the curfew-break, though later they maintained this was hardly their fault. They said it was the media's fault, and indeed the media had espied the issue women via their placards in amongst the traditional women carrying their own placards. And even though there were only seven of these issue women compared to the few hundred of traditional women, all the world's cameras instantly focused upon them. Wasn't either, that the traditional women craved fame and celebrity, that they wanted to be on TV as well as in all of the world's newspapers. It was that they didn't want to be identified as part of protests that weren't aimed at anything other than breaking the curfew and especially not with the issues these women talked ceaselessly on and on about. The normal women had been expecting, indeed dreading, that the issue women, once started, would take the exposure opportunity to harp on in a broad, encyclopaedic fashion about injustice towards and trespasses against women, not just in the present day but all through the ages, using terminology such as 'terminology', 'case studies show', 'incorporates the systemic, transhistoric, institutionalised and legislated antipathy of' and so on that completely these days these women appeared to be steeped in. There would be the injustices too, thought the traditional women, those big ones, the famous ones, the international ones — witch-burnings, footbindings, suttee, honour killings, female circumcision, rape, child marriages, retributions by stoning, female infanticide, gynaecological practices, maternal mortality, domestic servitude, treatment as chattels, as breeding stock, as possessions, girls going missing, girls being sold and all those other worldwide cultural, tribal and religious socialisations and scandalisations, also the warnings given against things throughout patriarchal history that were seen as uncommon for a woman to do or think or say. But no. Not that, which in the middle of a local curfewbreak would have been bad enough. Instead these local issue women spoke of homespun, personal, ordinary things, such as walking down the street and getting hit by a guy, any guy, just as you're walking by, just for nothing, just because he was in a bad mood and felt like hitting you or because some soldier from 'over the water' had given him a hard time so now it was your turn to have the hard time so he hits you. Or having your bum felt as you're walking along. Or having loud male comment passed upon your physical characteristics as you're passing. Or getting molested in the snow under the guise of some nice friendly snowfight. Or getting hang-ups in the summer about the summer because if you didn't wear much clothes because it was warm, if you wore a little dress, that would bring upon you all that general summertime street harassment. Then there was menstruation and how it was seen as an affront to being a person. And pregnancy too, how that couldn't be helped but all the same, an affront to being a person. Then they spoke about ordinary physical violence as if it wasn't just normal violence, also speaking of how getting your blouse ripped off in a physical fight, or your brassiere ripped off in a physical fight, or getting felt up in a fight wasn't violence that was physical so much as it was sexual even if, they said, you were supposed to pretend the bra and the breast had been incidental to the physical violence and not the disguised point of the physical violence, making it sexual violence all along. 'Those sorts of things,' said the traditional women.

'Spoken too,' they said, 'in all that language of terminology, and only to be laughed at, for everyone was laughing at them — the cameras, the reporters, even the curfew-makers — and no wonder, with all this linen they insist in taking out in public all the time.' What mostly got to the traditional women, however, was that anybody in the world watching would think that they, the sensible traditional women, were also these issue women. So frostiness set in, owing to this hijacking by the issue women of the curfew, and that was the state of affairs when the issue women said 'Over our dead bodies' to the renouncers. The traditional women, although irritated as one might be by idiots wanting to help wash-up but then clumsily breaking all the dishes, nevertheless felt they couldn't just let the renouncers do their usual deadly thing.

Which was why they went to see them, to see the renouncers. 'Don't be ridiculous,' they said. 'You can't kill them. They're simpletons. Intellectual simpletons. Academe! That's all they're fit for.' They added that to do away with the issue women, no matter how annoying they were, would be tantamount to unjust, inconsiderate and merciless behaviour towards the more fragile of our district; that by doing so, the renouncers would create one of those land-mark incidents such as would bring regret-ful consequences for their reputation in his-tory books later on. Instead the traditionals said the renouncers could leave the issue women to them, that they themselves would see to it, that they'd go downtown and have a private word with that eighth woman. This was said as diplomatically as possible, as if presenting to the renouncers not a directive but a favour or, even better, an urgent request for assistance and, although the re-nouncers in their turn knew the difference between a directive and a request for as-sistance, the fact that their survival as an armed guerrilla outfit in a tightly knit, anti-state environment depended upon local support in that environment, meant that they were quite willing to engage in polite brinkmanship too. They appeared to muse aloud, saying that those women being simpletons or not, and without fear or favour, they would not have the movement or its members jeopardised, nor would it be possible to make allowances for the seven should the eighth dare show her face again in the area. In the end, and after some backwards and forwards — and no matter how much the seven, meantime, continued to harangue about taking a bullet to defend their fellow eighth sister which the renouncers ignored and which had the traditional women telling the issue women just to be quiet and stop talking — both the traditionals and the renouncers seemed to close on some deal. Three of our traditionals then paid a visit downtown to the sub-branch eighth woman to explain the situation. 'We don't know what you've washed our women's brains with,' they said. 'We don't know if you're Mata Hari. We don't care what happens to you. What we don't want is for us normal women always having to drop our common tasks and daily rounds to prevent our daft women from being taken away by our paramilitaries. So we mean it. Stay out of our area.' The eighth woman agreed and that spelled the end of any outside issue woman with expansive worldviews coming to visit our totalitarian enclave and those three stories — the shed behaviour, the association with a state agent, and our seven women putting up the backs of not just our traditionals but also our renouncers — were the reasons why I kept away from these women myself. There was too much of risk, and besides, they were challenging the status quo while I was trying to go under the radar of the status quo. Plus they were being carefully reviewed for furthering signs of deterioration. Even if in some measure regarding their issues I might be in agreement, there was no way ever I was going to link with them. That was why I kept quiet in the lorry with real milkman, listening politely until he came to the end of his words.

This he did easily enough, the words petering out, probably owing to his own bewilderment over what those women stood for. After that, our journeying went silent, though we were now well away from both the ten-minute area and the usual place. We had reached and passed too, all my remaining landmarks — the police barracks, the house of baking-bread, the holy women's house, the parks & reservoirs, followed by the interface roads, then the street with the tiny house of third sister and third brother-in-law. After that we reached and stopped outside my front door. 'You go in now,' said real milkman. 'It's uncommonly dark, a densely dark night, but don't worry. I'll take care of what we talked about.' Here, he indicated the cat's head. 'Tell your ma,' he then said, 'if I've missed her at that poor woman's when I get round there, that I'll come and see her tomorrow.' I nodded and was about to ask again if really and truly he'd bury it and not pretend he was going to bury it, but then I knew I didn't have to ask that. 'Thanks,' I fumbled, and I was tired, suddenly tired, as if drunkenly tired. So exhausted did I feel that hardly could I get that last 'Thanks' out. I wanted to say it again, properly, meaning thank you for the cat, for bringing me home, for being ma's friend, for being a person in the background. I didn't though. Instead I got out of his lorry while he waited with the engine running. Then, with the sky now pitch black above us, I got out my key and slipped it — for the first time in what felt like ages — easily, without a shake, into the lock.

FOUR

That third encounter with the milkman was not the end of the milkman. Further meetings — real ones as well as the communally fabricated ones — also took place. At the real ones, and similar to when we met in the ten-minute area, the milkman didn't pretend any accidental bumping into me. There was no feigned surprise, no 'fancy seeing you here'. Instead it was, 'Ah, there you are,' plus other familiar expressions, all said casually as if we were fulfilling on some prior arrangement to meet up. These meetings took place everywhere. I'd pop to the local shops, he'd be there. I'd go into town, he'd be there. I'd come out of work, he'd be there. I'd visit the library, he'd be there. Even when I'd go to places and come out of them and he wasn't there, still it seemed as if he was there. Sometimes too, I'd recognise one of those district spotters and think, that child's been sent by him to spot me. Probably hadn't, of course. More likely the infant was doing its normal state-forces and military-insurgency spotting, or maybe it was having a day off from spotting. Thing was, my growing suspicions of almost everyone and everything was proof of how the milkman had got in. He'd infiltrated my psyche and now it was clear those first three meetings had never been the accidental encounters I'd tried to pretend to myself they had been. And now he was appearing, stopping me, standing in the way of me or falling into step beside me, all in the manner of some ordinary meeting up. This felt an injustice. In my memory-lapse moments I'd long for the ordinary things with boys, daydreaming of how nice it would be if maybe-boyfriend and I could meet in one of those regular fashions at the end of our workdays, the way I'd see proper couples meeting at the end of their workdays. The proper boyfriend would finish his work then stroll round to the City Hall to await his proper girlfriend. She too, would finish her work then make her way, in an equally ordinary entitled fashion, roundabouts to the City Hall to meet him. Quite a number of couples did this. I'd see them at it as I was going home from work and I'd know this was part of what made up proper coupledom. In some casual, comfortable, everyday manner they'd meet and do some casual, comfortable, everyday thing. They might go to a fish-and-chip salon for supper and over their meal, chat and exchange news on how their day was going. Although this ordinariness seemed a simple thing, I knew really it was the biggest thing, demonstrating that in proper coupledom there was nothing of the 'maybe' going on. Not so with us. My timetable and maybe-boyfriend's timetable didn't permit of this kind of intimacy. Really though, it was our 'maybe' status that didn't permit of this kind of intimacy. But now, with these escalating unwanted encounters, and in just that way he'd read my mind regarding the Greek and Roman class, again this milkman was picking up on my secret desires and dreams. But he was the wrong man. And this taking me for granted was without my acquiescence. Still though, he kept appearing, incapable of being averted; sometimes too, I'd see him, or think I'd see him, when downtown with maybe-boyfriend at the bars and clubs. These bars, these clubs, they were uncertain venues, risky venues, few in number too, owing to the political problems. In theory they were places anyone could go to, meaning mixed places, intended for all religions. There were smatterings of other religions apart from the two warring religions but in comparison with the warring ones, those others, whatever they were, didn't count. Also in these downtown socialising environments state-appointed undercover squads with their spying, their infiltrating, their hidden weapons and sessions of photography, were frequenters, meaning they were okay to go to, these bars, these clubs, for one drink say, or two drinks, but not the sort of place you'd want to end up drunk in. That was why most locals who were ordinary people — such as me and maybe-boyfriend — not up to anything political, might drop in to start with, to have a drink or two, to marvel at the idiocy of tourists, then to move on to more safely acceptable drinking establishments in the staunchly no-go areas elsewhere. In our case it was always his no-go area and not my no-go area because of the danger of ma weighing in with her assessment questions and marriage plans. Lately though, while downtown at the bars and clubs with maybe-boyfriend, I'd find myself glancing around, anxious that the milkman might be in here with us. I thought he might be watching us, spying on us, perhaps taking secret pictures of us, and especially I'd be worried because he'd made his position clear on my dating maybe-boyfriend. Yet here I was, still dating maybe-boyfriend, which didn't mean, however, I'd dismissed that bomb threat.

We'd had a fight about it, maybe-boyfriend and me, because the milkman was keeping up the pressure by continuing to highlight it, to make veiled threats, to count down time, to get his point over, basically: stop seeing the young guy or else. Again, he did this by mentioning maybe-boyfriend, then cars, then eldest sister whose husband — the one of her heart she didn't marry and not the sex-addict gossip whom, out of grief, loss and despair she did marry — had been killed that time by that defender-of-the-state bomb. 'Carbomb, wasn't it?' he'd say again. So it would be maybe-boyfriend. Then cars. Then sister. Then dead lover. Then carbombs. Then it was back to maybe-boyfriend till by the end his words were putting me in mind of Somebody McSomebody and his unrelenting stalk-talk. Eventually he'd get round to maybe-boyfriend *and* carbombs *and* the dead man who'd been sister's lover all in the same sentence, so impossible it was not to grasp what he was dropping big hints about. I did grasp. I drew the allusion, made the underpinnings and next I was picking that fight with maybe-boyfriend. At the time, and given the way my mind was going, it seemed to me this fight was entirely maybe-boyfriend's fault. Not a case either, this wasn't, of my not talking anymore, because here I was, talking. Unfortunately though, because of the loose status of our relationship; because he lived the other side of town so wouldn't have heard the rumour that I was now this milkman's new love interest; because I was confused and becoming enfeebled, shut down by the tactics of this milkman; and because I was eighteen and had never been demonstrated to in the healthy delivery of thoughts, needs and emotions, my explanations weren't coherent and nothing I attempted seemed to come out right. Still too, it seemed inconceivable to me that this milkman really and truly would kill maybe-boyfriend. Even I knew though, that people with ideological causes didn't always act in the name of their cause. Personal slants happened, singular irregularities, subjective interpretations. Crazy people. It wasn't either, that I thought the milkman couldn't rig a carbomb because I was fairly sure he could rig a carbomb. It was that still it was hard to believe it would be on that man's level to do that amount of coveting of me. Ever since he'd started in on this role of getting me ready, of putting me into confusion, edging me to the brink where, defeated, I'd surrender and step voluntarily as his woman into his vehicles, I wasn't sure anymore what was plausible, what was exaggeration, what might be reality or delusion or paranoia. Wouldn't have occurred to me either, that cultivating helplessness and a growing mental dispossession might all be part of this man's world of stimulation too. But they did happen. Carbombs did happen. Eldest sister was proof of this. She didn't go to her dead man's funeral because being married now to somebody else, she wasn't supposed still to be in love with him. Instead, on the day of the funeral of the man she was in love with, she sat in our house, our mother's house, not her own house, her face ashen, her eyes enormous, her hand in disbelief up to her mouth. She was staring at the clock, just staring at it, not wanting us near; not crying either, but saying in the most worst voice, *'Get out. Get out. Get out. Get out'* anytime any of us — even ma — went near. So I had fear for maybe-boyfriend, yet he stood there, not taking it seriously. I said did he have to drive his car and he looked at me and said, 'I'm a motor mechanic, but even if I wasn't, maybe-girlfriend, I don't have to drive my car but I want to drive my car.' 'What about . . .' I began, 'things.' 'Things?' said maybe-boyfriend. 'What things?' 'Things . . .' I said. 'You know . . . strapped to . . . strapped to . . .' 'Strapped to what?' '. . . undersides.' 'What d'ye mean, maybe-girlfriend?' Still he waited. 'What about . . .' I began again, '. . . bombs?'

Maybe-boyfriend, now enlightened, or thinking he was enlightened, said that sometimes yes, they happened, that of course they did, but that I must know myself they didn't always happen, that car-bombs, in terms commensurate with the population, hardly ever happened. 'Most people here don't get blown up by carbombs,' he said. 'Most people here don't get blown up. Besides, maybe-girlfriend, you can't not live your life just because some-body someday might kill you.' He made it sound easy which was proof he hadn't received the full particulars yet. I didn't know either, when he would receive them because apart from this encroachment upon me by the milkman, there were those other encroachments upon me by the community. The scandal of this milkman affair had mushroomed to the point where it was now rabid and raging and fast becoming a bestseller and because of it, because of all those compounding violations, I was finding myself more and more circumscribed into an incoherent, debilitated place. Maybe-boyfriend then said who was going to kill him anyway? It wasn't as if he worked in a defender area. He didn't even work in a mixed area. 'Look, love,' he said. 'You're only thinking this because of what happened to your poor sister's ex-boyfriend. Doesn't mean it's going to happen to everybody's boyfriend — probably less so too,' he joked, 'to *maybe*-boyfriends.' Again it sounded easy, as if such a thing, such an outcome, was very far from his view of his world. He tried to touch me then, but I pulled away, then stepped away, right away, from him. Before the milkman, maybe-boyfriend's touch, those fingers, his hands, had been the best, the most, the absolute of lovely. But now, since the milkman, any part of maybe-boyfriend coming towards me brought up in me mounting bouts of revulsion and a feeling that I might at any moment be sick. He was repulsing me, my own maybe-boyfriend was repulsing me, and even though I did not want to be repulsed and was trying my best not to become aware I was repulsed, I'd find myself blaming him for feeling it and for not being able to reason myself out of it. Instead I'd fling his hand, fling his fingers, push him off, tense up, have stomach pains. I knew too, that this was because of the milkman but I couldn't figure out how it could be the milkman. In all the small time since he'd set his sights on me and had started in on destroying me, still only that first time in the car had he even looked at me, never either, said anything lewd or mocking or of outright provocation to me. Most especially he hadn't laid a finger on me. Not one finger. Not once.

As for the community, and my affair with the milkman according to this community, I was now well in it, that being the case whether I was or not. It was put about I had regular engagements with him, rendezvous, intimate 'dot dot dots' at various 'dot dot dot' places. In particular we frequented our two favourite romance spots which were the parks & reservoirs and the ten-minute area, though also we were partial, it was said, to spending time, just the two of us — and presumably all the people who were spying on us — where the tall grasses grew over the ancient tombstones in the old part of the usual place. Ever so confidently, ever so arrogantly, I stepped into his flashy cars, it was said, for yes, many people had seen me. 'Picks her up for assignations,' they said, 'for their trysts, their lovers' appointments, and they go to these places.' 'When they're not there,' it was also said, 'they're fostering illicit togethernesses downtown at those risky bars and clubs.' 'Already he's married, you know,' whispered people and, 'Already he's covering her,' whispered back other people. 'Well, he is him,' they said. 'And as for her, doesn't she have that leaning of maybe-relationships instead of highly principled, rectitudinous coupledom relationships?' — which translated meant it wouldn't be long now before he moved me out of the family home and into some pad for established cinqasepts with him, the pad being located of course up the road in the red-light street. 'Mark our words,' said people, and again all this made sense within the context of our intricately coiled, overly secretive, hyper-gossipy, puritanical yet indecent, totalitarian district. But out of context, away from all that itchiness, the whispering, the passing of notes and where an unhealthy interest in sexual matters existed to the extent of sexual dirt being the most best for general gossip whenever you wanted a rest from political gossip, it would have been difficult to gauge how all these locals were arriving at the most detailed of information regarding me and him that they were. Their creative imaginings would reach my ears slander by gravitational slander. Then there were those other occasions when the more direct line of communication was attempted, such as when they'd chase me down to havoc me with questions, this time up close face-to-face.

My suspiciousness of questions had long existed before the rumour of me and the milkman. When asked one I'd think, who is this person? What's behind that question? Why are they going all around the houses, thinking they are deceiving me by going all around them? Why, in their supposedly hidden way, are they 'putting-on' with hints and pointed comment when I know they're attempting with this sample testing of my thoughts, opinion and inclination, to elicit a previously intended response from me and dishonestly to catch me in my words? I had noticed — certainly by the end of primary school I had noticed — that often it could be discerned when someone was up to something even when they thought they were concealing they were up to something. Wasn't either, that some inner or verbal aspect of themselves would be the only thing to give them away. Their true nature also would be revealed by the very contaminated, off-kilter atmosphere in which they chose to surround themselves. This energy field would accompany them as they made their way towards me, whereupon descrying them, my own skin would crawl and the hairs would move up on the back of my neck. It was the contrast between *that* — all those powerful yet invisible indicators — and the supposedly innocuous, parenthetical manner my neighbours assumed they were presenting to me that most would reveal to me they were not, for whatever reason, coming from the truth. Of course, I might not know why a person was dissembling. Could be that with certain individuals it wasn't to make game of me, to invoke immoderate emotion in me or to lure me verbally to my detriment. Might have been some personal concern of their own about which vulnerably and humanly they felt a need to keep silent, but on which nonetheless they needed clarification or information from someone else. With gossips and rumour-mongers however — and certainly with our gossips and our super-rumour-mongers — always it came down to scrutiny, to wangling, to listening for leverage, to the dedication public opinion here was invested in conjecture, not only abroad but within the Home Circle front.

So they'd embark on offensives and approach with their questions, but these were not straightforward questions, as in 'wherefore this?' or 'what about that?' Instead it was 'So-and-so said' and 'It has been said' and 'We heard our uncle's cousin's brother's daughter's friend who doesn't live in the area anymore said'. Some too, would make mention of the actual word 'rumour', as in 'Rumour says', before going on to personify rumour, as if it wasn't they who were launching or perpetuating Rumour themselves. With their seemingly innocent queries, often too, with assertions left hanging, they'd open their mouths in the hope of inciting me — in shock, in fear, in defensive disposition — into opening mine to give some juicy, easily to be expanded-upon response. Before they could utter a single 'So-and-so said', however, I'd have picked up on their covertness without betraying I'd picked up on it. The only way though, I knew how to counter them was by doing my own dissembling myself. I would do this in such a way as to get my reaction off the ground as swiftly and unsuspiciously as possible. This would be by feigning ignorance of their intention and giving a continuous *'I don't know'* to every probing query they put out. I'd launch my *'I don't know'* as the biggest player in my verbal defence repertoire and I'd be prepared to carry on saying it because another thing I'd learned by the end of primary school was that it was best not to open my mouth in the interests of truth except to a trusted few persons, this trusted-few becoming a trusted-fewer as time progressed in primary school and then I was in secondary school and by that time — age eleven through to sixteen — my trusted-fewer people had declined further so that by age eighteen — the time of me and the milkman as well as of this gossip about me and the milkman — it had got to the point where there was now only one remaining trusted-fewest person left for me to have faith in in all the world. I suspected that if I kept up this curtailing, this cauterising, all the distrust and systematic removal of myself from society, by age twenty it was more than likely I'd be at the stage of no longer opening my mouth to anyone, anywhere, at all.

So *'I don't know'* was my three-syllable defence in response to the questions. With it successfully I refused to be evoked, drawn out, shocked into revelation. Instead I minimalised, withheld, subverted thinking, dropped all interaction surplus to requirement which meant they got no public content, no symbolic content, no full-bodiedness, no bloodedness, no passion of the moment, no turn of plot, no sad shade, no angry shade, no panicked shade, no location of anything. Just me, downplayed. Just me, devoid. Just me, uncommingled. This meant that by the end of their roundabout goads and their many implied and searching significances, still they had nothing from me and I felt justified in presenting this unfruitfulness to them because it was clear to me by this time that in life some people did not deserve the truth. They weren't good enough for the truth. Not respectable enough to receive it. To lie or to omit therefore was fine. It was fine. That was what I thought. Then came complications. I had been aware that in the delivery of my *'I don't know'* I dared not show I was not as unintelligent of their codespeak, their eye signals, their attempt to traduce me, as clearly they were assuming. Knew too, I had to speak my three syllables in the most non-confrontational manner whilst concealing a crucial but unacknowledged preservation of distance between us at the same time. To have called them out otherwise — in this time, in this place — would have been tantamount to abandoning myself to mob-handedness or to some other intense despitefulness and I didn't feel strong enough to engage with that and with the repercussions of that. So it was a delicate and ongoing process not to reveal I had their measure or that my *'I don't know'* really meant *'Heel! Home! Get out! Get out!'* which meant I had to call upon a back-up manoeuvre. This was one from my non-verbal defence repertoire and I did call upon it, this manoeuvre at once stepping up to the mark. It didn't, however, do just that. Initially it came into its own and proved itself of invaluable assistance to me. Then, and outside of expectation, and without the least warning, it began to take over proceedings, overturning my *'I don't know'* as first initiative and implementing alternate strategies which belatedly I realised were incidental against my gossipy neighbours and more in the main against myself. I was attacking myself and it was my face, the expression on my face — one I had intended as temporary, as provisional, which surely and truly I believed could be nothing but provisional. I'd assumed that how my face looked, how I was making it look, how I presented it outwardly, was down to me, under the control of me, the *'I am'* deep in the council chamber. I thought this real me was in there, in charge, hidden from them but directing from the undergrowth. Thought too, I'd chosen a subordinate to assist me and not some rebel to turn tables and override me. That though, was what happened and it happened first with the face.

It got stuck. My careful rendering of *'I don't know'*, combined with a terminal face — nothing in it, nothing behind it, a well-turned-out nothing — I thought would bemuse the gossips, confound them, run counter to their expectations, so that eventually, frustrated, wearied, they'd call a halt to their persecutions, with everybody giving up and going home. I'd hoped the sheer nullity of me would lead them to doubt their inventions and their convictions, even to suspect that a renouncer — especially *that* Man of Men, Warrior of Warriors, our high-celebrity, local community hero — could ever have developed lust for such an inert, vapid person as myself. Wasn't even that I thought they'd think me stupid, or stop at thinking me stupid, but that they'd go further and come to the conclusion that I must not understand language in some prevailing, basal, social-code way. It was that I couldn't grasp what was being asked of me because the whole issue of emotional and psychological communication must be missing for me. I'd strike them as a textbook, some kind of log table — as in correct, but not really right either. This was what I'd hoped they'd think, that my dissembling and use of face would pay off and I'd be free, safe — at least from them if not from the milkman. However, both the milkman and the gossip about me and the milkman turned out to be a rapid learning on the job. I had not plotted for this. There'd been no time to plot and anyway, my mind didn't work best in plots, in blueprints, in join-the-dots prognostication arrangements. Instead I relied on instinct, on impromptu sidestepping, on a heightened sensitivity to what was out there for my reaction rather than some cold-headed, preplanned military precision for my reaction. Belatedly though, I realised that this must be as with informers here. At first they play into the hands of their police handlers then, by their subsequent and supposed stance of *'I'm not an informer so don't be thinking me an informer because I'm not an informer'* they play into the hands of the renouncers — I too, was beginning to lose my power of reason, my ability to see obvious connections and to retain even the most elementary sense of how to survive in this place. I can see now, of course, that no matter what I would have done or could have done, those gossips wouldn't have stopped, never would they have ceased and gone away, not until the man himself had gone away, after having me and had done with me. At the time though, I said my three words and I displayed my depersonalisation and did succeed in puzzling them. As a result, they became slovenly in method, intemperate with impatience, revealing ever more their true natures in their push to make me make sense. Never did it occur to them that my powers of acuity and deception might have exceeded their own powers of acuity and deception. People can be extraordinarily slipshod whenever already they have made up their minds. When it came to it, although I didn't betray I was emotionally or intellectually charged, that didn't mean I thought I was not so. Of course I believed myself sentient. Of course I knew I was angry. Of course I knew I was frightened, that I had no doubt my body, to me, was brimming with a natural reaction. At first I could feel this reaction which confirmed I was alive, that I was in there, inside my body, experiencing this under-the-surface turbulence. Thing was though, before I'd gained the understanding of what was happening, my seemingly flattened approach to life became less a pretence and more and more real as time went on. At first an emotional numbness set in. Then my head, which initially had reassured with, 'Excellent. Well done. Successfully am I fooling them in that they do not know who I am or what I'm thinking or what I'm feeling,' now began itself to doubt I was even there. *'Just a minute,'* it said. *'Where is our reaction? We were having a privately expressed reaction but now we're not having it. Where is it?'* Thus my feelings stopped expressing. Then they stopped existing. And now this numbance from nowhere had come so far on in its development that along with others in the area finding me inaccessible, I, too, came to find me inaccessible. My inner world, it seemed, had gone away.

Physically too, it got tiring, all that distrust and push-pull, the sniper-open-fire, the countersniper-return-fire, the sidestepping and twisting, with both me and my community appearing to freewheel our way to some final interface. Just as with the milkman, at the end of the day at home when I'd do my checking under the bed, behind the door, in the wardrobe and so on to see if he was in there, or under it, or behind it; checking curtains too, that they were firmly closed, that they weren't concealing him this side of the glass or that side of the glass, I realised things had reached the point where I was now checking to see if the community was concealing itself in those tucked-away places too. The extraordinary amount of energy I had on these people — as in trying to avoid them — meant, of course, I was attracting them, but I didn't understand the way of fixated energy then. It took its toll though, all that darkness and mutual games-playing, bringing with it the concomitant that even though the whole meat of my dissembling had been to keep separate by non-participation with them, here I was, making common cause with them. Too late I realised that all the time I'd been an active player, a contributing element, a major componential in the downfall of myself.

As for the gossips, and their response to my response, I knew I was confounding them as I had intended to confound them, even if I hadn't intended confounding myself as well. It transpired though, that they didn't care for confoundment and complained that my demeanour was improper, that it was resistant to ordinary treatment, that it was against the common weal, that I was almost-inordinately blank, almost-lifeless, almost-sterile, almost-counter-intuitive which was not and couldn't ever be, they said, normal for a person on this earth ceaselessly to be. As for their use of *'almost'* — *almost*-inordinately blank, *almost*-lifeless and so on — that of course, on my part had been meant. Although I'd said it was imperative to present myself as blank and empty, what I meant was *almost*-blank and *almost*-empty. This was because preciseness and clean-cut methods might work perfectly and give a certain bromidic satisfaction on paper, but they wouldn't do at all, or fool anybody for a second, in real life. Such meticulousness of planning smacked of aforethought, and obvious aforethought in this community — especially if you were trying to dupe it — was not a good thing. Unless you were dealing with the immensely stupid which I wasn't, it was best to muss things up, to crease things, to leave tea-stains, to place a small but partial muddy footprint not exactly in the middle of the issue but slightly to the side of, and hopefully suggestive of, an incidental to the issue. So that part worked. But they said I was ungenerous in my facial expression, stressing 'expression' as in singular, as in, I only seemed to have one. *Near*-expressionless too, was what they said it was. It was *near*-arid, *near*-solitary, *near*-deprogrammed and again I took hope from their not saying it was inscrutable. Inscrutability here, as with obvious aforethought, as with topsoil thinking, didn't work. At first they said they weren't sure if I was displaying an unamiable Marie Antoinetteness by being stuck-up, by thinking I was above them. Then they decided that no, probably this was some eccentricity in keeping with my character, most likely stemming from all that reading of ancient books I did while walking about. They said that overall, my not being one thing or the other was proving a drain on their resources, which didn't stop them though, from inferring me all the same. A bit eerie, a bit creepy, they decided, adding that they hadn't noticed before but it was that I resembled in my open-but-closed perspective the ten-minute area. It was as if there was nothing there when there was something there, while at the same time, as if there was something there when there was nothing there. I was a condition athwart, they said, transverse, not social, though they did mitigate this with, 'But perhaps that's only one side of her.' However, as they didn't believe there was any other side, that just brought them back to the beginning, to me having only the one.

As far as this communal drain upon me by the community went, and as far as went

the drain by me upon the community —
with their inferences disturbing me, my face
disturbing them, and with my numbance
doing all our heads in — thankfully I didn't
have to do *'I don't know'* or show my almost-
nearly-empty face, or expose my closed-up
state to them very much. This was because
most of the gossip about me and the milkman went on behind my back. But had the
situation been that bad? Had it really and
truly been the case that there was nobody,
that there hadn't been a single person to
whom in those days I could have gone,
could have off-loaded, who might have been
able to listen and offer comfort, support
and auspices? Had I really been as stubborn
and transverse and as ten-minute area as all
of the reprehenders of me had said I had?
Looking back, and excluding my friendship
with my one remaining trusted-fewest
person from schooldays, I think too, that
yes, I had. My distrust had been phenome-
nal to the point where I could not see that
probably there had existed individuals who
could have helped, who might have sup-
ported and comforted me — friends I could
have made, a support network I might have
been part of — only I lost that opportunity
through having no faith in them and no
faith or sense of entitlement in myself.

However, at the time, given my intention had been to keep the nerve and to hold it together in a place where everybody in their own way was also trying to keep the nerve and hold it together, impossible it would have been for me to have glimpsed, to have understood any concept of help or comfort then. Certain individuals did continue to approach me, however, and some of them might have been trustworthy, might have intended good offices. But I continued to withhold, even if not always from my usual fear and stubbornness. There was still my lack of certainty as to whether or not there was anything to tell.

That was the way it worked. Hard to define, this stalking, this predation, because it was piecemeal. A bit here, a bit there, maybe, maybe not, perhaps, don't know. It was constant hints, symbolisms, representations, metaphors. He could have meant what I thought he'd meant, but equally, he might not have meant anything. Taken on their own, or to describe each incident separately, particularly while in the middle of it, might not seem, once relayed, to be all that much at all. If I'd said, 'He offered me a lift as I was walking along the interface road reading *Ivanhoe*,' it would have been, 'Why were you walking along that dangerous interface road and why were you reading *Ivanhoe*?' If I'd said, 'I was running in the parks & reservoirs and he appeared also running in the parks & reservoirs,' it would have been, 'What were you doing, running in such a dangerous, questionable place and what were you doing, choosing to run?' If I'd said, 'He was parked in his wee white van up the entry opposite the college while I was with my French class looking at the sky enduring sunsets' it would have been, 'You left the safety of our insular area to go downtown to a mixed area to study foreign languages and view life as a figured representation?' If I'd said, 'He expressed condolences on my sister's loss of her murdered man while at the same time linking my almost-maybe-boyfriend to a constantly recurring carbomb,' they'd have said, 'How come you're not married and why do you go out with maybe-boyfriends in the first place?' Apart from the gossip — and even if there'd been no gossip — my belief from the outset was that not really would I have been heard or believed. If I'd gone to the authorities to have it officially recorded that he was stalking me, that he was threatening me, that he was making preparations for me, then to seek redress from these authorities as in, what were they going to do about it, our renouncers would have replied — well, I didn't know what they would have replied because he too, was a renouncer so why ever would I have gone to them? In a practical sense too, in what way would I go to them? Although I'd lived in this area which was run by the paramilitaries, which was policed by the paramilitaries, I didn't know how to approach these guys. I'd have had to enquire as to proper procedure from a community which, in its turn, was also stalking me and about which I would be putting in a complaint also. As for the actual police, the statelet's police, going to them didn't rate consideration because one, they were the enemy, and two, of all things crying out to have you killed as an informer in a renouncer-run, no-go area, approaching what was viewed as a highly partisan police force to complain about a renouncer in your area would have been, without doubt, highest on that list. According to the police, of course, our community was a rogue community. It was we who were the enemy, we who were the terrorists, the civilian terrorists, the associates of terrorists or simply individuals suspected of being but not yet discovered to be terrorists. That being the case, and understood by both parties to be the case, the only time you'd call the police in my area would be if you were going to shoot them, and naturally they would know this and so wouldn't come.

Everything would end my fault then, because of this lack of faith in my own conviction and of what my feelings were telling me. Was he actually doing anything? Was anything happening? If *I* didn't know, how could I explain to and convince anyone else? Instead I sensed that this doubt — of myself, of the situation — would be picked up on and would then lead to comment on my own credibility. Even if I were to be heard, people here were unused to words like 'pursuit' and 'stalking', that is, in terms of *sexual* pursuit and *sexual* stalking. It would be similar to saying 'kerb-crawling' as in those American movies, too outlandish, not at all the sort of thing that went on here. If such a thing was entertained to go on, hardly even then would our society take it seriously. It would have been on a par with jay-walking, maybe less than jay-walking, given it was a woman's thing, taking place too, during an era that was so stuffed with political problems that even a tiny demented person — our district's most successful superior poisoner — could walk around freely and weekly, poisoning people yet rate not a jot in the rankings. So the

Hollywood phenomenon of sexual prowling would have been overshadowed, as everything here was overshadowed, by the main topic of conversation in this place.

Yet others kept coming. Eldest sister kept coming, bringing with her the refrain of 'If you continue in liaison with this person' or 'You're doing yourself no favours', only to meet my cold determination not to plead my case or attempt in any way to appease her. By now we'd built up such an investment of hostility that we could not, and would not, hear each other out. Then there was her husband in the background, the horizontal wolf with something about the nostrils, the ears getting bigger and bigger, and pointier and pointier, with his hairy shankiness and hind legs and forelegs and snout and teeth sprouting, with claws, long black ones, floccillating ones, with his tongue egging her on, vexing himself unto death to have her keep on at me, to keep coming round to visit me, to insist on confidences from me. It was clear to everybody though, that first sister was too much in her own issues over her dead ex-lover so that hardly she was holding it together herself. Besides, I'd heard some new sexual preoccupation of his own had now taken hold of first brother-in-law and was fast reaching the level where he was drawing more than a little gossip and trouble towards himself. There was ma too, continuing her barrage of how I wouldn't get married, of how I was bringing shame by entering paramilitary groupiedom, of how I was bringing down on myself dark and unruly forces, bad-exampling wee sisters, bringing in God too, as in light and dark and the satanic and the infernal. 'It's like being hypnotised,' she said, 'or how you might imagine those people who are got by vampires in those horror films feel. They don't see the horror, daughter. Only the people outside see the horror. Instead they are in thrall, entranced, seeing only attraction.' Relations at work too, were not as they were. I had grown inattentive, drowsy at my workstation because I'd jump awake at night in my bed and not be able to return to sleep again. Partly these were urges that I should get up and again search my room to make sure he or the community had not got in since last time before bed when I'd searched it; jumping awake also, because of nightmares that I'd turned into the sickly, misanthropic Reeve from the 'General Prologue' to *The Canterbury Tales.* The house too, was having a go. Raps, noises, movements, agitations of the air, displacement of objects. It was banging and retorting and causing discordance — all to berate me, to warn me, to call attention to the threat that already I knew was surrounding me. And always this would be in my bedroom right in the middle of the night. A thump on the bedside table would wake me up. Things would rattle, such as a picture on the wall, or a hammering would break out on my floor right below me. Or maybe the bedroom door would start to shake. One time the spirits of the home tugged away my eiderdown and flung my feet and lower legs across the bed with such force that my whole torso almost tipped over and fell out of it. Ma shouted from her room, 'For the love of God, littlest daughters, I'm trying to have a night's reading here before sleep. What's all that banging?', with wee sisters shouting from their room, 'It's not us, mammy! We're sleeping. It's middle sister.' 'It's not me!' I shouted. 'It's the house. The spirits of the house. I'm sleeping too.' Apart though, from my guess that the house was telling me to do something, and that it was something about the milkman, I didn't know what it was expecting I should do. It had taken to awakening me, however, so that then I'd stay awake, with my corresponding lack of sleep at night-time leading to overwhelming sleepiness and dullness at my workstation during the daytime. It got to the point where twice now my supervisor had me into her office to have words. By now too, my French class had lost its sparkle, or I'd lost my eagerness for that sparkle. It became less exciting, more *'What's the point? There's no point'* and I became wearied, finding it more of an effort each week to get myself downtown to it. Then my legs hurt, so that bit by bit I pulled out of my runs with third brother-in-law. First it was the odd run, then more and more cancellations as the pain continued and a lack of coordination overtook me. It came that I couldn't anymore relax and feel myself in flow, couldn't breathe properly whereas before, the act of running brought breath through me, kept me in touch, filled me up. Something I'd taken for granted had altered, so that then I stopped running. Even the walking was coming to a halt. My balance went weird. It had grown lopsided, a lameness of stance setting in and overtaking me. At the time I tried to tell myself that it was *me* giving up the running, *me* not doing as much walking, that no one was forcing me. Then I gave up one of my days with maybe-boyfriend, the now-and-again day, telling myself that it was *my* decision, that nobody was making me, that Thursday wasn't important. It was the day I was least committed to my maybe-relationship, reminding myself also that this was, after all, only a maybe-relationship. Even so, and minus Thursdays, the milkman kept the car-bomb pressure up. He had started to weave in a new danger also, the threat of maybe-boyfriend possibly to be killed, either by the renouncers of his area or by everybody else in his area, owing to traitorship and informership. 'Ridiculous, of course,' he said, adding that people died here though from ridiculousness as well. With this, the milkman presented himself as saviour and as antidote. He alone, he hinted, had the power to make all that danger facing maybe-boyfriend go away. Then there were those lifts, the offers of lifts which he'd made and which still kept coming. Not just from him either. By now others in the area, his people, the cronies, those servitors of the conviction that they had to do as he bid them, would stop in their cars and offer to take me into town or out of town without any mention that the milkman had sent them. It was obvious though, from this overload of offers that they were acting on instructions. They'd plead with me, telling me I'd be doing them such a big favour if only I'd consent and get in.

Meantime, tension was ever mounting between me and maybe-boyfriend. Apart from my 'Will you stop driving your car?', and his 'Of course I won't, what you're asking me there, that's unreasonable, you're being unreasonable', we were both getting into fights about other things. If he was not going to get blown up by a carbomb, then he was going to be taken away by the re-nouncers as an informer for having the bit with the flag on. If not that, then those who weren't renouncers in his area but all the same, fanatics of the cause in his area, were going to come in their numbers and do him down over that selfsame imagined-flag thing. As for the rumour of the super-charger, of how it was unpatriotic of maybe-boyfriend to have it whether or not it had the flag on, because of it, according to maybe-boyfriend, he was now being photo-graphed in a minute, expert fashion by the state. I overheard him mention this to chef, saying that he believed, given this photo-graphing, he was attracting attention to himself even from outside his own area. 'Seems,' he joked, 'that owing to flags, emblems, traitorship and superchargers, I'll make a prospect to be turned informer by the state.' In contradiction to this, he also said it wouldn't be untoward if the statelet was not the party doing the photography but that the local paramilitary-renouncers were doing the photography. 'Could be keeping an eye,' he joked again, 'to see if already I've turned informer.' Then there were all those amateur photographers, the lay documentalists, the calendar-moment chroniclers of our troubled times. He said those boys with an eye for the chance, for the possibility of seeking fame and fortune in the future, were popping up everywhere, venturing out with cameras and tape recorders to capture and safeguard, they said, historical, political and social testimony for posterity. 'You never know,' they said, 'what might be considered the most sought-after paraphernalia of these sadnesses in years to come.' I knew, of course, though maybe-boyfriend didn't, that not only might he be getting snapped by the state as a potential informer, and snapped by the renouncers as a possible informer, and snapped by those backroom-enterprisers as someone who might be famous one day for being killed as an informer, but also that the state would snap him twice over as an associate of an associate of a man high on their list. As for the effect of the burgeoning rumour of the supercharger having that flag on, maybe-boyfriend's neighbours and acquaintances continued to edge away bit by bit. Much as they adored the supercharger and had had, for that little stretch of happy time, emotionally invested themselves in their passion for the supercharger, there were other things, such as 'soldier-lover', 'ensign-lover', 'country "over the water" lover', 'street justice', all of which had a bigger emotional impact on them than that. Life being short, sometimes incredibly short, why bring upon yourself accusations of collusion, of being an accessory, of implications in conduct unbecoming an inhabitant of the area? This was why it was considered best to sever even the slightest connection with maybe-boyfriend, though of course, his core friends did stay around. So did that other friend, the one purportedly from maybe-boyfriend's work, who lived 'over the road', meaning maybe-boyfriend's colleague from the opposite religion. It was said this person — Ivor — had shown willingness to vouchsafe maybe-boyfriend didn't have the bit with the flag on because Ivor himself had the bit with the flag on, with Ivor then offering to oblige his work colleague by sending over a Polaroid of himself in his own defender-run area holding up this bit with the flag on, all so maybe-boyfriend could defend himself should he end up on treason charges in his own area at a renouncer kangaroo court. Ivor said that although the renouncers could go fuck themselves as enemies of all that he himself stood for, he'd be delighted, it was said, to proffer pictorial testimony on behalf of his workmate to help him out of his current difficult spot. When I heard of this rumour of the existence of Ivor, realising my blunder too, at having invented him as an impromptu protection for maybe-boyfriend against the milkman, I was appalled at how easily an unguided thought, even one not expressed, could get plucked from the topsoil and still manage successfully to get through. And now here it was — out — having a life of its own, and I could only hope that, although Ivor at present was in the common round and unfortunately being added on to, eventually this rumour would go to dust and be forgotten, disappearing off the radar as if it had never been. Meanwhile, Ivor — and no matter how well-meaning he might appear or that he might promise to send over a hundred Polaroids and two hundred written testimonies in support of maybe-boyfriend — would not have been believed in maybe-boyfriend's district, owing to the fact that he wasn't one of them. Even if he'd existed — even too, overlooking the unlikeliness of his being willing to placate anti-ensign sentiments towards a flag he himself held dearly in his own community — as a *bona fide* witness he'd have proved less than no good at all. In the event, it was observed that Ivor sent no picture, no negative of a picture and no word of written testimony. Instead, and in spite of all his promises, he had done nothing and this served to reinforce the communal opinion of traitorous maybe-boyfriend having the bit with the flag on after all.

As I say, complicated. And all this spelled a serious turning bad for us, for me and maybe-boyfriend — in the way that the rumour about me and the milkman in my area was affecting me, and in the way that the rumour about him and the flag in his area was affecting him. Conjointly, these rumours and their effects upon us were turning bad also for our maybe-relationship. Under stress we were starting to fight and were communicating less with each other than the normal amount of sharing of ourselves that we didn't tend to communicate before. It was clear to me, that as well as my not telling him about the milkman and the stories doing the rounds in my community about me and the milkman, maybe-boyfriend had his own defensive front of silence, stemming from his stubbornness against me and against everybody, as his own way of shielding and keeping safe himself.

Bickering and squabbles then started in earnest, with the tension between us mounting as every day went by. Besides my 'Do you have to drive your car?' or my growing belief that matters might come to my having to obey the milkman and ditch maybe-boyfriend, I hadn't been able to work out any other solution to this problem at all. Maybe-boyfriend meanwhile, was getting worked up in his area, surprisingly not so much about the flag issue or the fear of being called to mortal account as an informer over the flag issue. It was that he was more worked up because the renouncers had called and asked for a cut at his door. This was to do with the supercharger, for it had been a subject of gossip for so long now that the latest rumour was that he was keeping the flag but selling the supercharger for a massive sum of money. So they visited him, his local renouncers, and asked for a cut though, of course, when I say 'asked', that they 'asked', that they wondered if possibly they could have some of the money, I mean they demanded it. If ever you've lived in a renouncer-run area, often you'll have heard, 'We need to commandeer your such-and-such for the good of the cause and the defence of the area.' That covered everything — your house, your motorcar, to their expecting a percentage on any discount you might receive on anything — a win at bingo, a Christmas bonus, practically even the saving on a marked-down Paris Bun at the bakery or discount on a tube of Smarties at the corner shop. All cuts and percentages of cuts you were obliged to hand over would, of course, be for the good of the cause and the defence of the area. So the local boys, the district renouncers, wanting cuts, calling for cuts, visiting at all hours at private houses for cuts, went on at this time which was why maybe-boyfriend feared them calling, feared them asking for a percentage of what they thought he'd sold which of course never would he sell because *he* was who he was and *it* was a Blower Bentley supercharger, but should he think of selling that supercharger, they said, and they said this — four of them in Halloween masks, three in balaclavas, all with guns, at seven o'clock at night on his doorstep — or should he have already sold it, they said, don't forget them and the need for proceeds for the defence of the area and the furtherance of the cause. They added also that should it be the case that somewhere in that catastrophe of a house of his was the actual caboodle of a whole Blower Bentley racing vehicle, again they'd have to commandeer it and here they paused and stared out from their masks at maybe-boyfriend which was when he knew, he said, it could only be a matter of time before they changed their mind and decided, why take a cut when they could take the whole lot? They went away then, he said, though before doing so, some guy appeared in the middle of this exchange who wasn't a renouncer. He had no gun, no mask, was wearing a suit and tie, a stranger to the area. It transpired he had sought permission the day before from the renouncers to enter the district. So he turned up and he apologised right away for his intrusion then, standing there amongst the local boys in their masks with their guns and with maybe-boyfriend on his doorstep, he introduced himself as a public relations man from the downtown arts council, adding that he wondered if it would be possible to stick a plaque on maybe-boyfriend's outside wall. He revealed this plaque and it announced in swirly gold writing that the international couple had once lived in this residence from nineteen-something until nineteen-something, before they'd gone off to be the most spectacular, internationally famous dancing stars in the world. 'It would make the area a bit more normal,' he explained, 'to have this plaque up, showing that it's not all doom and gloom and war in our little bit of the world, that we're not always just about shooting and bombing but that also we're about the arts and famous people and glamour.' He didn't go into detail about who he thought would come into that particular paramilitary stronghold to marvel at the plaque and talk about the arts and famous people and that was because no one would come in. In reality, the only people to see it would be the heavily patrolled and fortified units of the statelet police and the military from 'over the water', crashing in as periodically they did to ransack for renouncers, hardly people in the mental state to appreciate the plaque or to absorb that type of culture, or else it would be seen by the locals who wouldn't be enlightened because already they knew the international couple had once lived there. Maybe-boyfriend said he didn't want the plaque up, and the renouncers told the arts man that just because he apologised for intruding didn't mean he was no longer intruding. They added that someone calling himself an arts man — which was after all, some kind of government public-servant official, whether or not he had permission to come in — could just as easily be a spy for the state. At this point the man said, 'Fair enough, we don't have to put it up.' With that, and still buoyant, and with the plaque again under his arm, and after attempting to press his card upon maybe-boyfriend who refused it, he left — but they'd return for it, said maybe-boyfriend, moving swiftly back to his belief that the renouncers were determined to lay their hands on his glorious Blower Bentley supercharger, this thing that he'd won fairly and squarely and loved. So this compounded the strain between us because I couldn't help being astonished at his losing elementary wisdom, in that the renouncers coming for the supercharger, or for to have a cut of the supercharger, should have been the least thing for him to worry about. Given all the accusation of traitorship that was building up against him, it would be more conceivable that by now they would be calling to his house — in their masks, with their guns, probably also with an assortment of field and burial spades — not for to fetch the supercharger but for to fetch him. After all, many lives have been taken for less obvious betrayals than flying flags considered not to belong here even if you weren't flying them. So I said, 'Let them have it, maybe-boyfriend, because you must know anyway, because you can't not know, that if they want it, there's no way they're not going to take it,' which annoyed him. It was clear to me though, if not to him, there was the bigger issue of his life at stake here. It was as if he'd forgotten his life, all because of his stubbornness and besottedness with cars and his inability sensibly to prioritise and accept that sometimes you have to concede, have to let go, maybe you have to lose face, that some things compared to other things are just not worth sticking up for. But he didn't see it that way and that became one of the contentions between us so we had a fight over this supercharger in his living room one day. He had got into the habit of moving the thing round his house in the most furtive, obsessive manner in what seemed like every fifteen minutes to half an hour. He was hoping that with so much car about, so much hoarding-upon-hoarding, the renouncers would become perplexed, then wearied, then helpless as little babies, then they'd give up rather than persist in searching and again this astonished me. It seemed further proof of how far his mind was dwindling, his good sense slipping, in that he couldn't see they wouldn't instigate a search themselves for the supercharger but instead, with him at gunpoint, they'd demand he go fetch it at once from its hiding place for them. I said this too, but that further annoyed him, so it was in perpetual transit, this supercharger, on the run, currently taken from under the hallway's back floorboards which recently he'd dug up to make a hiding place for it, even though the night before, right up until breakfast this morning, it had been behind a false wall in the kitchen he'd made a few nights before that. Now, and only until he'd perfected some double-panelled, deceptive hidey-hole which he envisaged making in one of the upstairs rooms that currently he was working on, it had been placed inside some hollowed-out bit of car that he thought resembled a normal piece of compulsive car-hoarding, but already I could see he was casting around for where he was going to conceal the thing after the double-panelled hidey-hole sojourn planned for it upstairs. Meanwhile, there it was, sitting inside this giant bucket-like car contraption, with other sundry car parts plus a bathtowel, dishcloth and some of his own clothes strewn artfully, as in casually, over the top. The whole thing was standing on the low table between us, with this new ongoing tension also now between us. It was then I accused him once more of driving cars. I had barely got into doing so when he interrupted to accuse me for the first time of being ashamed of him because instead of letting him call to my door for me, I only wanted to meet him out of the way on those isolated interface roads. I retaliated with a charge of him liking cooking, of buying ingredients with chef, of actually liking cooking. Then he reinforced his proof of my being ashamed of him by delineating occasions of late when I'd recoiled from him, adding that on Thursdays I no longer stayed over with him, had become remote too, on our Tuesdays and on our Friday nights into Saturdays and our all day Saturdays into Sundays which of course was the case because of the growing repulsion I was transferring over onto him but which I knew in truth belonged to the milkman. At first I was stumped which gave him time to fit in extra charges of an unattractive numbed state he had observed was creeping over me, that he felt was starting to invade and possess me, saying it was as if I was no longer a living person but one of those jointed wooden dollies that artists use in — which was when I had to stop him because I couldn't bear for him to finish on my growing numbed condition only to start in on my face. Such became the stresses and strains, the building up of unforgiveness between us. There were other stresses too, when we were in his cars. Again I'd home in on why did he have to drive them, with him saying he was taking me home, that he was going to drive me home to my very door. Then I'd think, he's turning into the milkman, he's bossing me about, he's thinking he can control me, or else I'd think, he's saying he's had enough of me, so he's taking me home because he wants rid of me. 'Stop the car!' I'd pronounce. 'Stop the car on this deserted interface road immediately!' but he wouldn't want to stop the car. He'd say he didn't want me to get out but I'd say I'm walking and he'd say ach don't walk, which again would betray he was trying to lame me, to fell me, to cripple me, just like the milkman. So there was quite a bit of 'what's the matter with you?', 'you've got complications', 'so have you got complications', 'what's the matter with you?'. Then there was 'I'll give you a lift', 'I don't want a lift', 'I'll give you a lift', 'I don't want a lift' and to me this was a ruse by which he was no longer wanting rid of me but was now attempting to overcome his amnesia in order to further on our maybe-relationship, not however, further it into a loving, intimate proper relationship but into one of those stalking, possessive, controlling relationships, attempting to do so too, by bullying me which definitely was not the way a person seeking respectful coupledom should go about this. Meantime he'd say my contrariness in getting out of his car in the middle of a dangerous nowhere was a ruse, an unkind manipulation to torment him and emotionally to blackmail him in order to further on our maybe-relationship in some dark, unworthy way. 'Underhand,' he'd stress; also stressing that hitherto he would have considered such conduct below me and at this point I'd be forced to call him 'almost one year maybe-boyfriend' instead of the more intimate 'maybe-boyfriend' and I'd feel justified in distancing myself from him, though he must have felt similar because he'd refer to me even more formally as 'almost one year so far maybe-girlfriend' which meant that if we kept this up, soon we'd be addressing each other in terms most official and impersonal, such as might have been appropriate to the time before we met. That became the way of things, with increasing tension between us as he got wound up in his area and I got ground down in my area. Constantly I was getting things mixed up, back-to-front, blaming him for things that weren't blame-worthy or even if they were, he hadn't done them, and I think he must have been experiencing likewise given his own conduct and his words in his state of mind towards me. Meanwhile, somewhere at the back of this was the milkman wedged between us; also maybe-boyfriend being killed by this milk-man wedged between us. At back of all there was the image of my sister, my first, eldest, perpetually grieving sister, sitting in our house in that awful silence, with that look on her face on her murdered ex-lover's funeral day.

Because of these extra meetings — real ones and made-up ones — and because I was continuing not to reveal anything which was now a full-time, batting-away process with me, longest friend from primary school sent word she wanted to meet for a talk. Shun-ning telephone communication, she sent a message via one of those scouts, those liv-ing telegrams most secret of the area, to ar-range with me. I told him to tell her I'd meet her in the lounge of the district's most popular drinking-club at seven o'clock that night. I loved longest friend; at least used to love her, or loved still what I knew of her. It was that hardly now did I know her; hardly ever did I see her. One of the things about her was that her entire family had been killed in the political problems so far. She was the only one left, living alone too — though soon she was to marry — in the dead family house. As regards our friendship, this was the one person I could speak with, the one person I could listen to, totalling in fact the last trusted-fewest person who wouldn't drain the life out of me that I had left in the world. Like third brother-in-law she didn't gossip. Politically she kept her eyes and ears open. This was something she accused me deliberately of never doing, which I couldn't deny because it was true. I backed myself up by reminding her of my hatred of the twentieth century, adding that the unstoppable gossip in the district — also hateful — was more than enough for me. This was not the way of longest friend. Everything meant something to her. Everything was of use to her, or to be made of use, to be stored away for utility at some future opportunistic date. I would say that her information-acquisition, her silence, this stocking-up of hers — not only on factual reality but also on anecdotal and speculated reality — was questionable, also sinister, not a little scary. She would respond by saying this was a case of the pot calling the kettle black. Especially she told me this when we met up that night in the upstairs lounge of the district's most popular drinking-club. In case I didn't know, she said, I was more than a bit questionable, sinister and scary myself. I thought she meant by my not keeping my ears open, by not accruing information and disseminating local commentary, also because of my lifelong stubbornness in refusing to tell nosey bastards what it wasn't their business to hear. 'Why should I?' I said. 'It's not to do with them and anyway, I haven't done anything.' 'Lots of people haven't done anything,' said longest friend. 'And still they're not doing it, will always be not doing it, in their private coffins down at the usual place.' 'But I'm always only minding my business,' I said, 'doing my things, walking down the street, just walking down the street and —' 'Yeah,' said friend, 'there's *that* as well.' I asked her what she meant and she said she'd get on to that in a minute. First there was another point to be got through. Before that point, there was another point which was that ever since the end of our schooldays longest friend and I did not meet often. Whenever we did meet, our encounters were increasingly solemn and less and less cheerful. I can't remember when last they were cheerful. Even at her wedding, which took place four months after this meeting in the lounge, there was that same lack of cheerfulness. Indeed, so strong had been the impression of everyone present attending a joint funeral instead of one marriage that I couldn't shake it off and in the end had to leave the reception early, go home and lie on my bed, in broad daylight, in celebration clothes, depressed. Another point before the point was that between us there was an unspoken understanding that I did not ask her her business and in return she did not tell me it. We had stuck to this arrangement ever since she had started in on her business. That would be something like four years ago now.

So we were upstairs in the lounge and we ordered our drinks and sat at the back, and after a bit of not talking, which was not unusual in the initial stages between me and longest friend, she said, 'Knowing you, you've probably not done anything, but according to rumour, seems you've done everything. Now don't jump down my throat, longest friend, but tell me, what's the crack with you and Milkman?'

I noticed she called him Milkman and that she gave him a capital letter. To everybody else he was 'the milkman', with only the very youngest in the area believing he was a milkman, though even then, that didn't last long. If she was calling him 'Milkman', I now decided, that must be because he was 'Milkman'. She'd know more about it than any uninitiated outside influence and so, because of her inside knowledge, and because of our friendship, it was a relief to tell, though I didn't know how much of a relief until I opened my mouth and out it all came. I knew she'd believe me, because she knew me, because I knew her, or at least used to know her, so there'd be no need for anxiety or for having to decide whether or not to trust her. Nor would I have to make efforts to persuade her. I could just lay it all out exactly as it was. So I did. I told of his quick appearances and of his quiet pronouncements, of his knowledge of my whereabouts, of his knowing everything there was to know about my life. I told about his telling me what to do without openly telling me to do it. Then there were his swift leave-takings as startling as his arrivals, with my overwhelming sensation of falling into a trap. He was trailing me, tracking me, knowing my routines, my movements, also the routines of everyone I met up with. It was that he had some plan, I said, but was in no hurry, was going at his pace, though with the clear intention of one day carrying it out. Also his not touching I spoke of, even though it seemed always he was touching, and all the time the hairs being up — waiting, anticipating, dreading — at the back of my neck. I said then of the flashy cars and of the van, though I knew longest friend would know of those already, telling also of my instinct that warned never to get beaten down enough to step into one of them. I spoke then of the state forces and of their surveillance upon me because of their surveillance upon him. They took photos, I said, not just of me and him, but now of me on my own or me with anyone — persons met by chance or persons I'd arranged to meet up with. These hidden cameras would click, I said, with unconnected people then getting implicated, regardless that nothing was, or had, or was about to, go on. I mentioned then the emergence of the arse-lickers, the lickspittles, given that those individuals had started to appear, pretending that they liked me when of course they didn't like me. To my surprise, I even mentioned lascivious first brother-in-law. Towards the end there was ma and her sanctities and the holy people she had praying for me, then the elusive rumour-mongers who changed things if they heard things and who made things up when they did not hear things. Finally I ended on some possible future carbomb which just might kill the boyfriend I was in a maybe-relationship with. And that was it. I had said all. I stopped talking, took a big drink and sank back on the velvety cushioned bench, feeling lighter. I had told out to the right person. Definitely, longest friend had been the right person. The fact this had come out organically — even plausibly unchronologically — seemed to me to be proof of this.

So I was heard, and it felt good and respectful to be heard, to be got, not to be interrupted or cut off by opinionated, poorly attuned people. For the longest while longest friend didn't say anything and I didn't mind her not saying anything. Indeed I welcomed it. It seemed a sign she was digesting the information, letting it speak to her timely, to authenticate also in its proper moment the right and just response. So she stayed quiet and stayed still and looked ahead and it was then for the first time it struck me that this staring into the middle distance, which often she'd do when we'd meet, was identical to that of Milkman. Apart from the first time in his car when he'd leaned over and looked out at me, never again had he turned towards me. Was this some 'profile display stance' then, that they all learn at their paramilitary finishing schools? As I was pondering this, longest friend then did speak. Without turning, she said, 'I understand your not wanting to talk. That makes sense, and how could it not, now that you're considered a community beyond-the-pale.'

This I was not expecting and at once thought I could not have heard properly. 'What did you say?' I said and she said it again, delivering the news — which was news — that along with the district poisoner, the poisoner's sister, the boy who killed himself over America and Russia, the women with the issues, and real milkman, also known as the man who didn't love anybody, I too, was one of those intemperate, socially outlawed beyond-the-pales. I sat upright, shot upright, and I think my mouth must have fallen open. At least for a moment, for the tiniest time in weeks, even Milkman went out of my head. 'That can't be right,' I said, but longest friend sighed and here she did turn towards me. 'You brought it on yourself, longest friend. I informed you and informed you. I mean for the longest time ever since primary school I've been warning you to kill out that habit you insist on and that now I suspect you're addicted to — that reading in public as you're walking about.' 'But —' I said. 'Not natural,' she said. 'But —' I said. 'Unnerving behaviour,' she said. 'But —' I said. 'But —' I said, 'I thought you meant in case of traffic, in case I walked into traffic.' 'Not traffic,' she said. 'More stigmatic than traffic. But too late. The community has pronounced its diagnosis on you now.'

Nobody, especially a teenager, likes to discover they've been earmarked some freak-weirdo person. *Me! In the same boat as our poisoner, tablets girl!* This was shocking and not at all fair. It seemed too, that once again, everybody, bar maybe-boyfriend and — though I hated to admit it — Milkman, was homing in on my harmless reading-while-walking. These past months, ever since the beginning of Milkman, I was getting an education on just how much I was impacting people without any awareness I'd been visible to people. 'It's creepy, perverse, obstinately determined,' went on longest friend. 'It's not as if, friend,' she said, 'this were a case of a person glancing at some newspaper as they're walking along

338

to get the latest headlines or something. It's the way you do it — reading books, *whole books,* taking notes, checking footnotes, underlining passages as if you're at some desk or something, in a little private study or something, the curtains closed, your lamp on, a cup of tea beside you, essays being penned — your discourses, your lucubrations. It's disturbing. It's deviant. It's optical illusional. Not public-spirited. Not self-preservation. Calls attention to itself and why — with enemies at the door, with the community under siege, with us all having to pull together — would anyone want to call attention to themselves here?' 'Hold on a minute,' I said. 'Are you saying it's okay for him to go around with Semtex but not okay for me to read *Jane Eyre* in public?' 'I didn't say not in public. Just don't do it while you're walking about. They don't like it,' she added, meaning the community then, resuming that looking-ahead of hers, she said she was not prepared to get into amphibologies, into equivocations, into the auld 'over the water' double-talk, but if I cared to look at it in its proper surroundings, then Semtex taking precedence as something normal over reading-while-walking — 'which nobody but *you* thinks is normal' — could certainly be construed as the comprehensible interpretation here. 'Semtex isn't unusual,' she said. 'It's not *not* to be expected. It's not incapable of being mentally grasped, of being understood, even if most people here don't carry it, have never seen it, don't know what it looks like and don't want anything to do with it. It fits in — more than your dangerous reading-while-walking fits in. This is about aware-ness and your behaviour doesn't display awareness. So, looked at in those terms, terms of contextual environment, then yeah,' she concluded, *'it is okay for him and it's not okay for you.'*

I could sense her words, in one of those medieval, philosophical, 'relative versus absolute' dimensions, did have some ring of truth about them. Still, I didn't like the implication that I had contracted an incur-able beyond-the-pale. 'Just because I'm outnumbered in my reading-while-walking,' I said, 'doesn't mean I'm wrong. What if one person happened to be sane, longest friend, against a whole background, a race mind, that wasn't sane, that person would probably be viewed by the mass conscious-ness as mad — *but would that person be mad?*' 'Yes,' said friend, 'if they persisted in their version of life in the stacked-up odds of an opposing world. But that's not you anyway,' she went on, 'because there's this other thing.' I assumed — for why wouldn't I? — this must mean more Milkman, but friend said she didn't want to be harsh, that she didn't want to put me on the spot or to embarrass me. 'But what are you doing, longest friend,' she said, 'what are you thinking of, walking around with cats' heads?' This was when it came out I had dead animals on me. Perhaps for ceremonial, black-magic purposes? longest friend said the community was hazarding. Perhaps to invoke a ritual with piecemeal familiars in opposition to the pious women with their bells and birds and prognostications and auguries? Or was I pregnant? Had Milkman made me pregnant? *'Yes, that must be it!'* they were saying. *'Milkman's made her pregnant and because of hormones —'* 'Not cats' heads!' I cried. *'Cat's head!* Only one head! Only once!' Friend bit her lip. 'So you think,' she said, 'walking about while reading with your desk lamp on during riots and gunplay with one dead animal in your pocket instead of countless animals isn't going to tip the balance? Question is, friend, *why are you carrying a cat's head about?'* I took a breath, for how to explain? How to start in that I'd only carried it once, for one moment, and look — even then I'd been

341

spied upon. I didn't know how to talk anymore and I realised that even here, with longest friend, my one-time sister-in-thought, I was to have life drained from me after all. Here I was, having to persuade and prove credible to someone who'd always been in my confidence, someone whom I'd felt was authenticated in my heart even though as time went by — as four years went by — I could see the traffic was no longer two-way; that nowadays — didn't know why — because of that unspoken agreement between us perhaps? for my own good perhaps? — very little in the way of confidences tended to come back. I could say to her, I supposed, that I thought it must have been that bomb in the ten-minute area that did it; that it was Semtex or what would have been Semtex if it hadn't been an old-time bomb, that did it; that whoever left the bomb, or dropped the bomb from their bomber plane, did it, that I'd wanted to take the cat to the graveyard away from the brash, exploded concrete in order to offer it some green. I didn't say this because there was no way to do so that wouldn't have me come out like a madwoman. Plus the un-posed, unrehearsed candidness that had existed between me and longest friend since primary school seemed now to be at an end.

No longer did I want to explain, for I could see myself in the moment exactly as she was seeing me, as all of them were seeing me. Besides, I didn't know why I carried it. And now, quite suddenly, I felt sad. It wasn't that I was the one breaking ties and pulling first from longest friend but that longest friend had already done the pulling. Something of trust was over even if fondness remained but fondness was another of those maybes. So, leaving *that,* shunning *that* — for *that* was people, *that* was relationships, always what was to be expected — leaving also the cat business, I said, 'Can we get back to the main point now?'

Longest friend looked surprised — something she didn't do often. 'This is the main point,' she said, which had me, then, surprised. 'I thought Milkman was the main point,' I said. 'No,' she said. 'Why would he be the main point? He was the point before the point. This reading-while-walking, and your unreachable stubbornness at back of it, plus the dangers inherent in it, are the reasons we're meeting up here tonight. But you know' — and here she paused, for one of those illuminating, transcendent, contemplative insights seemed now to strike her — 'it might be as well,' she went on, 'I mean as in remedial — and even though it be in one of those unpopular "silver-lining, dark-cloud, learning-through-suffering" fashions — that this predation upon you by Milkman has happened. Your not wanting to be present but now forced by circumstance of Milkman to be present has been one of those reality checks that life has given you — to round you out, to step you up, to set you on the next stage of your journey. And as far as I can see, friend, the only thing that's done that for you *ever* has been Milkman appearing, as now he has, on your scene.' At this I thought, wasn't she the smug bastard and I said so and she said no, that we had not to get personal even though what was she being if not personal? She said we had to stay focused on the main point. This point was: how I was confounding the community with my reading-while-walking; how some people might not be terribly capable of being explained but that that didn't stop others explaining them anyway; how no one should go around in a political scene with their head switched off; how I was abnormally unnerved by social questions, by regular queries, even harmless requests for information even though I'd object and say I did uphold questions but no — she shook her head — I upheld only literature questions and even then, only

344

nineteenth-century or earlier questions. The point was also, she said, my refusal to abandon my facial and bodily numbance in spite of everybody knowing that numbance as protection didn't work here. Then there was the fact the girl who walks — 'The girl who walks?' 'Yes. You're the girl who walks. Sometimes the one who reads and other times you're the pale, adamantine, unyielding girl who walks around with the entrenched, boxed-in thinking.' Then she said she was going to get directive with me as if she hadn't been directive up to this point. 'It's not that you have to give actual autobiographical passages,' she said, 'but you do that reading-while-walking and you look nearly-blank and you give nothing which is too little and so they won't let go and move on to the next person. It's to bring the house down, friend,' she said, 'if you don't stop being haughty for they see you as haughty and that you think you'll get away with it because you're sleeping with —' *'Not sleeping with!'* '— considered to be sleeping with Milkman, also because in the movement that man's no lightweight so of course they won't — not with him behind you — have a direct go. You must know though,' she concluded, 'even you must appreciate, that as far as they're concerned you've fallen

345

into the difficult zone.' She meant the 'informer-type' zone — not that I was an informer. It was that miscellany territory where, like the informer, you're not accepted, you're not admired, you're not respected, not by one side, not by the other side, not by anybody, not even really by yourself. In my case though, seems I'd fallen into the difficult zone not only because I wouldn't tell my life to others, or because of my numbance, or because of my suspiciousness of questions. What was also being held against me was that I wasn't seen as the clean girlfriend, as in, he didn't have other attachments. He did have attachments. One was his wife. So I was the upstart, the little Frenchwoman, the arriviste, the hussy. Also, like the informer, when you're no longer needed, when you've been superseded, when you've served your purpose or been upended before you'd been able to serve your purpose, others, sometimes suffering the effects of their own presumption, have a tendency to want their own back. That was the difficult zone. It was of complex data, Any Other Business, even of contradiction, all reduced for convenience to a simple catch-all. But she was wrong. It wasn't that I fell into the difficult zone. It was that I was pushed.

'Okay. I'll stop doing it,' I said, and I meant here the reading-while-walking. I had jumped back to reading-while-walking to get away from stubbornness. If something had to go, I'd rather it was that. 'That's the spirit,' friend urged. 'Use your loaf, stop the stubbornness, work on your disposition, get off your high horse and show some friendly stray bits. Just something unimportant that would satisfy them rather than encourage them with silence. Then, if you also stop that unfathomable reading-while-walking, that should ameliorate the situation as well.' I nodded, but said the reading-while-walking wasn't going to be 'also'. It was going to be instead of. I needed my silence, my unaccommodation, to shield me from pawing and from molestation by questions. In contrast to friend, I myself was of the view that trying to placate with information to win them over, would not bring benefits of desistence but would encourage and lead them on even more. Besides, I didn't want to. Still I didn't want to. This was my one bit of power in this disempowering world. 'You'd better be careful then,' said friend, which was what everybody said. People always said you'd better be careful. Though how, when things are out of your hands, when things were never really in your hands, when things are stacked against you, does a person — the little person down here on the earth — be that? So I said about the books and the walking as compromise, which seemed easy in comparison. There wasn't even regret because by now I was no longer getting the old enjoyment from it. That experience of relaxing into it, of walking out the door and slipping the book out of the pocket, of sinking into the paragraph coming up after the recently left-off paragraph, had changed since the stalking, also since the rumouring, since even the state forces had got suspicious and were stopping me to take *Martin Chuzzlewit* for state-security purposes out of my hands. Then there was being watched as I was reading, being reported upon about my reading, being photographed by at least one person with or without the reading. How could a reader's concentration upon and enjoyment of a novel be sustained in the face of all that?

As for the state forces, friend told me not to worry about the cameras, the clicking, the data-storage, saying that even before Milkman there was bound to have been a file on me anyway. 'The whole community's a suspect community,' she said. 'Everybody has a file on them. Everybody's house, everybody's movements, everybody's connections constantly are checked and kept an eye on. It's only you who doesn't seem aware of that. With all their monitoring,' she went on, 'their infiltrating, their intercepting, listening at posts, drawing-up of room lay-outs, of position of furniture, of ornament placement, of wallpaper, of watch lists and geo-profiling, cutting feeds and feeding feeds, and "mother goose" and divination by tea-leaves and not least,' she said, 'with their helicopters flying over an alienated, cynical, existentially bitter landscape, it's no wonder everybody has files on them. If someone in a renouncer-run area didn't have a file on them, that would be a surety there was something dubious about that individual going on. They even photograph shadows,' she said. 'People here can be deciphered and likenesses discerned from silhouettes and shadows.' 'That's *very* attuned,' I said, impressed. Friend then said that even pre-Milkman there would have been a file with my name on it anyway because of my other associations. I was about to ask what associations when she interrupted. 'God. I can't believe this. Your head! Your memory! All those mental separations and splittings-off from consciousness. *I mean me! Your association with me! Your brothers! Your second brother! Your*

349

fourth brother!' And now she was shaking her head. 'The things you notice yet don't notice, friend. The disconnect you have going between your brain and what's out there. This mental misfiring — it's not normal. It's abnormal — the recognising, the not recognising, the remembering, the not remembering, the refusing to admit to the obvious. But you encourage that, these brain-twitches, this memory disordering — also this latest police business — all perfect examples they are, of what I'm talking about here.' She paused then to turn round and stare at me fully and I felt hurt but also panicked, as if at any moment she was going to hurl me into some dimension where I did not wish to go. 'No wonder,' she said, 'they're clocking and stopping you extra.' 'Not extra,' I objected. 'They're clocking and stopping me without previous stoppings because Milk—' 'No,' she said. 'They're stopping you because you've drawn attention to yourself with your beyond-the-pale reading-while —' 'No,' I said. 'If that were true, how come they weren't stopping me before Milk—' 'But they *were* stopping you! They *do* stop you. *They stop everybody!*' And here her tone became resigned rather than monitory. 'I think,' she said, 'that even at this minute we're entering another bout of your *jamais vu.*' 'What do you mean *my jamais vu*?' I asked. Then I asked, 'What do you mean *another* bout of *jamais vu*? Are you saying I have *jamais vu* and that frequently I have it?' which was when it came out that, similar to the way in which I would block as unfamiliar from my memory all my periodic attempts to establish a proper relationship between me and maybe-boyfriend, instead thinking each time to be the first time at furthering on our intimacy, here too, according to friend, I'd experience illusions of never having been stopped previously by the state security forces when it was obvious I was stopped by them, she maintained, all the time. Initially it was just routine, she said, cursory stoppings, the usual thing that they carry out on everybody who comes into and goes out of renouncer areas. But now — owing *not* to Milkman, but to my escalating beyond-the-paleness — I was being stopped not cursory but much more than cursory times. She ended this talk on surveillance and my disappearances into other dimensions by saying that just as with the camera, I shouldn't worry disproportionately as to what official gloss they might put upon my behaviour. Given I was now a beyond-the-pale, reputed to read-while-walking as if sitting down; prone, according to the community, to back-to-front reading, starting on the last page and working back to the front page in order to pre-empt narrative surprises because I didn't like surprises; given I put bookmarks in books, they said, or else turned down pages not correctly where I'd left off, but slyly at misleading places so as to deceive the public for personal round-about, paranoid reasons; given I was reported to have a counting thing where I'd figure cars, lamp-posts and tick off landmarks whilst at the same time pretend to give directions to invisible people — all while reading-while-walking; given I didn't like pictures of people's faces on books or on record sleeves or hanging in frames on walls because I'd imagine I was being spied upon by them; and finally, given I carried dead animals in my pockets, 'What's an affair with a major paramilitary player,' she asked, 'and who would give a damn anyway, taken amidst the craziness of all that?'

After this came the lighter side of the evening, the indulgent item at the end of the news. We had reached for our drinks and sipped, then sat back, with friend, apropos of just throwing it out, telling me it had been my first brother-in-law who had started the rumours about me. 'Shouldn't concern yourself with him though,' she said. 'He's currently being intervened on and soon is to have his own reality check.' First brother-in-law's reality check, unsurprisingly, was to stem from his latest sexual obsession. This latest had him visiting nuns — the community's full-on holy women — with masturbating questions disguised as harmless cultural queries about art. 'He brought up that sculpture,' said friend, 'you know, that statue, the one of the nun, Teresa of Avila, who had her own private levitation sessions?' I knew the statue she meant. Age twelve, flicking through a book in the art room at school I'd turned a page and seen a picture of that statue, jumping away with an actual cry when I realised what it was I was looking at. It had been unexpected. All of a sudden. A realisation I'd no premonition that day was coming to me. Those billowing clothes, nun's clothes, on her body, her inside them, suffocating inside them, them outside her, alive, maybe inside-out, swallowing her up. Those folds, those coils, those windings and volumes and living, moving layers, well, of course they frightened me. The picture itself repulsed me — yet it had held me. My thinking at the time, when I recovered from being repulsed and had gone back for a second, then a third, then a fourth, then a fifth look — and only on the fifth look did I take in that angel with the stick thing — my thinking was perhaps it would have been better, less scary, if the clothes had *not* been on her body. But what if they hadn't and she was in that contorted condition — bare arms, bare legs, bare bits all over — and that face, looking the way it was looking — helpless, abandoning, enjoying itself — or the opposite of enjoying itself — and her naked and praying — but that didn't look like praying unless — oh God — *that was what praying was*? On second thoughts, my twelve-year-old self decided, maybe it was better that the clothes, unsettling and voracious as they were, had been on her body all along.

'So, sisters,' had begun first brother-in-law, for he had gone to the convent with the intention of taking out his own magazine picture of that very same statue. Apparently this lover of art had been carrying it around for some time. 'About this emotive picture about a devotional statue. What do you make of the ecstasy, of the meditative, mystical, voluptuous — sweetly moaning as it seems to me — and yet excessively intrusive, jarringly orgiastic portrayal of the situation? Is this really' — and here he looked pensive, earnest, saying the next bit supposedly artistically and not at all sexually pervertedly — 'that this woman, in perfect union with God, this *nun* — such as you are yourselves — was perhaps rapturously aroused and self-pleasuring via the metaphor of levitation? And as for this seraph thrusting and thrusting and given your own experience —'

That was as far as he got.

He was seen through immediately of course, said friend, for the nuns weren't stupid, nor were they ignorant of art and even less so of his wink-wink, sexual dislocation-compulsion reputation. They had been praying for him. Indeed, he had almost reached number one at the apex of names of us people urgently to be prayed for locally on their long list. But now they threw him out. This was way past the stage of civilisation, way past quietly asking him to leave, of having courtesy shown him owing to his being a spiritual soul on life's path such as they themselves were spiritual souls on life's path. No. They threw him out — or rather, Sister Mary Pius, the big nun, she threw him out — after the rest of the nuns had had a slap at him first. After that, the head nun paid a visit to the sanctities — our pious women of the area who constituted intermediaries between the holy

355

women and the renouncers-of-the-state in our area. When the pious women heard the indecent news they paid a visit to the renouncers. That was when it was decided, said friend, that first brother-in-law's behaviour had better, for the first time, be put in check.

'The man is inexpugnable,' said friend. 'Yeah he is,' I said. 'Just what I was thinking. Only seems now he isn't. What'll happen to him? What'll they do to him?' — and it wasn't out of concern for him that I had asked. It was for first sister, his wife, my sister, though when third sister got to hear, she said absolutely she was glad he was to have his comeuppance, not glad either, in any compassionate 'may God have mercy on his soul' way. Because he was so into his wild torment, his strivings-through-sensation, his lack of modest thought, his insatiable addiction where everything and anyone — as long as it was female — had to be approached, had to be appropriated, he just couldn't stop himself. This would be too, us, his sisters-in-law, beginning as twelve-year-olds, or else other females in the area, or nuns as now it turned out to be. It was all about the sexual arena; the man knew not how to engage in any other arena. That was why third sister and I had tried to speak to the girls. Wee sisters, however, said they didn't need us to warn them to be on the alert as to something feverish, driven and greedyguts about first brother-in-law. That he had some sickly compulsion neurosis, they said, was very plain for all eyes to see. 'Only, what's that to us?' they added. 'Why are you coming to us, telling this us, warning of first brother-in-law us?' 'If he tries anything,' said third sister. 'Tries what?' they said. 'Even if he speaks to you in a seemingly innocent way on the subject, say, of the French Revolution —' 'What aspect of the French Revolution?' 'Any aspect,' said third sister. 'Or,' she went on, 'if he tries to get a discussion going on that marginalised scientific theory you three are keen on, the one about hydrothermal multi-turbulent —' 'You're outlining that incorrectly, third sister,' wee sisters began. 'What third sister means,' I interrupted, 'is that if he should sidle up with Demosthenes's disapproval of Alcibiades, or if he should appear suddenly and try to expound on the thesis of Francis Bacon really being William Shakespeare, which means —' 'We know what expounding theses means!' 'What middle sister is saying,' said third sister, 'is that if he gets into a summary exposition on Guy Fawkes's ordinary signature before he was tortured and Guy Fawkes's confession signature after he was tortured which means —' 'We know what summary exposition means!' 'Look, wee sisters, the point is,' I said, 'if he tries to lure you in on the pretext of anything — science, art, literature, linguistics, social anthropology, mathematics, politics, chemistry, the intestinal tract, unusual euphemisms, double-entry bookkeeping, the three divisions of the psyche, the Hebrew alphabet, Russian Nihilism, Asian cattle, twelfth-century Chinese porcelain, the Japanese unit —' 'We don't understand,' cried wee sisters. 'What's wrong with talking about them things?' 'What's wrong is that don't be fooled,' said third sister. 'None of that will be the business, won't be what he's really after.' 'But what's the business? What will he really be after? What is it you both mean?' We could see, third sister and me, that far from reassuring and protecting the children, we had alarmed and frightened the children. Third sister then said, 'It'll be something abusive, sexually invasive, a violating, creepy thing, always a verbal thing, but on second thoughts, never you mind. You three are too young to know of that yet.'

'He's to be had up,' friend said, and she

meant at one of the 'courts, for the 'courts, they happened. 'It's his first warning,' she said. 'Shouldn't be his first,' I said. 'He started in on me when I was twelve.' 'He might get a beating,' she said, 'which is skipping the warning, because of his propositioning of holy women.' 'The women with the issues,' I said, 'won't like that.' At this longest friend frowned and I thought at first it was because of this take on female hierarchy, that women all for God and having visions in billowing clothes should take precedence over other women, for who then came next — wives? mothers? virgins? The frown though, turned out not to be over the issue women's insistence on everything being fair which meant not patriarchal, but over my making reference to her business when we had that unspoken agreement that never was I to do that. She though, had been the one to start in on her business. This whole meeting in the lounge in the first place had been her on her business. Sending round that emissary, that spotter boy, to arrange between us had been her and her business. 'You started it,' I said. 'Had to,' she said. 'Because of your mental deterioration and because I reckoned that after all the harshness about your defects, you might want some cheering — hence your brother-in-law. But you're right. Let's leave this and stick to non-political issues from now on.'

After this our meeting in the lounge ended, and after that I had three further encounters with longest friend from primary school. One was at her wedding in the countryside four months on where I was the only one — bar the holy man officiating — not wearing dark glasses. Even the groom, and longest friend in her simple white gown, each had a pair on. Then I met her a year after her wedding, this time at the funeral of her husband. Three months on from that I went to her own funeral when they buried her with her husband. This was in the renouncers' plot of the graveyard just up from the ten-minute area, also known as 'the no-town cemetery', 'the no-time cemetery', 'the busy cemetery' or just simply, the usual place.

FIVE

The girl who was really a woman who went around putting poison in drinks poisoned me and I didn't know she'd done it, not even when I woke up with the most unbelievable stomach pains two hours after I went to bed. At first I thought it was more of those shudders, those tingles, the horrible sensations coming upon me since Milkman. But no. Tablets girl had slipped something into my drink. This had been in the club when I was with longest friend and we were finishing our discussion which I thought was to be on Milkman but which turned out to be on my beyond-the-pale status. Friend had then gone to the toilet and the moment I was alone at the table that girl who was really a woman snuck up. She accused me immediately of crimes against humanity, also of being selfish; also she poisoned me, managing to do all before I could tell her to fuck off. 'You should be

ashamed,' she said, but she was not referring to my love affair with Milkman, which
I assumed she was referring to because that
was all anybody — whose business still it
wasn't — referred to. Instead she was talking about my colluding with Milkman to
kill her in some other life. As well as her
death, apparently I was responsible for the
deaths of twenty-three other women —
'some of whom were definitely doing herbs,'
she said, 'just their innocent white medicine,
and some of whom weren't doing anything'
— and I did all these crimes during the time
we — the whole twenty-six of us — were in
this other life. She meant a past incarnation
sometime during the seventeenth century
and she gave dates and times and said he
had been a doctor, but one of those quack
doctors. Here she looked revolted that I
would align myself with, would become the
cat-familiar of, such a counterfeit man. She
said there was no point in my denying I'd
known of his impostorship. I had abetted
him, done black magic for him, cut up dead
animals for him, been a female accessory to
his murders of those twenty-three women,
plus her, in our picturesque village. 'We all
died, sister,' she said, 'because of you.'
Because of this, she said I deserved exactly
what was coming to me. It was at that point

I pulled myself out of her mesmerising fragmentations and said, 'Oh, for fuck's sake, fuck off.' When longest friend came back she asked what had gone on and I shook my head and said, 'Ach, it's that tablets girl.' Longest friend warned me to watch myself with tablets girl because, she said, 'that poor girl who's really a woman is getting worse'.

And that was the thing. Our most notorious beyond-the-pale was this girl who was really a woman, a small, slight, wiry girl, nearing thirty who put poison in people's drinks. For a long time nobody could draw any explanation from her on this matter. What was surmised about it had to be surmised by the community's embellishment on her initial lack of information, with most deciding she was doing what she was doing because of some feminist complaint. They didn't elaborate on the complaint but given, they said, the issue women from our district — another beyond-the-pale grouping — had been seen talking with tablets girl, priming her perhaps, brain-washing her into their movement, meant that obvious issues such as militant feminist ones could be the only reason for her continual attempts to kill us all. At the time the issue women denied this accusation, saying it was a misunderstanding of their objectives, also that the community hadn't a shred of evidence to bear it out. They added that tablets girl had already been poisoning people well before they'd decided to have a word with her and that they'd only approached anyway to try to understand and intervene. Impossible it was therefore, they said, to gauge in some offhand, irresponsible manner what this tiny person purposed by her poisonings. So back then interpretations continued, as did riffs and contentions on these interpretations. So too, did the poisonings continue, and mostly where they continued, where it was crucial to be on the look-out for her, was at the Friday night dance in the district's most popular drinking-club.

Especially crucial to keep an eye would be if you were on the dancefloor with your boyfriend or your mates, with drinks unattended at the table whenever she'd decide to come in. As it was, before she'd make her entrance, two other groupings always had to make their entrance. The renouncers-of-the-state would come in, in their black gear, their balaclavas and with their guns, to inspect for undesirables and underage drinkers. There would be many undesirables and underage drinkers but never once would anyone be hauled out and made to leave. It was a pretence. Everyone knew it was a pretence, a show of strength, one of those dresscode presentations that weekly had to be gone through. They would stride in, be determined, look around, flash hardware, finish their inspection then leave, and moments later, another grouping would enter and another pretence would take place. This would be the foreign soldiers, the occupying army from the country 'over the water'. They too, would be in their gear, their khaki, their helmets, with their guns and on the look-out for renouncers, those very same renouncers they'd missed just seconds before. Only occasionally would it cross our minds the extent of bloodbath that would ensue should these two groupings ever make it in together. Not once though, in all the years of Friday nights did that encounter take place. Hard to imagine it not happening, we'd say, therefore unconscious synchrony, some connected happenstance must unconsciously be taking place between them. 'It's Friday night,' one subliminal might have intimated to the other subliminal, 'so why not keep this simple? How about you go in first, then you leave, then we'll go in? Then next week we'll go in first, then leave, then you go in.' That must have been what happened because inconceivable they should miss each other by hairbreadths, not once, not twice, but easily a couple of hundred times. So these respective armies would enter, do their bit, scrutinise, show off, throw weight around, with everybody else, meaning us — young people on the dancefloor, young people at the drinking-tables, young people at the bar, kissing and canoodling in the shadows — ignoring them. As soon as tablets girl came in though, well, that was something else.

'She's in!'

'Hurry up!'

'Stations everybody! Careful! Oh watch out! Pills girl! It's pills girl!'

This would be hissed by every person in the club. At this point drunken panic would ensue and whoever had been designated that week as watchman or watchwoman for each group at each table would rush back to respective tables from the dancefloor, the toilets, the bar, the shadowed embrace in the corner, from wherever he or she at that moment happened to be. This would be to guard the drinks but even then the rest of us would remain on edge, totally attuned to her presence. We'd nudge each other, turn and turn about, follow her procession through the club, keeping all attention fixed upon her, while she, like some phantom, some horrific nightmare, would dander in and sidle around. You'd have thought, given our hypervigilance, that we, the majority, would have been best-placed to thwart tablets girl and protect our own health interests. When it came to it though, this lone combatant won hands down every time. No one knew how she did it but she had a way of getting substances in regardless of the person at the table. The person at the table, as could be evidenced by everybody, had dashed back conscientiously and grabbed in the drinks, keeping them close, taking no chances. Politeness wasn't pretended either in the urgency to get her away. 'Fuck off!' they'd shout, maintaining afterwards that it was best always to be frank in these poison situations. 'Fuck off!' they'd yell. 'Fuck off!' they'd abandon propriety. 'Fuck off!' they'd slip into appalling rudeness. By this time though, if they'd had to shout that many fuck-offs to the district's all-time most successful superior poisoner and still she hadn't gone from them, chances were they, and at least one other of their party, would be doubled over in pain, thrashing, clenching, trembling, contorting, dosed up on all kinds of expurgating substances, crying and begging too, from exhaustion, for death to overtake them, all to get it over with, and all before that long night into morning was through.

So she got herself thoroughly disliked, but contrarily, for all this disliking, tablets girl was pretty much taken in the district's stride. Even if it were a jumpy stride, a paranoid stride, a poisoned stride, because people might get furious, they might want to kill her. It never occurred to anybody though, that she should be barred from the district's most popular club. Nor either, that she should be hospitalised, jailed, that her family shouldn't let her out or, at least, should have a rota going to chaperone her whenever she did go out, that the rest of us shouldn't have to, every Friday night, go through this poison ordeal. Menace that she was, in that different time, during that different consciousness, and with all that other approach to life and to death and to custom, she was tolerated, just as the weather was tolerated, just as an Act of God or those Friday night armies coming in had to be tolerated. Declaring her a beyond-the-pale seemed as far as we, the community, could go. So always she was allowed back and always she came back and continued her poisoning. Then her trajectory changed and she started poisoning people on other days besides Friday, also becoming verbose as to why.

She had recently poisoned her own sister, said friend, though so far the family had it under wraps and were keeping very quiet about it. She had accused her sister of being some unacceptable aspect of herself. I said, 'This is getting complicated. Do you mean —' 'That's right,' said longest friend. 'Some split-off usurping aspect of herself.' Seemed there hadn't been enough room in the district for these contrary sides of her and so, from self-preservation — and given one part was a poisoner, the other part that wasn't a poisoner, her sister — had to go. Longest friend then agreed that yes, since tablets girl had started in on her explanations, the communal ability to explain her was indeed getting complicated and that perhaps if I'd stop walking about with a book at my face and got into proper reality, I might notice just how much the community itself was struggling to keep up. Everybody, of course, 'moved things on' here. There was a constant and unerring 'moving of one on' here, and this 'moving of things on one' happened pretty much all the time. The shifting sands of acceptable dislocations could easily be assimilated by the community's race consciousness, but when it came to those beyond-the-pales such as tablets girl (such as myself now too, though still I was baulking), they were a law unto themselves. Often the pales were said to flout convention, to move things not reasonably on one as everybody else did, but unapproved, unannounced, move things on two, or three, or even side-step their convolutions entirely on to some new, even more farfetched footing. That was what tablets girl, thinking her sister an oppositional side of herself, did.

Friend explained that the poisoned younger sister, the shiny one, had been poisoned right up to the hospital and in truth, well beyond the hospital. She had been poisoned to the extent of having most of her body in the ground. Of course she didn't go to hospital because, as with calling the police here — meaning you didn't call them — involving yourself with medical authorities could be viewed as imprudent as well. One set of authorities, pronounced the community, always brought on another set of authorities, and should it be that you were shot, or poisoned, or knifed, or damaged in any way you didn't feel like talking about, the police would be informed by the hospital regardless of your wishes and they would show up from their barracks right away. What would happen then, warned the community, was that this state-enemy force, on discovering which side of the fence you came from, would compromise you and present you with a choice. That choice would be: either you were to be falsely rigged up and hinted at in your district to be an informer for them, or else you were really to become an informer and inform on the renouncers-of-the-state from your district for them. Either way sooner or later, courtesy of the renouncers, your corpse would be the latest to be found up an entry with the obligatory tenner in its hand and the bullets in its head. So no. According to communal rules you didn't want to bother with hospitals. Why would you anyway, with safe-house surgery theatres, back-parlour casualty wards, homemade apothecaries and with more than enough garden-shed pharmacies dotted about the place?

As for tablets girl's sister, three-quarters in the grave, she did the best she could, with her family and neighbours also doing their best. Many severe purgings later, everyone attempted to say she was all right. While on the mend, it became clear this young woman's health and eyesight were dramatically now not what they used to be, so community justice, by way of the renouncers, once again got involved. The family, con-flicted, owing to blood connections with both victim and perpetrator, begged the re-nouncers to hold off retribution and to give tablets girl one more chance to redeem herself. The renouncers had promised last time that if tablets girl didn't stop her anti-social behaviour they themselves would stop it for her. Therefore now, in light of the ac-cused's latest disregard of their warnings, the time had come, the renouncers said, to carry their promise out. Longest friend then said the renouncers didn't act right away, but instead deliberated further owing to the beseeching of the family. Then they sum-moned the family and fore-advised them. 'Okay,' they said. 'One more chance, but that's all.'

We emptied our glasses then, and left the drinking-club and I went home and got into bed and fell asleep and stayed asleep until I was woken by something invisible wisping into my bedroom, wisping up my bed-clothes, getting in my open mouth and slip-ping down my throat. I jumped awake cry-ing, *'It got in! It made its way in! They got in while I was sleeping!'* But before I came awake properly and could work out what I was talking about, a burning sensation in my innards took hold. There was a pungency in my mouth too, which at first I thought was a tooth-filling behaving badly. Then I thought, that's no tooth! This is more of Milkman and of how his coveting is affecting me now. Cramps then took hold, exhaling the air out of me, squeezing it from me, with my muscles going nuts and turning me rigid. Then I fell out of bed, still rigid, my insides turning to stone. I crawled out the bedroom on forearms and knees, bumping the door with my head because I couldn't lift my head because of the rigidity of my torso. I didn't know what the head-bumping meant, didn't know what the door meant, didn't know either where I was going except that I had to get out and get help.

On the upstairs landing new pains set in, these of a darting, crisscross fashion. Because of them, I was forced to give up crawling somewhere between my bedroom and the bathroom, all the time hearing strange sounds which I thought were voices on a radio made to go slow. I found out later they'd been my groans and, 'Guess what! They woke up everybody!' cried my younger sisters. They were speaking with relish, these sisters, and this was four days on from the poisoning when I was in bed, on the mend, recuperating. They recounted these groans to me, demonstrated a selection for me, described also the events of the middle of that night to me, adding that I looked white — 'but not that awful white you look usually'. 'More like milk,' said oldest-youngest sister. 'A bottle of milk,' said middle-youngest sister. 'Like white milk that's been painted extra white,' suggested youngest-youngest sister, 'so that it glows in the dark.' A three-way fight broke out between wee sisters over whether this 'glowing in the dark' aspect had been true or fabricated. Also they fought over when this extra whiteness had materialised. Had it been *before* our mother and the neighbours purged me or *after* our mother and the neighbours purged me? For yes, ma and the neighbours purged me, ma being first to reach me on the landing and to put her arms out and around me but, because of what was happening within me, I hadn't heard her come up. I felt her strong arms though, felt her warm breath, and knew in that moment that it was good beyond God to have my mother near me. Gripping the hem of her nightdress, then crawling along this nightdress, then inching into the belly of this nightdress, I knew I would be safe, that I would not now be alone.

At the same time as saving me, of course she had a go at me. Along with her rapid physical examination and quick-fire questions to me — Was I cut? Was I knifed? What did I eat? What did I drink? Did someone out of the ordinary give me something out of the ordinary? Was I in a fight with someone? Had I been kicked in the head earlier by someone? Were all my trusted friends trustworthy? With what had I been poisoned? — came also her first judgemental remark. 'Well, what do you expect, wee girl,' she said, 'if you go round stealing other people's husbands? Of course those women are going to try to kill you. For all your so-called knowledge of the world, how come you don't know that?' I didn't know what ma meant by my knowledge of the world. My knowledge of the world consisted of fucking hell, fucking hell, fucking hell, which didn't lend itself to detail, the detail really being those words themselves. Ma, though, hadn't finished the husband-and-wife bit. Next came more 'what do you expect' only this time with variations on my sometimes having affairs with lots of husbands, sometimes with all husbands, sometimes just with one husband, with Milkman. 'Fool girl. Oh foolhardy! Foolhardy!' she cried. 'You a teenager with him more than twice your age too!' Here she paused to hoist me up against herself to get me down to the bathroom. Then she continued her accusations and her jumping to conclusions, adding grimly, 'All the same, when this is done with, daughter, I want you to list me all those wives' names.' During this time I was still curled in a ball, unable to straighten, unable to stand, with waves of pain building, then pushing from below, then shooting up — still in that crisscross manner — through me. So she lifted me in this ball, bidding me to keep an arm round her neck whilst holding best I could with the other hand to the banisters, urging me too, to reveal to her the poison — 'But what did they give you? Do you know what they gave you?' — with at last my managing, 'No wives, ma. No husbands. No affair with Milkman. No poison.' Then — not listening because a new thought was now in her head — she turned herself to stone.

'In the name of God!' she cried. 'Are they correct? Is everybody correct? Have you been fecundated by him, by that renouncer, that "top of wanted list" clever man, the false milkman?' 'What?' I said, for it had been singular, that word she'd used and genuinely for a moment I had not a clue what she meant by it. 'Imbued by him?' she elaborated. 'Engendered in. Breeded in. Fertilised, vexed, embarrassed, sprinkled, caused to feel regret, wished not to have happened — dear God, child, do I have to spell it out?' Well, why didn't she spell it out? Why couldn't she just say pregnant? But this was like ma. It wasn't as if I hadn't enough on my plate, without having to take time out from poisoning — which still I hadn't realised was poisoning — to guess her latest removed remark. She didn't stay on difficult pregnancies either, for ma could give herself horror stories one right after the other. Next came abortions and I had to guess them also, from 'vermifuge, penny-royal, Satan's apple, premature expulsion, being failed in the course of coming into being' with any doubt dispelled by, 'Well, daughter, you can't disappoint me anymore than you've already disappointed me, so tell me — what did you procure and which of them drab aunts did you procure it of?'

This was news to me. I hadn't known there were drab aunts in the area, that the renouncers would permit them or be unable to stop them. Typical too, of ma, the fount of knowledge, to reveal to me, as always she did, astounding detail about the underside whilst at the same time accusing me of knowing it already. Once again, she was showing no faith, didn't believe I could be true, that I was true, that I might have enough wit of my own not to take up with such a man as Milkman, all of which didn't inspire me to inspire her with confidence in me, for why should I? Last time I tried she called me a liar, demanding — even though I had been doing it — that I give her the truth. She didn't want the truth. All she wanted was confirmation of the rumour. What was the use therefore, in trying to settle the attribution, to get her to see that these spasms, this stiffness, this unable to straighten, unable to stand, weren't down to poison or to any of her imaginings but instead were an intensified version of the usual? I was being sick because of Milkman stalking me, Milkman tracking me, Milkman knowing everything about me, biding his time, closing in on me, and because of the perniciousness of the secrecy, gawking and gossip that existed in this place. So ma and I were at cross purposes, as always we were at cross purposes, but then I did attempt because in that moment, which was a lonely moment, more than ever I longed for her belief in me, for her properly to perceive me. 'No wives, ma,' I said. 'No husbands, no foetus, no drab aunts, no poison, no suicide' — adding on that last to save her the trouble of adding it on herself. 'Well, what is it then?' she said and in the middle of pain, in the middle of poison, gloriously I felt a comfort go through me, a sense of solace descend on me, all because she'd paused in her admonition to consider I might be telling the truth. It could be easy to love her. Sometimes I could see how easy it could be to love her. Then it was gone and she broke off from hesitation, from prodding and hoisting and falsely accusing, to call to wee sisters. The three sisters were out of bed, standing behind us in their nightclothes at this point.

She commanded them to help and of course younger sisters were overjoyed to do this. They loved drama, any drama, just so long as it was sheer and they could be part of it, or at least bear witness to it. They rushed over and took hold exactly where ma instructed and between the four of them, got me along the rest of the landing, down the step at the end of the landing, then into the bathroom where wee sisters let go. They thought they were supposed to let go, so I fell along with ma onto the floor. It was sharp and painful, that fall, and at first I cried out with it. Then I realised this floor was good. It was cold, smooth, welcome, but short-lived also, because my body once again began to assert itself. It got back onto forearms, onto knees, in preparation for some imminence. Ma, meantime, was issuing instructions to wee sisters to go and get the keys of her backyard pharmacy from her bedroom and to bring them to her right away. They rushed off as one, which was how wee sisters did everything, and ma, turning back, kept pressing my middle while ordering me to think! think! If not 'chagrined', not 'vermifuged', not 'pennyroyaled', was there anything of eating? Anything of drinking? Anybody hanging around who shouldn't have been hanging around, but with me now unable to answer at all. Still contracted, still in that odd shape, stiffly I flung myself towards the bath, towards the floor, towards the toilet, then over the floor again. Something enormous was coming and it seemed my body wasn't hopeful of getting it out.

Sisters came back with a jangling of keys and ma jumped up shouting, 'Back in a minute' to them. She told them not to leave me, not to take their eyes from me, to make sure I didn't go on my back or fall asleep and to come and get her if I turned blue or if anything happened except throwing up. She rushed away then and the sisters crowded round and I felt their zeal more than the heat from their bodies. I couldn't see these bodies because my forehead, in another bout of relief, was pressed again to the cold floor. A respite only, I knew, and I knew too, that I must enjoy this simple pleasure before the onset of more flinging. Immediately though, wee sisters set asquawking. They shook me. Prodded me. 'Stop that! No sleeping! Mammy says it's not allowed!'

Ma returned with an awful-smelling, dreadful-looking, monstrous pint-size concoction. So also appeared neighbours, bearing demijohns, bell-jars, green, brown and yellow warning jars, balsams, philtres, phials, herbs, powders, weighing scales, pestle and mortars, huge pharmacopoeias, plus other 'keep it in the family' distillations of their own. They had materialised out of nowhere which was usual with neighbours on occasions of 'not going to hospital'. Like ma, they were prepared, with nightdress sleeves rolled up. First there was a conference held in the bathroom with the women standing over me, speaking to and fro across me. I heard most everything with wee sisters filling in blanks later on. They were debating the course of action, with the purists among them saying it was not good policy to induce vomiting if it hadn't been ascertained what it was they were dealing with. Others said to take a look, that it was clear this was no time to be precise and godlike, that a makeshift, slapdash approach would be entirely in order here. 'Speaking of entirely,' said one of the neighbours, 'this is entirely similar to that poor girl who had been poisoned by her sister.' 'What poor girl?' said ma, and tones of voice, according to wee sisters, dropped low at this point.

'Only the other day,' began the neighbour, 'and you must keep this quiet, neighbours, those of you who don't know, for it hasn't properly been leaked yet into the community, but that wee girl who's really a woman had another of her fractures. She poisoned her sister, the shiny one. Some of us were in at the purging and take it from us, it looked pretty bad.' The neighbours nodded because most of them, it seemed, had been in at the purging. But ma hadn't. And wee sisters hadn't, and the impact of this news hit them pretty hard. Especially so wee sisters. Much as they loved drama, they loved tablets girl's sister even more than drama. With this news of her poisoning, and regardless of the excitement at being allowed up in the night to attend the adult equivalent of an Enid Blyton midnight-feast adventure, in this case there was now a blight on the adventure, one being experienced not only by them. In spite of her shininess, her amiable disposition, her all-round goodwill and pretty much asking-for-it openness, tablets girl's sister was liked by everyone, including everyone in this bathroom. That night then, in the bathroom, wee sisters, on hearing the news, became worried, also did ma look worried. The four of them were shaken. Indeed all the women looked shaken. They paused for an eternity to take in the gravity of what had happened to this radiant young woman, forgetting in eternity's interim, that another, perhaps not-so-radiant young woman, was lying dying at their feet.

Then another neighbour said, 'All that is of note but in truth, the situation here isn't comparable.' As she spoke, she brought everyone's attention back to me on the floor. 'The other seemed to me,' she said, 'far worse than this one.' And here the neighbours who'd been in at the earlier purging concurred that the state of me wasn't as bad as the state of the poor other. Owing to their misperception, however — that my condition could only be down to vengeance on the part of the wife of Milkman — they didn't realise the significance of their own words. Ma didn't either and, in the moment, unbelievably neither did I. Not even when tablets girl's sister came into my mind whilst on the floor did I register this obvious trail of breadcrumbs. Of course I'd felt sorry for the girl when longest friend told me of what her mad sibling had done to her, but this had been in the manner of feeling sorry for a person whom you'd heard had undergone some dreadful experience without thinking for a second you were about to undergo the very same experience yourself. So it had been a 'by the by', a fairly dismissive feeling sorry on my part for tablets girl's sister, a heedlessness not badly meant but not an emotion of true understanding or of felt compassion either. As for my view of my condition, it would have been preposterous to consider that this tummy ache was down to poison when it was nerves — even if nerves in a worse state than ever they had been in since Milkman — and it was at this point ma did the unthinkable and mooted the hospital, stating she was not prepared to let her daughter die just because societal convention dictated she was not to call an ambulance. Her words were as a bombshell. The neighbours gasped. 'Enough! Oh enough!' and they begged her not to go on.

'Are you mad, dear neighbour!' they cried. 'Think upon it. You can't take her to hospital. Apart from the district mores of not going should there be something wrong that might require a police report, there's also the fact of your daughter's reputation preceding her, which most certainly it will do if you take her there. If that police confederation of felons get wind they have mistress of *you know who* down at the hospital, they'll think themselves handed best bait to reel in one of the most shadowy renouncers of all.' 'Why would they pass up on that?' another neighbour continued. 'Your daughter's only young, easily to be manipulated and intimidated. They'd frighten her, dangle her, implicate her, twist things and — *damn their hearts, dogs in the street* — not going along with them, as well you know, wouldn't save her either, the mere hint of informership being more than enough here.'

'Then there's yourself,' enjoined another, 'poor widow, household of girls, husband dead, one son dead, another son on the run, another son gone errant and yet another son creeping in and out of the area as if he was up to something. Then there's your eldest daughter in unspeakable grief, your second daughter banished by the renouncers, your third daughter perfectly perfect apart from her french which officially is the bluest in the area. And now there's this daughter possibly to be had up for traitor-ship. Consider the wee ones' — they indi-cated the wee ones, standing beside them, absorbing into themselves every word. 'No,' they shook their heads. 'No hospital. This one will have to pull through. And she will pull through,' they persisted. 'Don't you be worrying, neighbour.' Here, they patted ma and put their arms around her. 'Don't forget,' they concluded, 'it's not as if we don't know what's wanted here. We've all of us, including yourself, been through these improvisations, these rudiments, these homespun prescripts many, many times before.'

I agreed with the neighbours, though not from the premise of my reputation preced-ing me. The only reason such a thing was preceding was because they had made it up and put it there. Mistress of *you know who* would have been silly if Milkman himself hadn't been determined on just such a posi-tion for me. Also, in a district that thrived on suspicion, supposition and imprecision, where everything was so back-to-front it was impossible to tell a story properly, or not tell it but just remain quiet, nothing could get said here or not said but it was turned into gospel. Given this community then believed this gospel, what chance was there that the state, dealing with the disdain and inflexibility of a no-go area, would not grab at nonsense and photograph it, film it, put it in files, out-context it, and easily believe it as well? As for informership, the police could lift you anyway. Everyone knew they could lift you and try, at any time, to turn you. That would be regardless of whether or not you called an ambulance. Calling an ambulance shouldn't have been an issue but it was an issue because that had been decided as the way of things then. All the same, I myself didn't want an ambulance, didn't want the hospital. Nor did I need them because — *how long must I say?* — this wasn't a poisoning. The neighbours, however, weren't viewing it like that. They suggested purging, that if I were to have all my guts up and out onto the ground, they said, that would be acting on the safe side. 'After all,' they continued, 'seems her body itself is trying to evict something. We'd only be helping.' Therefore, purging and guts out it became.

They intervened on the state of my insides, as well as on my next bout of flinging and whatever high dose of purgative they put in there, it did something which did make me throw up. Over the course of the night I was made to ingest everything, then bring up everything, and in between I went from rigid to rag-doll at least seventeen times. At first I tried counting how many times as a way to distract my mind, to pretend this was an exercise in remoteness. I counted out loud, wee sisters said, then they said that either I lost count or I began to figure my numbers in a muttering fashion. I remembered some tearing sensation at my throat and at my abdomen and at first naively thought all that could happen would be a normal, unpleasant throwing-up. During this vomit session I'd bring up my last meal, then after that all that would be left to come would be bile. No. First there were the stomach contents. Then came many bouts of low-down, intestinal brown contents. Then, when I could no longer cope with the brown contents, only then came the bile. After that, there was more. There was dry heaving. An awful lot of dry heaving. All those stages too, increasingly against gravity, soon had me longing, begging, for the closure of my eyes. As it was, I could hardly keep them open. Got to sleep, I'd think. Got to lie down. Die soon. Why won't they let me die soon? It seemed really, it was these women with their purging and intermittent praying, and not the poison, that were the cause of my dying in our bathroom that night. There was no let-up. They had split into two groups, one taking on the purging while the other handled the praying. Then they'd swap and only after much prolongation and exhaustion, did the nicer part of the evening bit by bit ensue. This existed in brief lulls, increasingly turning to longer lulls, each occurring after the purgers' every administration to me followed by my body getting the poison out of me. Only then, when they'd withdraw to convene on next steps, could I remain on the floor, relieved, untampered-with, alone. Here, I'd contemplate the floor — the light dust on it, the odd hair on it, the specks of my recent emesis on it — and I'd consider the only true things in this world were these basic conditions of floor, dust and so on and that they, and only they, could sustain me forever. Sometimes though, I'd change my mind and it would become the panel of the bath, or the toilet bowl or the friendly bathroom wall against which occasionally I'd find myself, that I'd consider just as dependable of sustaining me forever too.

First time I awoke it was daylight and I was in my bed, mentally conjugating the French verb, *être.* I was running through the persons, tenses and cases of it in my mind.

Second time I awoke, I was still in bed, thinking, well, if that's the latest effect he's had on me with his sexual prowling, I don't know how I'm going to escape from him now. Third time I awoke it was from a dream of Proust, or rather, a nightmare of Proust, in which he turned out to be some reprehensible contemporary Nineteen-Seventies writer passing himself off as a turn-of-the-century writer, which apparently was why he was being sued in court in the dream by, I think, me. At that point again I fell asleep then final time I awoke — for I continued this waking and sleeping many times before waking up properly — I knew I'd turned a corner and was now on the mend. The reason I knew this was because of Fray Bentos. I was doing an elaborate Fray Bentos Steak and Kidney Pie fantasy in my head. I had got the tin out of the cupboard, took off the lid and put it in the oven. Then I set out a plate, knife, fork and mug of tea for myself. Even in bed, in my head, the aroma of that pie was making my mouth water. Thank God then, in the next second, it was done. I got it out of the oven, fainting with anticipation, and was about to tuck in when my bedroom door burst open. It was wee sisters. Again as one, they sprang into the room.

'She's awake!' they screamed, and they screamed this in my face as well as to each other. Right away they announced that ma was out and that they had been put in charge. They listed what I wasn't to do which was to fall out of bed, to try to get out of bed, to eat or drink, also I was not to attempt gallivanting. This was when they spoke of my being sick, also when they enacted for me my groaning. Then they moved on to the state of my skin's sickly, palely whiteness which was when I interrupted to say I was starving and threw the blankets off to get out of bed. This produced squawking. 'Not allowed!' they cried. 'Mammy says!' they cried. And I said, 'Okay. What's to eat then? Go and see and bring me something.' But they pushed me back and placed the bedclothes over me. To distract me they said they'd tell the exciting story of the renouncers. That morning while I'd been sleeping, the paramilitary renouncers-of-the-state from our district had called to our house.

Wee sisters had heard the door. Then ma and wee sisters opened it. Men were on the step. They spoke in low tones, saying something had happened in the area and that they wanted to speak to me about it. Ma said, 'Well, you can't speak to her. She's been sick, in bed too, sleeping, or doing her French languages while recuperating. But what happened? Tell me what happened.' The men said to send the nippers down the back. Ma told wee sisters to go down to the living room and to close the door and be no part of this conversation. She pushed them along the hallway to start them off. Wee sisters sneaked back, this time into the parlour at the front of the house where they pressed their ears to the curtained windows. The renouncers though, still spoke low.

'So what if she was in the club at the same time?' they heard ma interrupting. 'Lots of people go to that club. That drinking-club,' she said, 'is the most popular in the area. Doesn't signify that just because my daughter was in there that she'd know of these things.' Ma then said that I'd been abed four days, poisoned, and for them to ask the purging-women, with the renouncers replying that they'd leave for now and that certainly they'd speak with the purging-women — also that they'd be back if the testimony of the purgers proved unsatisfactory. Then they went off and ma took herself to the neighbours to find out this new crack. 'So now we've cheered you up,' said wee sisters — though from my latest anxiety I could not see how they could discern this

— 'it's your turn, middle sister, to read to us.' At this they produced storybooks which I hadn't noticed till that moment they were holding. These were: *The Exorcist,* taken from ma's stack of books by her bedside; *The Tragicall History of the Life and Death of Doctor Faustus,* taken from I didn't know where; and the children's adaptation of the adult *Call Yourself a Democracy!* which began: *'Which statelet up until five years ago could search homes without a warrant, could arrest without a warrant, could imprison without a charge, could imprison without a trial, could punish by flogging, could deny all prison visits, could prohibit inquests into deaths in prison after arresting without a warrant and imprisoning without a charge and imprisoning without a trial?'* Weird wee sisters, I thought. Too many Shakespeares. Real milkman's right. Must have a word with ma about them. Meantime, sisters had placed these books on the eiderdown on top of me. After that, they clambered into my single bed under the blankets beside me. Youngest wee sister, at the headboard, wrapped her arm best she could around me, while oldest wee sister and middle wee sister also squeezed in, holding hands, waiting to be read to down at the footboard end.

Later that day when wee sisters were out

on adventures and ma was back, she came upstairs to see me. She looked solemn, which meant more bad news was coming. She said, 'That poor girl who goes around poisoning people — she's dead. A sweep-patrol of soldiers found her up an entry with her throat cut so somebody killed her.' My first reaction was not, as one might expect, 'What did you say? Unbelievable. How can she be dead when she's the one trying to kill people?' Nor was it a plain, 'Who killed her?' because although I'd heard ma's words, my head couldn't take in the part about somebody having killed her. The mere introduction of her into the conversation had been enough to set me off. Ach, she's done it again, I thought. Who's she poisoned this time? I didn't want to know though, not really, because these things go on so long that you end up getting listless with them. I was sorry, of course, for whoever it had been, but that was in the way I'd been sorry when longest friend told me of the poisoning of tablets girl's sister. It was another of those removed sorries, the un-concerned sorries, with no true pull of involvement — least not till I realised with a bolt of lightning that the person poisoned had been me. Then it was, *how blind I've been! What an idiot I am!* For now that it was clear, it was absolutely bloody obvious. She was a poisoner. She'd been in the club. She'd come over to me in the club, pestering me about having killed her plus others whilst in cahoots with Milkman or something. Her new method of working too, as everybody knew, was to talk incessantly her hypnotic, inventive stories at you. That way she got you, her next victim, hooked and involved. Disquieted yet fixated, you focused on her words, meaning — and despite knowledge of her *modus operandi* and of all of her poisoning history — you didn't take in what her hands were up to. That was what she wanted. Very deft, very furtive, very making herself invisible, blending into everything, dissolving away to nothing. Some people said she was a cunning wee innate, fierce feminist-tract person, except still she wasn't a feminist according to the real feminists because the women with the issues here said she was mentally ill.

They said it was now obvious she was periodically using, not just legitimate issues of gender injustice, but also other legitimate issues of any kind of injustice as a front to cover up her madness. Just the way, they added, anybody can use anything to cover up madness — education, career, homelife, sexlife, religion, physical fitness, stuffing your face, starving your face, child-rearing, freedom-fighting, governmental administration of a country. All this poor woman was doing, they concluded, was her individual rather than collective version of that. The women with the issues had told the renouncers earlier that it was pointless to keep warning tablets girl to stop doing what she was doing because she couldn't stop what she was doing and that she needed intervention — just not their type of intervention. They then went on to say that as the renouncers had elected themselves rulers of the roost here, how about they leave tablets girl to them, to the issue women, and instead investigate one of their own? They could do something, suggested these women, about that middle-aged letch in their movement who went around preying upon and grooming young women. The renouncers responded by saying they would not be drawn into equivocation, nor would they be dictated to. 'You had your go with tablets girl,' they said. 'And you failed, even ending up, so we heard, with a few of yourselves poisoned. So out of the road, we'll deal with it' — meaning, of course, deal with it in their time-proven, unmistakable way.

So the renouncers issued their warnings,

saying that having poisoned too many people, tablets girl was now not allowed to poison a single other person, but she did and the last one, I then found out, hadn't even been me. After me came somebody else, a man, and she poisoned him thinking he was — I don't know, Hitler maybe — with the man up all night, and the man's wife up all night, along with their neighbours, purging him. Afterwards, the wife had gone to the renouncers to tell them what tablets girl had done. Before the renouncers could take action, some mystery person took action. This was according to ma, sitting on my bedroom chair across from me, relaying in shock this buzz of the grapevine to me. They'd come to our door, she said, because their mission was now no longer to kill tablets girl, but to discover who had killed her. Every person recently having dealings with her was required to go to the renouncers and give clear account of him or herself. Exceptions had been made for me — who'd been seen talking with tablets girl in the drinking-club some nights earlier — also for the man mistaken for Hitler, with the renouncers coming to us as we were both still too ill to get out of our beds. The poisoned man had been able to prove he hadn't killed her because his family and purgers bore witness to his incapac-itation. My mother, on our threshold, then told the renouncers that our family and our purgers, on my behalf, could assert the same thing.

The renouncers didn't come back, satis-fied that I too, had been laid up during the murder of tablets girl, and strange it was that still I hadn't registered this person was no longer living. Instead my stubbornness at my mother, because of her stubbornness at me, prevailed. It was clear she had ac-cepted that the man mistaken for Hitler could conceivably have been poisoned by tablets girl, yet her belief in the rumours of my involvement with Milkman was still so strong, and her faith in me so weak, that there was no way in her mentality I could be permitted to be poisoned by her as well. At the same time as feeling relief that my bad night had been down to tablets girl and so had had nothing to do with the effects upon me of Milkman, an irritation at my mother for not seeing what was in front of her was steadily building up. As she contin-ued to talk about the death, having forgot-ten, it seemed, that eight times out of ten 'poor tablets girl' was responsible for the district's intentional poisonings, I snapped and came out, not with the most pertinent remark, but best I could manage in the moment. 'Look, ma, she's not a wee girl. She's older than me. She's a woman!' with ma responding, 'Ach, you know what I mean. She was tiny and titchy and everybody knew there was something wrong with her. Even if she hadn't been killed, that wee girl would never have grown up.' It was at that moment the realisation of tablets girl's death came through.

And ma was worried. She said that if the renouncers hadn't killed her — and they said they hadn't, with there no reason why they would say they hadn't if they had, given they'd been going around declaring they were going to kill her — this could only mean an ordinary murder had taken place. Ordinary murders were eerie, unfathomable, the exact murders that didn't happen here. People had no idea how to gauge them, how to categorise them, how to begin a discussion on them, and that was because only political murders happened in this place. 'Political' of course, covered anything to do with the border, anything that could be construed — even in the slightest, even in the most contorted, even something the rest of the world, if interested, would view as most unlikely — as to do with the border. Any killing other than political and the community was in perplexity, also in anxiety, as to how to proceed.

'I don't know what we're coming to,' said ma, and yes, definitely she was worried. 'We're turning into that country "over the water". Anything happens there. Ordinary murders happen there. Loose morals happen there. People marry there, have affairs, but their spouses don't care about these affairs because they're having their own affairs also — so why get married? They don't say why they got married. Then they get divorced, or don't bother getting divorced but instead just marry their own children. Then they have children by their children. Then they abduct other children. You can't walk out your door over there but you're falling over sex crimes.' I had never seen ma like this, in shock, getting hysterical, which is what happens, I suppose, when you have ordinary murders in the vicinity of people not used to them. 'Ma,' I said. I tried to stop her, tried to intervene on her. 'Ma! Ma!' Ma looked up, confused, then she struggled to re-focus. 'Tell me, ma,' I said. 'What else did you hear about tablets girl?'

She knew nothing else, apart from the state police getting involved, with next to nobody in the community speaking to them. A few double-talked them, another few merry-danced them. Snipers, no doubt, were getting ready to shoot them. As soon as the heavily fortified patrol with their own countersniping unit and the corpse were gone though, the community as always wouldn't shut up. There was more of that 'Can't be an ordinary murder. We don't have ordinary murders. Must be a political murder only does anybody know in what way it could be political?' And that was the state of things, or so I thought when almost two weeks later I decided to take myself to the chip shop.

Since recovering from being poisoned I couldn't stop eating. Neither could I stop having fantasies of eating when I wasn't actually eating, my mind presenting sweet and savoury special-effect shows in my head. There was more Fray Bentos, but now also Farley's Rusks, Sugar Puffs, pilchards in tomato sauce, custard cream biscuit sandwiches, Mars Bar sandwiches, potato crisp sandwiches, wilucs, pigs' feet, dulse, fried liver, dolly mixture in the porridge — former baby treats, childhood treats, most of them usually now to me, disgusting. It was only when I felt the urge for chips, just chips, nothing but chips, that I thought, ah, proper food. Back to normal again now.

I left the house with the usual worry I now

carried as to sudden appearances of Milkman, reached the chip shop in the heart of
the area without Milkman appearing,
pushed open the poky saloon doors and immediately was in the middle of all that lovely
chip smell. So much was I in it, savouring
it, wallowing in it, that I didn't realise at
first the strange atmosphere surrounding
me, which was similar, I realised later, to
not noticing I had been poisoned until long
after a sensible person would have noticed
they'd been poisoned. This chip shop situation proved exactly like that.

There was a queue, a big long one, wind-
ing round two of the salon walls and I
joined the end of it. Immediately others
came in and joined the queue behind. Most
of these people I knew to see but not to
speak to — middle-aged women, coming in
for the suppers, some men, some children,
some teenagers. Nobody I knew personally
though, was in there at the time. While waiting, I settled in to enjoy the smell, also I did
more *'je suis, je ne suis pas'* in my head, as
well as mentally counting how many people
were in front of me. As I was doing this,
however, the people I was counting began
to drop out of line. A few left the shop immediately, with most stepping to the side or
else to the far end of it. This meant I

reached the counter nineteen people before I was supposed to reach the counter and as I did so I had a sensation that those behind had fallen away as well. Soon I was the only person in the queue, though this queue, unaccountably, was still present in the chip shop. Behind the counter, one of the two serving women in a big white apron came towards me and placed herself directly in front. Her arms were akimbo and she didn't ask my order, didn't look at me either as I gave it. Instead she seemed to direct her gaze somewhere to the side of my head. Not quite worried, but a little bit of something, I watched as she moved off to get the chips for me and wee sisters. It was then I became aware of the silence and, given I'd always lived in this district and had since child-hood, without properly acknowledging it, been attuned to the currents, subtleties and rhythms of this district, I can only think slowness after my recent illness was the reason I was so behindhand at this point. It was at my back, the silence, making shivers at my back, and I couldn't turn, though my mind began racing. *Don't let it be Milkman. Oh please, don't let it be Milkman.* Then I did turn and it wasn't Milkman. It was everybody else. Every single person was staring at me in the shop.

Some instantly looked away, down at the ground, others into their hands or up at the big menu displayed on the wall by the counter in front of us. Others stared openly, I think even defiantly, and I thought, shitsies, what is it I'm supposed to have done now? The penny then dropped and I sensed this was something to do with tablets girl. Not the poisoning of me by her which I knew everyone by now would have heard about. I meant her death. But surely they can't think, I thought, that *I* had anything to do with that. At this point the serving woman returned and put my chips down on the counter. I turned from the others, lifted the packets and fumbled to hand my money across. The woman had gone. She had turned her broad back and already was at the far end, standing also in silence beside the second serving woman. No one else was being attended. No one was asking to be attended. Everyone was waiting, it seemed, for what was to happen next.

The renouncers said they hadn't killed her. Then they made enquiries to find out who had killed her. Then, claiming sudden urgent border engagements, conveniently, it was said, they dropped their sense of diligence and backed off. But these people never backed off. That was their reputation,

their hallmark, their stock-in-trade unstop-
pability. Because of this, the community
came to the conclusion that it must have
been one of them who'd killed her after all.
Not politically, of course, because with the
renouncers' sudden silence, with their quiet
withdrawal, the abrupt end to their fierce,
minute perquisition and especially without
their usual admittance to deeds done when
they had been done, tablets girl could not
have been killed politically. So not from
border motives. Not to save the country,
defend the area, keep anti-social behaviour
out of our area. It had been Milkman. He
had killed her. Ordinarily, not politically, he
had killed her, and all because — so it
seemed to this community — he hadn't
liked that she'd attempted to kill me.

That might have been true or might not
have been true, but the chip shop thought it
was true and, in that moment, surrounded
by all these people with their minds made
up, I thought it true as well. A highranking
hero of the community had committed a
foul, an ordinary murder, all to avenge some
malapert hussy. Now, I am not greatly naïve
which means I've discovered that you live
your life lots of days with things a bit out of
joint, a bit moved-on, but not unmanage-
able, indeed only to be expected. But then a

particular day comes when conditions across the board — with or without your knowledge, with or without your consent — completely have been changed around. Things have been moved on, yes, but not just by one have they been moved on but by considerably more than one. Before this, it had been my insides disoriented, pains in my stomach, quivers in my legs, my hand shaking as I put the key in the lock. Paranoia indoors too, it had been, in case he might be in my wardrobe when he wasn't, in case he might be in my cupboards when he wasn't, in case he might be under my bed. Each time he'd gotten close . . . closer . . . even closer, but I couldn't tell, not till now, if his stamp was still coming on me or if all the time already it had been on me. Longest friend had warned, 'You are not inferable. You cannot be deduced — *and they don't like that.* You're stubborn, friend, sometimes stupid, incredibly stupid, for you prepossess people with your lack of give not to like you. That is dangerous. What you don't offer — especially in volatile times — people will make up for themselves.' 'Not all people,' I argued. 'And anyway, my life's not theirs. Why should I explain and beg excuse from them when it's they who have invented this history and who even now are as bad dogs, watching and waiting to take over?' As for their view of me as loose, as wanton, as shameless, I said, 'When it comes to it, longest friend, in reality I'm probably more Virgin Mary than any of —' 'You're eighteen,' she said. 'You're a girl. No back-up — not unless you want Milkman as back-up. So give them something — *anything* — even if they don't believe it, especially because they'll enjoy not believing it. At least then, they won't hold your high position with him against you.' But I didn't. Couldn't. Didn't know how to. Didn't believe there was still time to. Too much of rumour, of implication, also of *'mind your own business'* had gone on for redress from them now.

So I was learning something, but in the rapidity, especially of emotions, I didn't know what it was I was learning. Didn't know what to do either, so I did a stupid thing. Amidst the silence and the staring, I took the chips, kept my money, then turned and walked out of the shop. I didn't want these chips, didn't want now my own money. Of course I should have left them, chips, money, both, on the counter and purged myself of that situation, but it's hard to think of obvious things, of high-minded, honourable things, during the real-time of unexpected shocking things. How do you know after a time anyway, what is normal and high-minded and what is not? So I took them and I didn't pay for them and this was partly out of an angry *'Yes, Milkman. Go. Kill. Kill all of them. Go forth. Attend me. I command you'* and partly it was out of sensibility and anxiousness for their feelings. It was not wanting to get into trouble with my elders as an eighteen-year-old daring to disrespect and correct their behaviour. So I lost presence of mind and allowed myself to be pushed into obtaining chips with menaces. Most damning therefore, my own behaviour, this handling of the chip shop badly, no matter there'd been a compelling of me by everybody in it exactly to handle it badly. I knew now though, what they'd known for some time which was that no longer was I a teenager amidst a bunch of other teenagers, coming into and going out of and gallivanting about the area. Now I knew that that stamp — and not just by Milkman — had unreservedly, and against my will, been put on.

Six

After hearing of the murder of tablets girl but before that encounter in the chip shop, I was still in bed recuperating when three phone calls came through. Two were about me and first was from third brother-in-law. He had heard about the poisoning but wanted to know from my mother, who had answered, why I was not going running. He said I'd missed our run a day earlier, that I'd missed other runs, that I hadn't called round to discuss this or to get into any altercation with him over it. Then he added there'd been such a falling-down in standards that he was bewildered by what was happening to women these days. Ma said, 'Son-in-law, she's not going running. She's in bed, poisoned,' with brother-in-law saying he understood about the poisoning, 'But is she coming running?' Ma said, 'No. In bed. Poisoned.' 'Yeah, but is she coming running?' 'No —' 'Yeah, but —' Wee sisters said ma's eyes went into Heaven at this point. She tried again. 'Son, we can't be doing this all day. She's in bed. Not going running. Poisoned. Not running. In bed, poisoned,' with third brother-in-law — exercise fixation overriding thinking mechanism — about to ask if I was going running but this time ma pre-empted with, 'God love you and everything, son-in-law, but is there something wrong with you? You know yourself she's been poisoned, the whole district knows, yet here I am, spending twenty hours relaying to you that her stomach's been expunged or whatever that word is, with me having to sit up two nights with her in case the expunging hadn't taken, yet you're not assimilating but instead are behaving as if I haven't explained at all.' With just the slightest falter, brother-in-law said, 'Are you saying she's *not* coming running?' 'That's the ticket,' said ma. 'And tripping up? What's tripping up got to do with any of this?' 'Falling-down,' corrected brother-in-law, 'of standards, of women.' Here ma covered the mouthpiece and whispered to wee sisters, 'The boy makes no sense. Funny wee being. Then again, that whole family's funny. God knows why your sister married into it.' Then she uncovered the mouthpiece for brother-in-law was concluding, 'Well, first there's her way of walking and reading books which is not understandable. Then that excuse about legs no longer working — also not understandable. And now she's not running. If she's persisting in this incomprehensibility, mother-in-law, tell her she knows where to find me when she comes to her senses. Meanwhile, I'm away on here to run by myself.' Ma said, 'Okay, son, and I agree about the book-walking but as it is, she's still nearly dead so I'm keeping her in bed yet,' after which they said goodbye which took another five minutes because kind people here, not used to phones, not trustful of them either, didn't want to be rude or abrasive by hanging up after just one goodbye in case the other's leave-taking was still travelling its way, with a delay, over the airwaves towards them. Therefore, owing to phone etiquette, there was lots of ' 'Bye', ' 'Bye', 'Goodbye, son-in-law', 'Goodbye, mother-in-law', 'Goodbye', 'Goodbye', ' 'Bye', ' 'Bye' with each person's ear still at the earpiece as they bent their body over, inching the receiver ever and ever closer on each goodbye to the rest of the phone. Eventually it would end up back on its hook with the human ear physically removed from it. There might be further insurance goodbyes even at this stage, out of compulsion to seal and make sure the matter, which didn't mean the person who'd gone through the protractions wasn't contorted in body and exhausted in mind by the effort of detaching from a phone conversation. What it did mean was that that conversation — without any anxious *'Did I cut him off? Will he be hurt? Have I hung up too soon and damaged his feelings?'* — had finally reached its traditional end. When I was told of this I was glad — given I was not yet strong enough to bear, then browbeat the prescriptive mindset of brother-in-law — that ma had been the one to take that call.

Ma then took the second call which I was not glad about. It was from maybe-boyfriend and it didn't go well. First, it was unprecedented for I didn't know maybe-boyfriend had my number. He never called me at my home and I never called him at his home, nor did I have his number or even knew whether or not he had a number. Telephones didn't feature much for me, nor had I thought they featured for maybe-boyfriend. One reason I had nineteenth-century literature as back-up was so I wouldn't have to get into any modern-day, fraught, involved stuff like that. Our arrangements were such that we made them at the end of each last meeting and we stuck to them. This was the case, partly because of phones being generally distrusted — as technological objects, as abnormal communication objects. Mainly though, they were not trusted because of 'dirty tricks', unofficial-party-line, state-surveillance campaigns. This meant ordinary people didn't use them for private things, meaning vulnerable romance things. Of course the paramilitary-renouncers didn't use them either, but I'm not talking about them here. So phones weren't trusted; indeed we only had one because it had been in the house when we moved in and ma was wary to have it removed in case the people who came to remove it weren't really telephone wiremen but instead state spymaster-infiltrators in disguise. They'd take the phone away, warned neighbours, but in the process they'd plant other things, things evidential of us being tight-in with renouncers when we weren't tight-in with renouncers. Despite two of my brothers having been renouncers, we were averagely in, the normal amount in, that too, more at the beginning than we were these latter days. Now, though still in principle approving their initial objective and in no way prepared to denounce them publicly to a state to which she did not

413

ascribe validity, depending upon the latest of what they had done and her current level of ambivalence towards them, ma had no qualms denouncing them to their face — proof more or less, I suppose, that we weren't tight-in. So our phone hung on the wall by the stairs and people used it sometimes. Thing was though, you had to open phones everywhere and every time you wanted to use one in order to see if there was a bug inside. On the rare occasion when I did use one I did this checking too, though I'd no idea what a bug looked like, or if it would be in the phone, or outside on the overhead cable, or at the telephone exchange if exchanges still happened. In truth, I was just going through the motions with the bug thing, which was what I suspected others, also regularly taking their phones apart, were simply doing as well.

So I didn't have his number, if he had one, and I thought he didn't have mine because of the convolutions to be got through by having them. Mainly though, the not having each other's numbers was because of the 'maybe' category our relationship was in. This 'maybeness' was why I didn't tell about tablets girl poisoning me, why I didn't tell about Milkman pursuing me, why I didn't tell about the district gossip overriding me.

It didn't occur to me to tell because why would maybe-boyfriend in our maybe-relationship want to know, or think either of us should presume permission to disclose, thoughts, feelings and neediness about that? Also, what if I attempted and he didn't hear? What if he was unable to take in the weight of what I myself couldn't take in the weight of? But he rang and ma answered and he asked for me and she said, 'Oh no you don't. I don't care about your conjurations or how great a renouncer you are or how gallant in action or what your hero standing is in the community. You're a be-fouler of young girls and a depraved, fraud milkman who gives bad names to people who are really milkmen. You're not going to speak to her. You're not going to vitiate her. You stay away from her. Take yourself and your bombs — *you married man!* — off.' This she said without care, without couching, without the least concealment should third parties be listening. She hung up then, with no goodbyes either, no wearing herself out with *adieux* for his benefit. During this I was in bed but could hear perfectly all she was saying, mistakenly thinking, as she was, that it was Milkman himself on the line. With all his skill at surveillance, of course he'd be far more likely to have my telephone number than even myself or my 'almost one year so far maybe-boyfriend' would be likely to have it. And now here he was, reaching with his unstoppable predations right inside my home. I thought of maybe-boyfriend then, and did so with longing, wishing for the first time since being poisoned that he was here, in this house, in this bedroom, right next me. If only he'd contact me. Those thoughts didn't stay long though, because of the one that followed. This was of ma and of how impossible it would be if ever she were to meet him: *'So, young man, and when is to be the wedding? And, young man, when are to be the babies? And it is true, young man, is it not, that you are the right religion and that you are not already married?'* Yes. Awful. I pushed him out of my mind, not because he didn't matter but because he did matter. How lucky he was though, to have had parents who long ago had run away.

Third call was for ma and it was one of her pious friends, Jason of the Names, ringing in a hurry. Jason said something had happened outside the usual place. One of those state killer squads, she said, had ambushed and shot real milkman, then they took him to the hospital, the hospital being the very place where everybody knew, owing to stigma of informer status, that if you had political ailments it was never safe to go. 'He didn't have a say, friend,' said her friend. 'There was no choice. They just took him after they shot him. But switch on your wireless to get the latest for they're saying he was a terrorist. Can you imagine? *Real milkman! — the man who doesn't love any-body! — a terrorist!*' At that point wee sisters said ma dropped the phone.

She ran up to my room then, saying she had to go to the hospital, that she had to get to real milkman. Would I be strong enough to get up, she said, to look after the wee ones and the home? 'Is he dead?' I asked, surprising myself for never was I one to ask that question. She said she didn't know, but that those hellhounds, those ac-cusers and roamers throughout the earth, going to and fro and up and down in it, had taken him to hospital after shooting him but that it was unclear if Jason meant because he was dead he'd been taken to hospital, meaning the morgue adjacent to the hospital. Or was it, she said, that Jason meant he was unconscious, maybe dying, so couldn't protest he didn't want to go to hospital. Or maybe he didn't mind going to hospital and insisted on being taken to hospital because as everybody knew, real milkman was contrary for doing exactly what the renouncers-of-the-state in our district had ordered people in our district not to do. 'Don't know,' said ma, then she said, 'They're saying he was a terrorist. They're searching his house right now, digging up his backyard, trying to find things terroristic buried there.' 'It's all right, ma,' I said, getting out of bed. 'You go and do what you have to and I'll look after us and everything.' At that, she leaned over and kissed me, then she leaned down and kissed wee sisters who had followed her up the stairs. They were clinging and crying and begging and pleading, 'No, mammy! No, mammy! We wish you didn't go!' She told them they were good daughters but that they must now do as I, their middle sister, instructed them. After straightening up and extracting their grip, she took a little money from her purse for emergencies, slipped it into her skirt pocket, then handed me the purse with the rest of her money inside. In that moment I knew exactly wee sisters' state of mind, of clinging, of crying, of begging, of pleading. Ma had handed her purse over only on two former occasions. First had been when the state police had come to fetch her to identify the body of her son, our second brother. At that time, she'd handed the purse to eldest sister, not trusting what she might do, then what might be done to her should those anthropomorphisms, she said, taunt her with, 'Serves you right. Serves your broodling firstborn right too, in his little militia, for daring to go partisan against us.' Second time of the purse had been when the renouncers in our district had come for second sister, to kill her or otherwise to punish her — not so much for marrying into the enemy, as for her face in insulting the area by coming back to visit her family *after* marrying into the enemy — or else it was to get her to expiate herself for marrying-out by setting up her husband to be killed in an ambush by them. On that occasion, ma hurriedly pushed her purse at third sister before running to the hutment where they were adjudging second sister. She took with her my dead brother's spare gun from upstairs which I hadn't known was up there, and which I knew too, she hadn't a clue how to use. The renouncers took it off her, then they gave her a warning, with second sister then flogged and told she was never again to come back to the area. And now I had the purse. 'Just in case,' said ma as she put her coat and headscarf on. Wee sisters were bawling by now and I was down on my hunkers with my arms around them, trying to comfort them. Ma was looking grim, exactly as she hadn't looked, I couldn't help noting, when her husband, our father, had been dying in hospital. So I couldn't blame wee sisters. Felt too, not panic, but a state of mind easily to be tipped into panic. I didn't want to think about it, but what if wee sisters were right and she did get into a fight and was herself lifted, ending up imprisoned, never to return after all?

She did return, but not till after dark, by which time wee sisters were in bed, lulled to sleep by Rice Krispies, Tayto Crisps, Paris Buns, bread-in-the-pan, halibut orange tablets with extra sugar on everything. Then there was *Who's Afraid of Virginia Woolf?* which was their choice of matter, not my choice of matter. It ruffled me terribly, being twentieth century but I found it wasn't really the dialogue or the story wee sisters were interested in, but the fairytale title, which simply they wanted to hear over and over again. I slipped it in therefore, every third phrase which calmed them down and now they were sleeping. Leaving their door ajar, I crept downstairs to the living room and sat in the armchair in the silence of the half dark. I thought of putting on the radio to hear if he was dead but I could not ever bear radios: those voices announcing; those voices murmuring; those voices repeating on the hour, on the half hour, in their special urgent extra bulletins, all those things I didn't want to hear. I hoped he wasn't but nearly always in these situations they were dead. Why disturb myself therefore, by facing prematurely all my mind could still have leeway from? I hadn't reached that point, the critical point, where not to know became more unbearable than getting to know. I was still at the *'hold off, not yet'* stage of proceedings and it was while I was in it that I heard ma's key go in our lock.

Although the room was now proper dark, she knew I was in it, as a person knows these things, by invisible influences maybe, by mental construction or clear-sensing maybe. She too, didn't draw the curtains or put the light on. Instead she sat opposite, still in her coat and headscarf, and said he was alive, that his condition was stable but that she didn't know what 'stable' meant and that because she wasn't family even though real milkman — his only brother years dead — now had no family, they wouldn't give her, or any of the other neighbours who'd also turned up at the hospital, any information other than that. She veered off then — not unusual — a mind suddenly compelled to convolute and address issues which might be relevant but to the listener seemed not relevant. She began to speak of someone, some girl she used to know. This was in the long ago, she said, when she too, had been a girl, and this person she knew had been her second longest friend, someone I'd never heard of, someone ma had never spoken of. But now she was saying the two of them had ended their friendship and parted company because this friend had taken vows to become a holy woman, going to join the other holy women in their holy house down the road. Ma sighed. 'I couldn't believe it,' she said. 'We were nineteen, and Peggy gave up life — clothes, jewellery, dances, being beautiful — all that that stood for — just for to become a holy woman.' This wasn't the most tragic though, according to ma, of what this Peggy person had given up. As ma talked on, I became confused and wondered if she was speaking of this Peggy, who might not have existed, because, in truth, her first and genuine longtime friend since childhood — real milkman — had after all been shot and killed that day. This might be a substitute, some story, one of those blinds for, *'He's dead, daughter. He is dead. And now, how will I face*

that?' Instead a mind unravelling, determined in its unravelling not to take in bad
consequence, inventing anecdotes to delay
the consequence, refusing to attend even at
the moment of the delivery of the — Ma
interrupted my thoughts on her thoughts to
say, 'Thing was, daughter, I wanted him
too.' She was speaking certainly now of real
milkman, saying all the girls had had pashes
on him, all the girls being none other than
those women of the reverences, those
middle-aged supplicants in our district, one
notch down from the actual holy women
and women too, who would have been no
notches down if only they hadn't slipped up
by having men and sex and offspring at
some time. 'Clear as day I remember,' said
ma, 'when they heard about Peggy deciding
to enter holy orders. They laughed at the
absurdity of it, at the sheer good luck of it,
at the timeliness of it for, with Peggy out of
the way, who was there, after all, to stop
them now?' Ma said that made her angry,
but also that she was angry at Peggy who
had turned one hundred per cent contemplative and in her habit, her mystic state,
her marriage to Jesus, no longer distin-
guished real milkman from any man, no
longer cared what people thought or said. 'I
was puzzled,' said ma, 'because she'd loved

him, I knew she'd loved him, yet she renounced him, also her physicality with him, for yes, daughter' — and here ma lowered her voice — 'in those days there was respect and much less disclosing and emotionalism and indiscretion than there is these days, but I knew she'd slept with him and at that time too, you never did that.'

So God was great and all, according to ma, but imagine giving up real milkman for Him. That was what she said. Ma actually said this and it was revelatory coming from her mouth straight into my ears. Here was my mother, one of the Top Five pious women of the district, coming out with the unbelievable *'God's great and all but'*. This was scandalous, also exciting, even rather refreshing — that a person of the sanctities was showing herself to be not one hundred per cent of the sanctities, or else there was nothing for it but that the sanctities would have to adjust in meaning to include the lower half of the body now as well. So we were right. My sisters and I were right. Ma *had* had trysts and assignations with men in her youth at 'dot dot dot' places — or had attempted to have them, or at least wasn't against having them. In her deep recesses she upheld them. Death is truthful, and 'ambushed and shot and nearly dead' is also truthful. I would never have got this low-down about ma and real milkman and Peggy and the district's upper echelon of advanced pious secular women if real milkman hadn't been shot and nearly killed that day. And here she was, continuing on. It made them happy, she said, when longest friend took the veil, though not for long as conflict between them then ensued in earnest. 'They vied for him,' she said. 'And I too, daughter, I vied for him.' I kept quiet here because I wanted her to finish, didn't want her coming to her senses, remembering who she was, who I was, also that other man, the dead man, my father whom she'd married. 'But an awful thing happened,' she said, 'something not considered by myself or by any of the others.' This awful thing turned out to be that real milkman, in accordance with his usual oppositional contrariness, decided the issue of his own marital status himself. If he wasn't to have Peggy, he had decided, he wasn't going to have anybody. As for the source of his name — ma moved directly next to that.

Along with everybody of my generation, I thought he was known about the area as 'the man who didn't love anybody' because he'd gotten cross that time and shouted at children — unloving, anti-social, bad-

425

tempered — the district had said he was. Also, that he hadn't been a team player, that he'd proved unsupportive of the efforts of the renouncers. 'They were for our good, those guns,' said people, 'and the local boys had had to hide them somewhere.' Uncooperative therefore, the consensus also was. He was prone to arguments too, again mainly with the renouncers — over their death threat to tablets girl, over their flogging of our second sister, over their trying to kill guest speakers coming to the feminist shed to give talks on worldwide women's issues. He'd even argued over kneecappings, beatings, protection rackets, tar and featherings — not just others' tar and featherings, but also his own. You could see the dilemma he was creating, said people. He went about not being peaceful, not being tactful, but instead stern and conscious and aware and unyielding. Naturally, these were the reasons my generation were given to understand had brought about his 'not loving anybody' name. There was his other name, of course, that of 'real milkman' but that came into play only latterly as a way to differentiate him from the one I was supposed to be in love with. But now it transpired, listening to ma, there was another, older reason for his name. 'When Peggy broke his heart for

God,' she said, 'he broke every other girl's heart by marrying nobody and by refusing to get over her.' He carried on being handsome, though now in that marred, loss of innocence, bitter tinge of acerbity way, so that at first he was 'the man who was incapable of loving anybody but Peggy'. Then he became 'the man who deliberately wouldn't love anybody but Peggy'. Then, during his ash-and-wormwood, ergot-diseased, hard-hearted phase, he was 'the man who'd set a grim policy never to love anybody, especially Peggy' which, for brevity's sake, got shortened to 'the man who didn't love anybody' which, until 'real milkman' came along, had been graven onto stone as his name. Undiminished too, that name was, said ma, by his deeds of goodness for still he did deeds of goodness. He'd helped Somebody McSomebody's ma, who was also poor dead nuclear boy's ma, after her husband's death, then after her daughter's death, then again after each of her four sons' deaths. Then he'd helped ma when da died, then when second brother died, also when second sister got into trouble with the renouncers over her rebellious choice of a spouse. He'd helped me too, after that meeting I'd had in the ten-minute area with Milkman. So he'd gone to the aid of others, many others, tablets girl too, who'd rebuffed him, though surprisingly she hadn't poisoned him. The women with the issues also he'd helped when communal attitude towards them was one of mockery and chastisement for storms in teacups when eight hundred years of the political problems were still to be sorted. So he did all this helping, and he did it too, from some wider perspective, some higher state of consciousness. All the same, it counted for nothing as far as his name in our community went. 'A waste,' said ma. 'Such a man. Such a fine, fair, honest man. And his looks, daughter —' Here she veered off to ask if I was in accord that he was the spit of the actor James Stewart, also of the actors Robert Stack, Gregory Peck, John Garfield, Robert Mitchum, Victor Mature, Alan Ladd, Tyrone Power and Clark Gable. I couldn't say I was in accord but people in love, I knew, saw crazy things all the time. 'Eventually us women had to leave off,' she said, which had me looking at her, which then had her, even in the dark, sensing that I was looking at her. Hurriedly she tried to amend. 'Not *me,*' she said. 'I didn't mean *me.* Already long ago I'd got over him.' But no she hadn't. Oh no she hadn't. It was during that night then, for me, that something clicked into place.

'Of course I got over him,' she persisted, and she raised her voice here in an attempt to prevent my new insight from penetrating. 'If I hadn't got over him, daughter' — this was supposed to be proof — 'why ever would I have married your da?'

Why indeed? Once again, I was back to pondering this 'marrying of the wrong spouse' business. I don't mean the outgrowing of what was once a successful union, with each partner contributing and committing to each other, celebrating each other until they reached a natural end of their shared path together when they'd part with or without love and a blessing before moving on to somebody or to something else. I mean this business of people marrying people they didn't love and didn't want and where someone from the outside might look in and shake their head and say that somebody ought not to be in such an intimate position in another somebody's life if it turned out they were the wrong somebody. In the general local thinking though, there were reasons for this. One was the political situation here in which the spouse you really wanted might not have a premature, violent death, but then again, he or she might have. Why invest your heart in the one person in the world you loved and wanted to spend your life with when maybe not that long down the road they were going to abandon you for the grave? Another reason was fear of being alone because of the social stigma that automatically attached to it. Marry anybody therefore. He'll do. Yer man there will do. Or she'll do. Pick yer woman. Then there was being bullied into it because you have to fit convention, because you can't let people down — the date's been set, the cake's been ordered, haven't you even gone and booked the honeymoon? Then there was fear of oneself, of one's independence, of one's potential, so avoid that path by marrying somebody not on it, somebody with no feeling for it, somebody who wouldn't recognise it or encourage it in you. Then there was not going for the one you want because by doing so, you might cause envy and anger to arise in others, others whom you knew wanted this person too. There were other reasons for the wrong spouse — fear of losing control through letting the desired into your subsoil, or marrying somebody close to the one you wanted but who didn't want you so have their best friend, their colleague from work, a relative, even the person living next door to them. Of course there was the big one, the biggest reason for not marrying the right spouse. If you married *that* one, the one you loved and desired and who loved and desired you back, with the union proving true and good and replete with the most fulfilling happiness, well, what if this wonderful spouse didn't fall out of love with you, or you with them, and neither of you either, got killed in the political problems? All those joyful evers and infinites? Are you sure, really, really sure, you could cope with the prospect of that? The community decided that no, it couldn't. Great and sustained happiness was far too much to ask of it. That was why marrying in doubt, marrying in guilt, marrying in regret, in fear, in despair, in blame, also in terrible self-sacrifice was pretty much the unspoken matrimonial requisite here. That was why too, I protected myself by not getting married; further, by sticking to maybe-relationships in spite of my intermittent longing for, and futile attempts to mould me and maybe-boyfriend into, a proper relationship. These were all the reasons then — certainly an ample selection of them — for the so-called accident of marrying the wrong spouse. And now I knew da *had* been the wrong spouse because although she'd blamed him, always had blamed him — for his depressions, for staying in bed, for going into hospital, for dying, for not being in love

431

with her — it wasn't da. It was that she'd been in love, still was in love, with real milkman all the time. As for da, had he known he was the wrong spouse? Had he cared, been broken-hearted, not only because he'd been falsely positioned but because he'd allowed himself to be falsely positioned? Or had da known that ma, through all those years of marriage, even before marriage, had been for him the wrong spouse too?

Now, nearly two weeks on, ma was still away at the hospital seeing to real milkman, with me at home seeing to the girls. Their panic had subsided, given now they understood she hadn't gone forever, hadn't disappeared, been disappeared, stolen away to spooky places such as the hospital or the jailhouse, that she wasn't dead with her body buried in some secretly dug-out, then hurriedly filled-in grave. They accepted that for a while she'd turn up sporadically and that on those occasions they could be with her; also, that in the meantime they could run rings around me which was then what they did. 'Mammy says we can have this.' 'Mammy says we can go there.' 'Mammy says we can stay out till four o'clock in the morning.' I let them away with some of these mammies, and at night-time I read to them because wee sisters loved being read to. It was at this time also, because they demanded them and because I too, was getting pangs for them, that I went that early suppertime into the heart of the area to purchase (in a manner of speaking) those damn chips.

I pushed open the poky saloon doors and went in and had that unpleasant experience of being made an accessory-after-the-fact of tablets girl's murder which, of course, by the time I was back out in the street I had decided probably had nothing to do with him at all. This was more of their sensationalism, more of those makings-up, those lies of theirs that they wanted to be true and so in their heads and in their gossip they made true. Anyway, if I was an accessory, who were they to talk, because all of them would be accessories too. I pushed open the doors and went in, and then, not long after — in shock, in shame, with free chips, also with that angry *'Kill them, Milkman. Kill all of them. I hate them. Hurry up and kill them'* — I came out again. I walked along the street from the chip shop and headed round the corner, thinking, so is this how it is to be now? I meant the start of getting things for nothing. I'd witnessed over time that select others in the area got things for nothing.

They'd go into shops, have silent, sometimes unfriendly though mostly always over-anxious and over-friendly shopkeepers pushing free packages at them. So was this to be my role in Milkman's infrastructure now? I was to be hated, feared, despised, but crucially to be kept in with. If that were the case — all this giving to me of things, delivering onto me of things, more and more things, whether or not I wanted them — what then, I worried, should be my next move? Should I get it over with, take the free things, pile them in the corner and never once look at them? Should I be firm, not coerced, not bullied, slap my money on the counter? Or should I leave with self-respect intact without buying or accepting anything? If it were to be the last, I'd keep control, but I *had* taken the chips so already they had control. This meant there was nothing for it but that I'd have to venture out of the area in order to do the messages — not just the tiniest of items either, but probably the whole weekly shop. Also I wasn't trained for this, in how to oppose it, how to surmount it. Should he die — should Milkman die — or be jailed, or dis-appeared — because the renouncers thought nothing of now and again disappearing each other — or should he even reach the point of just no longer desiring me, I'd plummet in the ratings, and they, the shopkeepers, in turn, would want reprisals for all that arse-licking as well as demanding all their packages back. So I walked on, despondent in my thoughts, bleak in outlook, thinking, *what's the point? What's the use?* and with a pile of negativities growing up inside me. It was then too, that that unpleasant physical floatiness in my body once again assailed me, my legs no longer having feeling and my feet no longer touching the ground. I could see them moving, but I could gain no sensation of them moving. Once more too, I got that impression of being naked and exposed from behind. What's happening? I hate this, I thought, and here I ceased walking and took hold of some railings. This was when, as if on cue, another bout of those quivering anti-orgasms passed through me. So it was to be shock upon shock, one shitty thing after another shitty thing until, it seemed, I should get the message. But what message? How was it my fault that they had decided that he, for me, had cut her throat?

Then I remembered the chips. I was still holding them, encumbered by them, so I chucked them. Then, when they were on the ground, I ruined this noble gesture by thinking, now why'd I go and do that?

Should I pick them up? I wondered. They're not dirty, still in their wrappings. I could dust them off, give the sign of the cross over them and bring them home to wee sisters? The matter was settled, however, by a pack of street dogs appearing out of nowhere, bolting to the chips, fighting each other for them, with the victors, within moments, wolfing them down. The violence of the dogs brought a gasp from over the way and I looked and there was tablets girl's sister, the one who, like me, and by the same person, had recently been poisoned unto death. Again like me, she was holding on to railings, looking startled, looking too, as they said she was, as if at the beginning of her poison ordeal instead of having already undergone the purge of her poison ordeal. She was squinting over, first at me, then at the dogs and I saw it was true too, that ever since her poisoning they said she hadn't recovered her shininess — also that she could no longer properly see. They said she didn't use a stick and here she was, not using one. Instead she was adapting what was left of her eyesight, plus walls, palings, lamp-posts, hedges and it was in that manner she negotiated her passage, bringing her face close to objects and feeling her way along. 'She's fine, out and about' was the communal prognosis upon her, also the communal euphemism for 'mended though broken', itself another euphemism for 'in urgent need of medical care and attention', all of which the person in need unfortunately was not going to attend hospital to get. As for her shininess, I now had my own confirmation that it was damaged, patchy, hardly to be discernible. Apart from a few dithering blinks and the odd, sullen twinkle, she could have been any one of us with our heavy, slumbering loads. There were few people on the street at this hour because most were indoors, having their tea, watching the news, and those who did appear were walking straight by her. Some deliberately didn't look; others halted, slowed down, paused, then crossed the road abruptly to where the dogs were still fighting, choosing that route as the least unsettling by which to pass by. One or two hesitated, as I was hesitating, not because we didn't want to help, but because tablets girl's sister, in her diminished shininess, in her encroaching darkness, might now rebut offers of help. Then too, a person might want to help but not be able to, owing to a state of clinging to railings herself. Those hesitating across from me then made up their minds. They too, crossed the road, so then there was only me and tablets girl's sister. There were the dogs, of course — some fighting, some licking, even eating the chip-papers. Then I saw two men just up from us and they too, were fighting, physically fighting. The reason I hadn't seen them earlier was because no sound was issuing from them at all. They were at it in silence, absolute quietness — fists up, lunging, jab-punch, jab-jab-hook, undercut, evading, leaping around, grabbing hold of each other. This was strange to behold but what was stranger was that each of these men, during their physical exertions, had a lazy, long cigarette dangling from his mouth.

I let go of my railing and went over to tablets girl's sister. I told who I was for it didn't seem clear she could discern me. I asked if she wanted a hand but didn't believe she'd say yes and was unsure she'd even answer, one reason being that, like the others in the chip shop, if she thought I'd had a hand in the slaying of her sister, why would she think I'd think she'd want a hand from me now? Two was more of that marrying in doubt, the wrong-spouse business. Indeed some were saying that this new taint of darkness which had befallen tablets girl's sister had not been down so much to her poisoning by her sister as down to a gradual giving-up of her spirit after being dumped a year earlier by her long-term boyfriend. Given who had dumped her, almost in fact, jilted her, given too, my blood association with this person, my mind in that moment just couldn't go there. But I did offer to help and she said, 'What'd you do? I saw movement and now there are dogs and I can't get past them.' Already she was turning to take the long route the opposite way. Presumably this meant railing after railing, hedge after hedge, broken lamppost upon broken lamppost until she got round to her own house. 'Throwing chips away,' I explained then I said, 'Don't go that way. Men are fighting that way.' At this she paused, then said she was struggling to make things out. Especially street signs, she said, and she indicated with her hand, saying they were palely written. I looked to where she was pointing but there were no street signs. In this district, where most streets were identical, the renouncers, to slow and confuse the enemy, had removed every single street sign, something she should have known, so that had me wondering if her brain had been affected by the poisoning as well. 'I was counting my way,' she said, and still she peered, her hand holding to the railing. 'I couldn't remember if I'd turned into

—' — here she mentioned two streets, neither of which she'd turned into. Her own street though, was only three streets away. I explained where we were and intended asking if she'd like for us to walk together. Instead both of us spoke at the same time. Our words went to essentials and I'd warned myself beforehand not to be selfish by saying what the very second later I went and did say which was, 'I didn't kill your sister. Nor am I responsible for you being rejected by your true lover.' Meanwhile, her words were, 'We found a letter in my sister's room the other day.'

This letter had been found by tablets girl's sister during a concerted search undertaken by her family. They were determined to uncover where tablets girl kept her potions and her poisons, all those tools of her trade. She had a constant supply and it couldn't, not all of it, always be on her person. Must be concealing them, they thought, somewhere about the house. While some of them tackled the far reaches of the coal-hole, the glory-hole, the toilet cistern, the attic and so on, tablets girl's sister had gone for the unlikely places. Places, she said, where American Indians, full of wisdom and insight and with an ancient affinity to the environment and its elements, would hide in plain sight and not be found. In translation obviously this meant the living room. Tablets girl, the poisoner, shunned even the most basic of familial get-togethers, so that meant never would she have ventured in there. So tablets girl's sister went straightaway into the living room and cast around for the most unlikeliest spot in this most unlikeliest of rooms to discover where best her sister could have concealed her poisons. Again the American Indian answer was obvious. Lying across the top of the settee that day — as it had been lying for five years and counting — was the once beloved family rag-doll. This doll had been passed down the children until it had reached the last child before he turned eleven and had discarded it. Although someone in that family must have thought that one day, one day soon, yes, one day, when he or she had dealt with all the other, much more pressing, essential housework, they'd get around to putting or to giving that doll away. Because it had been such a minor item, practically a fixture and fitting, that day so far had not come. The cleaner in the family then forgot, so the doll continued to lie there in full view over the settee until it became invisible. So tablets girl's sister went over and picked it up. Inside the belly of this doll, between the sexual chakra and the solar plexus chakra was a big nappy-pinned entrance and exit. Tablets girl's sister opened the pin, extracted it from the belly of this doll and inside found not tablet girl's actual poisons but instead a letter folded into eighths. It was written in her sister's hand and seemed to be a private missive written by some aspect of tablets girl to another aspect of herself. *My Dearest Susannah Eleanor Lizabetta Effie,* it began. Here tablets girl's sister paused. As with all members of that conscientious family, she was disinclined to poke about in another's personal belongings. Ordinarily never would she have done so except the family was under the bigger obligation to hunt out and destroy their relative's murder weapons and, with the renouncers on the doorstep, threatening to kill this relative, they felt they'd no choice but to get a move on. Whilst the rest of them then continued above and below and out the back, dislodging floorboards, making holes in walls, searching under rafters for the phials and the potions, it was with qualm and scruple that tablets girl's sister, perching on the edge of the settee, opened out the folds of what amounted to thirteen pages of the smallest, neatest, blackest handwriting. She inhaled deeply. *My Dearest Susannah Elea-*

nor Lizabetta Effie, it began.

My Dearest Susannah Eleanor Lizabetta Effie,

It is incumbent upon us to list you your fears lest you forget them: that of being needy; of being clingy; of being odd; of being invisible; of being visible; of being shamed; of being shunned; of being deceived; of being bullied, of being abandoned; of being hit; of being talked about; of being pitied; of being mocked; of being thought both 'child' and at the same time 'old woman'; of anger; of others; of making mistakes; of knowing instinctively; of sadness; of loneliness; of failure; of loss; of love; of death. If not death, then of living — of the body, its needs, its bits, its daring bits, its unwanted bits. Then the shudders, the ripples, our legs turning to pulp because of those shudders and ripples. On a scale of one to ten, nine and nine-tenths of us believe in the loss of our power and in succumbing to weakness, also in the slyness of others. In instability too, we believe. Nine and nine-tenths of us think we are spied upon, that we replay old trauma, that we are tight and unhappy and numb in our facial expression. These are our fears, Dear Susannah Eleanor Lizabetta Effie. Note them please. Remember these points please. Susannah, oh our Susannah. We are afraid.

'Golly,' I said.

'Yes,' tablets girl's sister said. 'And there was more.'

Not to prolong or belabour, the biggest worry, the worry that we hold, and one that if only we didn't have it, even if we should retain all our other fears, still would we be indescribably happy, that which has condemned us profoundly, changed us negatively, stopped us surmounting trifles such as the fears already listed, and it is that weird something of the psyche — for do you remember, our Susannah, that weird something of the psyche? Of Lightness and Niceness that had got inside us, that was inside us and which, as you recall, possesses us still?

'She meant me,' said tablets girl's sister. 'Before the poisonings took off, and I mean really took off — I'm referring to the olden days when sister was poisoning just the odd seasonal person — and don't forget, she was my big sister, my older sister, so I had to respect her for her years — but I went to talk to her but because I'd no understanding, not only of the extent of her fears, but of the very existence of her fears, I went to her room and I blundered in my words. I didn't know I was blundering but I made things worse. Didn't see what was staring me in the face. Did nothing with my attempts but arise in her suspicions of me. I tried to elicit the wherefore of her poisoning, unravel the distortions, have her right mind restored to her. She said it was impossible, that it was perilous to focus on good things when there were bad things, all these bad things, she said, that could not be forgot. She said old dark things as well as new dark things had to be remembered, had to be acknowledged because otherwise everything that had gone before would have been in vain. In my ignorance,' went on tablets girl's sister, 'and even though I'd no clue what she meant by "in vainness", I said could they not have been in vain then, regretfully in vain maybe, but crucially that they could be set down now, that she could walk away from them now? That was when she poisoned me for the first time.' 'First time?' I said. 'Yes. She poisoned me five times, though the first three times I thought were just periods.' This younger sister then said that she and her older sister had another cup of tea and a chat on a second occasion. This time, while tablets girl once again made the tea, the younger sister once more heard her speak of bad things that had to be held on to. She realised that her sister was yet entrapped within the issue of the bad things. This time it was how they were not to be let go of, otherwise that would mean forgiveness could get in by the back door. She couldn't forgive, tablets girl's sister said tablets girl said, least not while she hadn't received the sorries. 'I said,' said tablets girl's sister, 'and again I said this in spite of not knowing who these sorries were to come from or what the unforgiven were to be sorry for — but I said I had an instinct that awaiting the sorries was part of the war-thinking and I asked if she could stop waiting for them, because otherwise to wait around for them would only destroy her even more. She said she couldn't move forward, that she had to receive the sorries before anything could be possible, and I said she didn't, that she really, really didn't, and that was when I thought I'd taken a very bad bout of menstruation for the second time.' On the third time when they had had tea and a talk together, it seemed, said tablets girl's sister, that they'd left off that whole subject of 'in vain' and of the unde-livered sorries, also of whether or not to forgive, and had moved instead to identity, legacy and tradition. 'I said to her that it seemed to me,' said tablets girl's sister, 'that she was minding to a very great degree, adhering far too much, giving more atten-tion perhaps than was meet, to separating herself, to isolating herself which was what she was doing whenever she did her poisoning. "What about co-existence?" I asked and she said things had to be respected, that besides, if she were to focus only on shiny aspects, then everyone would think there were no other aspects. They'd forget, she said. Consider everything fine and they'd leave her the only one remembering. I didn't know what these things were that she was talking about. I said that her identity seemed to be coming from an extreme edge so could she not let herself have doubt instead of reinforcing this edge, which was when I took an excruciatingly bad, crampy period for the third time.' On the fourth time tablets girl's sister said she realised her sister had been poisoning her and after that, they stopped having tea and chats together. 'I still thought though,' she said, 'there must be another way.' By then, the renouncers-of-the-state in our district had threatened tablets girl which was when her family began searching for the murder weapons. 'That was when I found the missive,' said the sister, 'which started in that vein of fear and went on for pages and pages, an awful lot of thirteen, smally written pages.' Eventually though, it ended:

With love and very much worryies and con-

*cerneds for your present and your ever future
safety, from,*

Yours, while still being really truly frightened,
*Faithful Terror Of Other People And Not Just
On Difficult Days.*

*Faithful Terror Of Other People And Not Just
On Difficult Days* hadn't pulled any punches.
There'd been no sustained correspondence
either, said tablets girl's sister, meaning one
of opposing strength, of some brave foray
by an inner oppositional party attempting
to outdo and wrest back a situation of terror to one of hopeful resolution. Instead
there was one loose sheet from *Lightness
and Niceness,* and even then, with constant
interruptions from *Faithful Terror Of Other
People And Not Just On Difficult Days. Dear
Susannah Eleanor Lizabetta Effie,* this Lone
Ranger sheet of paper began.

Dear Susannah Eleanor Lizabetta Effie,
You don't need me to tell you —
IT'S FRIGHTENING! O SO FRIGHTENING!
*— that everything you see is a reflection
of —*
ALL SO TERRIFYING!
*— your inner landscape and that you don't
have to —*
*HELP! HELP! WE'RE GOING TO DIE!
WE'RE ALL GOING TO DIE!*
— believe in this inner —

448

*MY STOMACH! MY HEAD! O MY INTES-
TINES!*

— landscape. Instead we can —

*REMEMBER OUR HELP KIT, SUSANNAH!
OUR COMFORT KIT! OUR SURVIVAL SELF-
DEFENCE KIT! OUR WAY TO FIGHT OUR
CORNER KIT! OUR PHIALS AND OUR PO-
TIONS AND OUR SHINY BLACK PILLS! OH
QUICK! REVENGE! WE WANT THEM TO
FEEL OUR PAIN AND . . .*

So it was that *Terror Of Other People* over-
ruled, disordered, then finally assassinated
Lightness and Niceness. *Lightness and Niceness* had come in other guises: *Oneness,
Shininess, Syster.* It had come in under *Syster.* So it was logical. *Syster* had got inside
her. She needed *Syster* not inside her. *Syster,* therefore, had to go. That was how come
tablets girl's sister was poisoned for the fifth
and almost the fatal time. Then I was
poisoned. Then the man mistaken for Hitler
was poisoned. After that, tablets girl herself
violently died. *Terror Of Other People* probably thought that with her dead, it, itself,
could carry on living. It would party it up,
let its hair down, continue to be fearful.
Never do they realise, these psychological
usurpers and possessors, that in dispensing
with the host — with the one being above
all whom they need for their own survival

— inevitably they are also dispensing with themselves. I stared at tablets girl's sister then, and she was of an ill pallor, sweat on her brow, difficulty breathing, eyes wretched with impairment and with her tiny hands clutching still to railings. She was plucking at them as in a fever. Maybe she was in a fever. And she was tissue-paper thin, not only in her body but in every aspect of her. Wired she was, undercurrents becoming overcurrents, sensitivities and early warning systems, all her surveillance detections overwhelmed and overwhelming. I'd gone to help but I didn't know how to help. If anything, I felt myself pulled in. She said my name then, my first name, and that felt warm, friendly, it felt a relief, far from my expectation of 'You killed our sister!' Then it was, 'You see how frightened she was? I never knew how beleaguered because she was my big sister, no matter too, she had that whole enemy situation going on.' I answered with a nod then realised she might not have seen it. So I said, 'Yeah,' and I was wondering what else to add because, just as with real milkman in his lorry, I felt I wanted to add something, to do something. Before anything occurred to me though, her ex-lover showed up.

I felt him behind me before I felt the

hands upon me. It was third brother, my third brother, whom I hadn't seen in almost a year. Hardly now, or for long, not since his marriage also nearly a year earlier, did he appear in this area. He would come to visit ma, bring her money, but he'd arrive in a hurry and get out in a hurry, taking her and wee sisters with him, picking them up — *quick! hurry!* — dropping them off — *quick! hurry!* — driving them somewhere on a jaunt. He'd take them downtown, said wee sisters, or up to the hills, or to the seaside if it was sunny and always they'd stop for treats and bouts of indulgence — 'ice-cream and chips and lemonade and sausages'. 'When the merry-go-rounds are here,' they added, 'we go there too, and he puts us, even ma, on all the attractions.' He also took them across town from time to time, they said, to have tea in his own house with him and his new wife. This new wife had been unexpected. She hadn't been seen coming — not by ma, not by us, not by the community, not by third brother and certainly not by tablets girl's sister, the long-time girlfriend whom for years he'd been in love with. As for me and him, we hadn't met since his marriage because he'd come to the house every second or third Tuesday, exactly the day of the week I spent after work over at maybe-boyfriend's. But here he was, having come up behind me, putting his hands on my shoulders before I'd a chance to turn and realise it wasn't Milkman, wasn't the lynchers from the chip shop, wasn't *Terror Of Other People* or the revenant of tablets girl herself. It was him, third brother, and I felt the vibrations of his approach and wasn't alone either in picking up on them. Tablets girl's sister had sensed something as well. She broke off from her talk about her sister's great terror, which had been mistaken for her sister's great anger, and she started, then cried out, 'Who's that? Who's there? *Who is that?*', her voice urgent and demanding, yet also excited, hopeful, because she knew before I did who was standing behind me; knew even before brother said, 'Step aside, twin sister, I'm coming through.'

He had to step me aside himself though, for I was too overwhelmed to do my own stepping. Even though he'd spoken to me, I could see already he'd forgotten my existence, was looking past me, making moves directly towards the only girl he'd ever loved. On hearing his voice, tablets girl's sister uttered another cry, one hand flew to her mouth, the other reached out, possibly to ward him off, possibly to take hold of him. Then she dropped her hands, tried to step back but couldn't because already she was at the railings. Instead she stepped sideways and I knew by this point I was all but forgotten by her as well. This was the second reason I thought she might have rebuffed the help I'd offered. Given I was the sister of the ex-lover who'd ditched her to go and marry some expedient unknown, might she not have wanted any reminder of this terrible event from her past? So it was back to the wrong spouse, in this case to that of third brother's wife being the wrong spouse with tablets girl's sister meant to have been the right spouse. That was how it looked to us — to my family, her family, everybody in the community. Yet they hadn't married because third brother had gone and done the usual unquestioned, unconscious, self-protective thing. Being loved back by the person he loved to the point where he couldn't cope anymore with the vulnerable reciprocity of giving and receiving, he ended the relationship to get it over with before he lost it, before it was snatched from him, either by fate or by somebody else. Nobody said anything sensible to him at the time because who would have been that some-body? So it was that brother attempted to evade his great fear of theoretically losing what he wanted more than anything and to make do with a substitute instead. Unsurprisingly, tablets girl's sister had something to say about that.

'Go away,' she said. 'You went away, exboy lover, so now you just go away.' Her voice was trembling, her body shaking, definitely she was angry and it was with difficulty she was trying to focus; clear too, that she couldn't properly make him out. As for me, I remained invisible to both but that didn't stop my mind racing. Was it too late? Had he burnt his boats? Had he ruined everything? Or was she going to relent and let him make repair? With the intention of repair, it seemed, third brother didn't go away as commanded. Instead he stepped closer and although he hadn't yet touched her, he was now speaking to her, imploring her. Without editing, without refining, because he was too far gone emotionally for any self-conscious evaluation, he was saying something about '. . . mistake . . . fool! . . . Big fool! Buck idjit! Didn't know what I was thinking, what I was doing . . . Stupid . . . Wrong person. Because I loved you . . . Afraid. Risky . . . Played for safety . . . Sold out the dream . . . Oh idjit! . . . Oh fool! . . . Dammit! . . . Wrong person . . . Fuckit . . . Immature!' There was something else on 'not cherishment', then something about 'cherishment', something on 'love, my love' and 'couldn't cope' and 'idjit, madman, big idjit, the happiness, couldn't . . . wouldn't . . . big bastard idjit'. I think he was meaning himself. After that, it was 'this love business' and how he'd compromised, how he'd 'settled', telling her he was shaking, that here he was, standing before her right now, shaking. 'Cannot you see me shaking?' he said. Then he said, *'Fuck! You can't see me shaking! You can't see! What did she do? What did your sister do to your eyes?'*

This stopped him in his tracks and I think it must have been recently he'd heard that tablets girl's sister, his ex-girlfriend, had been poisoned but without anticipating the extent of this poisoning, not having been around many poisoned people perhaps at close quarters to have grasped it wasn't always only the alimentary tract that got destroyed. Tablets girl's sister, however, by now was well into her stride. 'You broke my heart,' she cried. 'You made me miserable. You made you miserable and any way you look at this, you can't have made her — whoever she is — not miserable. So go away, go away,' and again her hands came out. Again his hands came out, and she tried, and he tried, then she tried, then she halted. Then he tried again, then she pushed him off. Generally, there was halting and pushing, hands coming out, arms coming out, hands pushing away and more than one verbal 'go away' but with no going-away happening. Then, from him there were further declarations of love, further fools and damn fools and damn idjits. 'If she'd killed you!' he cried. 'What if your sister'd killed you! You could have died and I would never have . . .' and though he wasn't really shaking, not physically, definitely there was turmoil churning up from inside. Not that she could see, but it was unmistakable not to hear what he looked like. It was true, certainly, that he had compromised, that he had settled, become sullied, jaded, so that maybe in less than another year of not following his heart, not allowing his heart, he was to be turned into one of those buried-alive, hundred-per-cent, dulled-to-death, coffined people. But in the middle of this declaration of love and of his innards shaking there came upon him a change in tone. Now there was urgency, a sharpness, an admirable fearlessness, even anger. He asked again what her sister had done to her and had anyone taken her, his beloved, to get help? So now it was the doctor. Had she been taken to one? What had been done to help her? Had anything been done to help her? But tablets girl's sister interrupted, rebuffed his concern over the trifle of what her sister had done to her. 'For what care you what's been done to me when you didn't care what you did to me yourself!' There was more somethings here, this time from both, followed by pushing from her, then a taking hold of his shirt, a taking hold of him, an almost laying her head onto — But no! Instead it was rejection of his shirt, rejection of him, then further pushing, but then a taking to the shirt again, stepping close, closer, another closer, more closers. Then she leaned over, leaned in, leaned her head onto her forearms, already at home on his heart. She closed her eyes then and breathed him into her, her lover, ex-lover, her lover, at which point third brother must have thought permission was granted. He brought his arms up — too early! — not granted. With a cry she pushed him off once more.

So there they were. She pushed again, weaker pushing, and already his arms were out — wiser, waiting, alert for the cue, for the subtle indication that this time would be the right time, all of which, of course, was not meant for my ears to hear or my eyes to see. Ordinarily, I would have been shocked, disgusted, at the thought of anyone — especially me — standing feet away from and having a good gawk at two overly wrought, emotional lovers. But I had become glued, couldn't stop myself, didn't want to stop myself and besides, they'd started it and were continuing it. And now, permitting him to bring his arms around her, while she herself held on to him while managing at the same time to push away at him, she admonished, saying, 'I think I hate you,' which meant she didn't because 'I *think* I hate you' is the same as 'probably I hate you', which is the same as 'I don't know if I hate you', which is the same as 'I don't hate you, oh my God, my love, I love you, still love you, always, always have I loved you and never have I stopped loving you'. Then, taking her face out of his chest, to push or not push, both of them ceased activity. There was a second of nothing, a blip of suspension, then they fell — no more talk, no more dramatics — with relief into each other's arms.

They were kissing now, tightly embracing; he, leaning her over, supporting her by her back, her waist — and her, arms about his neck, letting him hold her, letting him support her, letting him lean her over. Soon indeed, it seemed he was kissing her backwards off her feet. It was one of those *you'll never be kissed like this until you smell like this* Christmas French perfume advertisements and here too, I noticed — though they didn't — others had come to view them as well. The majority of these people had broken off from the small crowd which had gathered to observe the strange spectacle of the men fighting down the street. They were still at it, those men, in silence, doing so too, with those cigarettes dangling. Perhaps it had been a fight too quiet, too prolonged, too puzzling, a disconcerting fight, difficult to gauge, one which worked largely perhaps by association of ideas, some modern, stylistic *art nouveau* encounter. Being a conventional audience, however, used to chronological and traditional realism, the majority began to doubt that those men, indeed, were fighting at all. That was why they lost interest and broke away to come down to us, and most of these neighbours were now nodding, and nodding sagely. The woman beside me nodded sagely to the woman on the other side of me, who acknowledged her sage nod by herself nodding sagely. 'I knew it was guilt,' said the first, now talking to me. 'That explains your brother's behaviour, his furtiveness in sneaking into the area and the same on his rushing out of the area. Guilt. Only guilt. Nothing to do with the political problems, with renouncership or with any possible suspicion of informership. All guilt — also remorse — and a bad conscience at what he'd done to her. But do you have any idea' — and at this all of them turned to me — 'what his wrong wife is going to say about that?'

That was something else. Brothers. My brothers. I had four brothers, three really, and one of them, the second one, was dead. I still counted dead second brother because still he was my brother. I counted fourth brother also, the one who'd never been my brother but who instead had been second brother's longest friend since their days at the baby school. Always he'd lived with us, this fourth brother, even though he had his own family — two parents, two brothers, seven sisters — still had them too, residing just four streets away. At age fourteen, having left school, he'd continued to live in our house, though by that time he'd joined the renouncers. Second brother also had joined the renouncers. Even now, with second brother gone, fourth brother in theory still lived with us as part of our family, although at present he wasn't in our house because he was on the run. They said he'd taken motorbike for the border after shooting up that patrol during which deliberately he'd killed four state people and accidentally three ordinary people — one adult and two six-year-olds, standing at their countryside bus-stop waiting for their bus. No longer now did we see him, although it was said he was somewhere down there, in one of those counties in that country 'over the border'. As for first brother, eldest brother, well, by tradition, it was expected that if anyone in a family here was to go and join the movement, it would be the firstborn son who'd go and join the movement. So much was this believed that when ma's second son, my second brother, who had joined the movement, got killed while himself in a shootout with the state forces, the policemen, when they came to fetch ma to identify the body, kept getting it wrong and calling him her firstborn instead. In the case of ma's actual firstborn, my first brother, he didn't join the renouncers but instead fell over drunk one night in town and broke his arm. He took himself to the hospital and said it had been the fault of a loose paving stone and put in a claim and was believed by those in charge of believing or not believing and was awarded a whack of thousands.

461

He gave a lump sum to ma, then, regarding the country and its political problems, said, 'Fuck this, I'm outta here,' and went to the Middle East for a bit of peace and quiet and sunshine instead. Before going, he offered to take the brothers with him, but second brother and fourth brother, deep in their renouncership, said they didn't want to go, and third brother didn't want to go because he was in love with tablets girl's sister. So first brother went alone and no one has heard tell of him since. So this brother, first brother errant, went and did his thing. And second brother, my late brother, he did his thing. Fourth brother was currently doing his thing. As for third brother, jilting his right spouse then marrying the wrong one, then doing nothing about it till now, delineated — least also until now — all that could be said about him.

After completing the Jean Paul Gaultier kiss, and oblivious still of us, the audience, third brother swept his true wife off her feet and up into his arms. He said one word, 'Hospital!', then, switching from earlier declarations of love and self-idiocy to 'urgent need of medical care and attention', he turned and carried his love to his car. 'Shouldn't take her to hospital,' murmured the crowd, now shaking their heads. 'Hospital's wrong, entirely wrong. There's nothing so wrong as a hospital. There'll be forms to fill in. Questions asked on who poisoned her. Then the *Schutzstaffel* will be sent for and them two will be forced into informership.' They turned to me then. 'They'll recognise your brother, you know. They'll know who he is, that he's your dead second brother's brother and your fugitive fourth brother's brother and it'll make no difference that he himself is no renouncer. Being an associate of a renouncer,' they said, 'a family member of a renouncer, will be seen as proof that he's connected as well.' With this they waited for me to respond. As for me, I just wished they'd give over about the hospital. Lots of people here bucked the trend now, broke the hospital embargo and took themselves down there regularly. The hospital was busting with people from my area who weren't supposed to be in it. Before long it'll be day-trips to the hospital and booking your holidays down at the hospital. Now was the dawning of a new era, at least concerning hospitals, and the sooner these neighbours realised that, the sooner we could all adjust and move on. I knew of course they wouldn't dare mention what they were edging around, which was that third brother would also be recognised as the brother of the sister who was sexually involved with that major paramilitary player, the one who not long ago had been background person in those killings of judges and judges' wives and who'd killed too, the most major of poisoners our district had ever known. Instead these neighbours skirted that whole murder business, also the business of myself having been the inducement to the 'ordinary murder' aspect of it. Instead they reiterated the turning by the police of third brother and his girlfriend into informers. Meanwhile, this brother, deaf to sageness and to disapproval and to the dangers of opening oneself to informership, placed the love of his life into the passenger seat of his car. He threw himself over the bonnet and straightaway was in the driving seat where at once he gunned the engine. The car roared up the street and screeched round the corner into the interface road that led to the hospital. After that, all sight and sound of my worried but now happy third brother, with his newly happy but perilously ill former ex-lover, disappeared.

That was that. All action over. Far more than enough of it too, for me, for one day. I didn't like action because hardly ever was it good action, hardly ever to do with things nice. So now I was going home and the adjusted plan for the rest of the evening was that wee sisters could eat cake. After cake, they could go out on adventures and I myself would stay in, have a bubble bath, eat cake too, in bath, put feet up during and after bath, finish off *Persian Letters,* possibly with it disintegrating in steam and water-dribbles owing to sogginess which didn't matter as in a few pages I'd have done with it anyhow. After that, if ma still wasn't back by wee sisters' bedtime, I'd read them some Hardy for they were well into their Hardy phase. Before that it had been their Kafka phase followed by their Conrad phase which was absurd given none of them had reached ten. So I'd read to them even though it was the hideous century of Hardy and not the acceptable century of Hardy, but I'd do it then, to round off the evening, I'd get into my own bed and start in on my eighteenth-century *Some Considerations on the Causes of Roman Greatness and Decadence* which, published in 1734, was pretty much, I reckoned, how all books should be. So it was a simple and sequential plan, no involutions, easy of implementation, but I got in the door and wee sisters came out

the back living room holding oriental para-
sols with tinsel wrapped around themselves
from the Christmas box kept out of the way
on top of the wardrobe and their first words
to me were, 'Somebody for you called
maybe-boyfriend rang up.' This surprised
me because it was unprecedented that
maybe-boyfriend should have my number.
He never called me at my home and I never
called him at his home, nor did I have his
number or even know whether or not he —
Wee sisters by now were continuing on. 'We
informed this person you were at the chip
shop getting us chips, middle sister' — they
looked for the chips but in my hands there
were not any — 'then we requested his
telephonic number for you to return the call
but he said, "If she's only gone for chips, if
that's all she's gone for," and said he'd ring
again in half an hour. He rang thirty-seven
minutes later but still you weren't here. You
were taking a long time getting our chips,
middle sister' — again they looked for the
chips, frowns of tiny proportion forming on
their faces — 'so we suggested once more
his telephonic number and once more,
"Don't bother yourselves," this person, your
maybe-boyfriend, said. Then he asked if we
were your sisters and we answered yes but,
middle sister, *where are the chips?*' They

had gone to the heart of the matter so I explained about the no-chip situation without giving any truth in my explanation. Instead I offered a vague non-committal about the chip shop not having any, even though I knew non-committals and vagueness never sat easily with them. To pass quickly on, as well as to counter any disapproving comment they might make about my moral probity in telling lies to them, I slipped in that they could have whatever they wanted from the kitchen cupboards — hoping that outstanding treat-foods would be in the kitchen cupboards — then I closed the chapter on the chips by announcing that tablets girl's sister and third brother were sort of, kind of, back together again.

That was the right manoeuvre, a brilliant piece of sidetracking. Wee sisters loved tablets girl's sister. So much they loved her that always they'd run towards her, jump up, throw themselves at her, swing on her arms, on her neck, give hugs, laugh, receive hugs and this would be every single time during the time she was the girlfriend of third brother. So it was within reason that when third brother threw her over, they too, were heartbroken, to the extent of crossing third brother off their Christmas list for almost a year. Nine months, three weeks and up until half a day before the end of Christmas Eve he'd been struck off, after which they relented and put him on again. This exclusion period covered the times too, when he was taking them, along with ma on Tuesdays for those jaunts, those merry-go-rounds, those convivial entertainments, with no understanding, it seemed, of the extensiveness to which he'd been unforgiven, nor of the criminal misconduct in which they had held him, or of how close he'd come to getting no reindeer card, no men's pair of socks, no men's shoelaces and no men's soap-on-rope from wee sisters that particular Christmastime around. And now news of the reconciliation had done the trick. This was best news, not least because tablets girl's sister reciprocated wee sisters' love entirely. I'd never met anyone so indulgent of three little individuals discoursing earnestly on the invention of the encyclopaedia, the whirlwinds of the Faeroe Islands, the diatonic scale, prefectures in China, the non-local universe, the theories and facts of material science or on the cultural destruction of the courtyard of the Ca' d'Oro. Tablets girl's sister did so indulge. She delighted in wee sisters, listened to them, encouraged them, took them seriously, read their voluminous notes and asked sensible questions, which pleased them. So now, with the couple back together, there was rejoicing, with queries no longer on locus of chips but now on locus of tablets girl's sister and third brother. Not realising, however, the extent of the effects of poison, just as third brother and I at first also hadn't realised the ravaging of poisoning, wee sisters were unaware of the precarious state this lovely girl they loved was in. I left off being exact about that as well, about how currently she was at death's door and even now was down at the hospital with third brother, having the poison seen to. Instead I said probably they could see her and be reunited in just a little while. Meantime, and as long as it was available in the kitchen, I said they could have supper made out of anything, then they could go out and play until very, very late with the added bonus of my reading twentieth-century Hardy to them later on. This was satisfactory and so that was where we were — wee sisters opting for Smarties, Farley's Rusks, boiled eggs, something called 'easily expressed mints' with various other nuncheon-type snack things — when maybe-boyfriend, for the third time that evening, for the fourth time ever, rang up.

'Well, go and have them then,' I shouted,

meaning their aliments because, as the telephone rang and I answered, wee sisters were about to set off for the kitchen. Then, when maybe-boyfriend said, 'It's yourself,' I covered the mouthpiece to shout further, 'And close the door behind you and don't listen to this telephone call!' As this was the first time to talk with maybe-boyfriend — with any maybe-boyfriend — via the telephone, I felt inhibited, so I didn't want any overhearers to our conversation, meaning wee sisters in this instance, listening in. Of course there was also the security forces with their electronic surveillance but as for them, if they were listening — because maybe no one was listening — there wasn't a lot in the moment, bar not speaking to maybe-boyfriend, that I could do. So I shouted to wee sisters to eat their nuncheons out the back, then to leave by the back, then I sat on the stairs, uncovered the mouthpiece, placed the receiver back at my ear and said, 'Maybe-boyfriend.' I was glad it was him, very glad, even though it was weird to talk on the telephone. Only eight times, seven, maybe six, ever had I done so. Maybe-boyfriend said, 'You took a long time getting those chips, maybe-girlfriend,' and his voice sounded like him which meant lovely, which meant male, which meant welcoming, and he was bantering about the chips, with my taking it at first to be banter. So the telephone call started fine, but by the end — by the time we got through the bit about my ma calling him a terrorist, the bit about his being under further siege, not solely now from that supercharger and flag rumour, but also because of some new rumour involving him way over in his district but for which he seemed to think I was responsible way over here in my district — I was reeling and reassessing his remark of *'took a long time'* as not really some affectionate opening banter. Before long I became sure it was an attack upon me after all.

He asked what had happened. Why had I missed our Tuesdays and our Friday nights into Saturdays and our all day Saturdays into Sundays because, apart from my ending our sometimes-Thursday nights together, neither of us had missed a date during our almost year-long maybe-dating so far? I told him something had come up and that I'd had to stay and look after our house and wee sisters. I didn't share about real milkman getting shot, or ma being transformed into her true self because of real milkman getting shot, or about my being poisoned, or about tablets girl being murdered, or about Milkman intensifying his predations upon me — indeed, about Milkman. Nor did I share about the community and its fabrications, or the particulars of that carbomb which still remained a live issue between us even though still he was persisting in shrugging it off. There was the chip shop experience too, that I didn't share, with its attitude of *'Here! Take these chips, but don't be thinking you'll get away with this, hussy!'* and it wasn't because of stubbornness that I didn't share. Even so, it started to seem to me that perhaps I could tell, that perhaps my business could be — if maybe-boyfriend wanted it to be — his business also. Still I held back though, thinking, well, what if I did tell? What if I do tell? What if I manage to get it out and, just as with the carbomb, he dismisses and shrugs it off? At this point in my life — and again, because I was confused and shut down by Milkman, and by the community, also because of this uncommitted status of me and maybe-boyfriend; because too, I'd been watching my back so long I'd no conception I was missing out on my own good opportunities; because of all that then, I construed that the hurtful impact upon me of his shrugging it off would be worse than not revealing at all. So I downplayed it, thinking even at this point that that was how I had to play it, but maybe-boyfriend said, 'But what happened? What is this thing, maybe-girl, that's come up?' After a startled moment, my mouth fell open and despite all my long-held reasons for not telling, spontaneous words came out of my mouth. I heard myself speak of ma's friend being shot, and of her being down at the hospital a lot now — which was when maybe-boyfriend interrupted to say he would come over, did I want him to come over? I only wished my spontaneity had carried itself further and I'd been able to say what I wanted to say which was yes. He could come over. He could be here. Come also, without ma haranguing, without questions of marriage or babies or of accusations of being Milkman. Even if she'd been here, ma was so distracted now with her own heart issues, it was unlikely she'd even register maybe-boyfriend was in the room. So it wasn't thoughts of her that were stopping me now, causing me to hesitate, to deprive myself of maybe-boyfriend. It was — *well, what if he does come over and he gets to hear?* I found myself back, then, with eldest sister, sitting silent in ma's front parlour on the day and hour of the funeral of her murdered ex-boyfriend. I knew it was

473

unbelievable that I should let myself get pushed into becoming what the gossips were saying I'd already become but, according to the latest in the area, it was the case I'd been in relationship with Milkman for two months by now. That meant it was time to cheat on him, they said, so I was cheating on him, having a dalliance behind his back with some young car mechanic whipper-snapper from across town. Because of this new rumour then, I hesitated to get my thoughts straight before answering. Having told out some — the easier bit, the bit that didn't involve me but only ma and real milkman — it was now time, I decided, to tell out to maybe-boyfriend all the rest. Before I could do this, however, maybe-boyfriend misconstrued my hesitation and pounced, saying I didn't want him to come over, that never had I wanted him to come over — to pick me up, to drive me home, to spend time with me in my district. At first he said he thought it was because of the ru-mour of him and the supercharger which had made me ashamed to be seen with him; that perhaps, just as with the gossips over his way, I had even started to believe him an informer too. That had been before the other rumour, he said, for even across town in his own district he had heard of that other rumour — the one about his daring to vie for the affections of a renouncer's girlfriend. 'And *that* renouncer,' he said. '*The milkman* renouncer. So, maybe-girlfriend, what have you got to say about that?'

Immediately the tenseness was back, the one which had been building between us owing to the respective rumours in our areas. And it now seemed these rumours were converging, with his viewpoint shifting from 'my not wanting him to call because I was ashamed of him' to 'not wanting him to call because I was in relationship with Milkman', and my viewpoint shifting from 'not wanting him to call because of ma demanding marriage and babies' to 'not wanting him to call in case Milkman took his life'. As for telling out, it boded no good to tell, I had decided, for look, hadn't I just started to open up and there he was, getting into a fight over it? Instead of answering — for why should I answer when, just as with the others, he was initiating by accusing? — I withdrew again, closed up, piqued and angry, and it was at this point that the revulsion again took hold. Oh no, I thought. Not that revulsion, not at maybe-boyfriend. But yes, within seconds maybe-boyfriend had once again started to change. Instantly he

475

became less attractive, less himself. Then not attractive, not himself. Instead more and more Milkman. Then I got the shudders, which was the first time with maybe-boyfriend to have got them. Then I thought, hold on a minute. How'd he get my number? What sneaky, spying, stalking thing did he get up to in order to obtain my telephone number? 'How'd you get my number?' And the moment I attacked with this question, the revulsion subsided and I remembered again who he was. *You're silly,* I said to myself. *What does it matter how he got it?* It wasn't even that I didn't want him to have it, for weighed in balance I did want him to have it. Not for getting rung by him. It was more that his having of the number, his wanting to have it, presaged in my mind a certain closeness, a growth of trust. But he took my question at face value as the attack which, in the moment of asking, unfortunately it had been. 'From the phonebook, maybe-girlfriend,' he snapped and snapping had not been in the old days usual for maybe-boyfriend. 'What phonebook?' I said. 'Christ all Friday, maybe-girl! Are twentieth-century phonebooks off-limits also?' which was, for the first time, from him, a slur on my reading tastes. So, him too, I thought. Him too. My own maybe-boyfriend treacherously also. Stabbed by him also. 'So I rang a few numbers that had your surname listed in your area,' he went on, 'because you know, you've never given me your address, maybe-girlfriend' — and here was bitterness, distinct bitterness. 'Eventually, after a few wrong numbers,' said the bitterness, 'I rang another number and got a woman who was your ma.'

The tone now was frosty, to be described as resentment-tinged, disgruntled, frosty. He said nothing else about his coming over, but did stay on the Milkman theme. 'Maybe-girlfriend,' he said, 'what have you been saying about me and this renouncer to your mother?' 'Nothing,' I said. 'That's what my ma does. She makes it up herself.' 'She said I had bombs,' he said. 'Called me married and a befouler, then she hung up and wouldn't let me speak to you. So tell me, what did you say to her?' 'I told you,' I said. 'Nothing. It's her. I'm not responsible for her. That's what she does.' 'You must have said something,' he said. 'And why must I have?' I said. Here again, was the admonition, with my having to refute, to explain, to be responsible for other people's misconceptions. Then he carried on in his pronouncements, saying he'd heard this middle-aged guy was middle-aged. He also stressed that the middle-aged guy, the auld lad, might be middle-aged but certainly he was no light-weight in the movement. Did I know what this hardcore pensioner got up to in the — 'Stop saying that,' I said. 'And I'm not see-ing him. Not involved with him.' 'Does he know, maybe-girlfriend,' persisted maybe-boyfriend, 'about me?' I couldn't believe this. It seemed now he was processing things along at such a trot that he was overtaking the keenest gossips of both my district and his own district. 'I know we've never talked about this before,' he said, 'about us being just maybe-boy and maybe-girl in an "al-most one year so far maybe-relationship" which means probably, it's okay for us to date other people — but a renouncer, maybe-girlfriend — I mean, *that* renouncer? Are you really sure you wanna go down that road?' I was hurt at this, that he didn't seem to care that each of us could date others whilst being almost one year into our own maybe-relationship. I myself, at the start of me and him, had tried out a few other boys with the view, I suppose, to one of them becoming maybe-boyfriend but then I stopped because maybe-boyfriend became maybe-boyfriend and we upped our days and nights together and besides, those oth-ers had fallen short. They'd asked too many

478

questions, testing, proving questions, obviously a checklist — to evaluate, pass judgement, see if I was good enough — not questions coming from interest in wanting to know who I really was. So I evaluated these guys right back and came to the conclusion it was they who weren't good enough for me, meaning I ended before we'd begun what might have been a possible maybe-relationship. As for maybe-boyfriend's remark — that of double-dating, of treble-dating — did that mean he himself had been multiple-dating? Had he been seeing some girl or girls during all this time we'd been having our maybe-relationship? Was he sleeping with them as he was sleeping with me because that was just how unspecial I was? Was he involved with them still, all these numerous, numberless females, even too, after he'd asked me to move in with him up the road in the red-light street?

'— then she accused me of bombs and hung up.'

This was him, continuing on the subject of ma which brought me out of my own painful subject of him and other women. 'But not before she let me know,' he said, 'that one of those marvellous blokes in her standing I was not.' 'She thinks you're someone else,' I said. 'I know,' he said.

'That's what I've been telling you.' Here he sounded derisive and self-righteous, so I said, 'You'd better not push it, maybe-boyfriend. It's not my fault my ma has the whole six volumes going, that all of them have the volumes going. There is no Milk-man — well, there is *Milkman* but no me and —' 'Don't bother explaining,' he said. 'I already know.' And it was that languid, dismissive, oh-so-world-weary 'don't bother explaining' that did it. How dare he say 'don't bother explaining' as if I was bother-ing him constantly, wearing him to the bone with attempts at explanations, as if he hadn't right there and then been doing all this pronouncing in order to drag explana-tions segment by segment out of my throat. So it was because of his remark that I launched into my own retaliation. 'Don't take your supercharger butcher's apron,' I said, 'out on me.' That was dirty, very dirty, below-the-belt, disgusting, disgracefully dirty, not something I'd ever say to anybody — not even to somebody I hated who might just happen to have a quintessential 'over the water' Blower Bentley supercharger tucked away in their house of informership that had not just one flag of contention from the country 'over the water' on it, but heaps of flags of contention from that country, which maybe-boyfriend, I knew, had not. Not one of my finer days then, but I'd been provoked by his manner, by his accusing me of going with the paramilitant. So I put the boot in, though sorry after that I had put it in; not immediately sorry, however, not to put it in again. I did this by following up my almost-immediately regretted remark with other retaliatory observations, also almost-immediately regretted. 'You cook,' I said. 'You do coffeepots and sunsets when not even women do coffeepots and sunsets. You replace people with cars. You keep a cramped house with challenging rooms and you talk about Lithuanian films.' Then he said, 'You read while you walk.' 'Here we go,' I said. 'Haven't finished,' he said. 'I like that you do that reading-while-walking. It's the sort of quiet, out-of-sync thing you would do, thinking too, that nothing was odd or that anybody was noticing. But it is odd, maybe-girlfriend. Not normal. Not self-preservation. Instead it's unyielding and confounding and in our type of environment it presents you as a stubborn, perverse character. I didn't want to say this but you're saying things so I'm going to say it. It's that you don't seem alive anymore. I look at your face and it's as if your sense organs are disappearing or as if they've already disappeared so that no one gets to connect with you. Always you've been hard to second-guess, but now you're impossible. Perhaps we should stop now though, before this gets even worse.'

So we decried each other's insufficiencies, did hauling of reckonings — one of those fights — but I did agree with him that yes, we should stop. At the back of my mind all through this phone altercation, I felt unease that someone was listening, which might be nothing as I'd had that feeling of someone listening, someone watching, someone following, someone clocking everything, no matter where I was, what I was doing, who I was with, all through these past two months. I was on edge and more and more convinced that all some individuals did, that the whole mission in life for some people, was covertly to listen, but perhaps this was my overwrought imagination and nobody was listening, nobody interloping at all. We ended our call then in a stilted, formal manner, with my saying that soon as I could, I would go over to him, with him sounding as if he couldn't be bothered, as if he didn't believe me, as if he didn't want to see me. This was followed from both sides by one single, solitary goodbye, then a hanging up. After I'd hung up, I continued to sit on the stairs and, even if belatedly, my new spontaneity again began to stir itself. It told me to stop all that self-pitying and to go over to maybe-boyfriend, reminding me that I liked maybe-boyfriend, that maybe-boyfriend had been my first sunset, that he'd been the only one I'd slept with, that I had stayed with him at least three nights a week until Milkman had threatened to kill him, after which I brought it down to two nights, and that I did this, this staying-over, when prior to maybe-boyfriend I'd never stayed over with anybody before. Regardless then, that we were in a maybe-relationship instead of a proper coupledom relationship; regardless too, that we kept getting amnesia every time either of us broached furthering on our maybe status, I was to go to him, to go now, said my spontaneity, to tell out to him face-to-face all this misunderstanding we'd been having and to communicate properly and get this mess cleared up. After I did that — and if maybe-boyfriend let me do it without again jumping on the defensive — he might then tell out — regarding that supercharger affair and the informer affair and now also this latest renouncer-girlfriend tittle-tattle — all that was happening over his way with him. Depending on how it went, he could then drive me home, for I had to get back for wee sisters. Regardless of ma, however, and regardless of Milkman, he could drive me, not to the usual demarcation point on the outskirts of the district, but this time right into the district and straight to my door. He could come in too, stay awhile, stay overnight — as long as he was okay afterwards with Milkman trying to kill him. He was an adult, a grown man. I could leave that decision to him. So, said my spontaneity, maybe-boyfriend was my maybe-boyfriend; Milkman was not my lover. At the time of affirming this conviction, the resurgence of truth felt lucid and uplifting. Somewhat unaware in my feverish excitement that instead of lucidity and upliftment, however, I might instead be swinging from one extreme of despondency and powerlessness over to the other extreme of sudden and incongruous jollity, I scribbled a note for wee sisters. It said, *'Put on your nightclothes. I'll be back later to read you Hardy as promised.'* With that, I threw on my jacket and rushed to the bus-stop up the road.

There were three reasons why I didn't walk. One was, I was in that overwound, falsely buoyed-up state which I mistook for resolve and happy conviction. Therefore, I was eager to get over to maybe-boyfriend's as quickly as I could. Two was, that even now, even with this springiness and excitement upon me, my legs, even just for walking — not for running, just for walking — still were not back to their best. Three was, at the back of my decision to make clearance with maybe-boyfriend, I was uneasy still of going out my door and encountering Milkman. It seemed then — though I did not question this — that I did not want my newfound regeneration tested, perhaps defeated, by him once again appearing on the scene.

I got off the bus in maybe-boyfriend's area, took the cut-through that led round to his street and his big front door was busted. It was leaned-to but it was busted. What did that mean? I pushed it gingerly and slipped round into the tiny hall. From there I went to the living room which was empty of people though car parts were strewn about, scattered, crashed here and there, suggesting the hoarding had taken on some haphazard, noisy, even violent quality rather than maybe-boyfriend's usual stacking-upon-stacking, or else some disturbance of his normal day-to-day hoarding had taken place. I was about to call his name but then I heard chef's voice issuing from the kitchen. He was murmuring his usual cooking instructions to his imaginary apprentice.

'Here. Try it this way. No. Leave off that. This way, this way. There, that's better. Put the dishcloth to them while I get this together, then I'll rinse —' I headed towards the kitchen to interrupt chef to ask what had happened to the front door and to enquire as to the whereabouts of maybe-boyfriend, but then I halted for chef's imaginary companion at that moment was murmuring back. It was *something something,* couldn't make it out, but I made out the voice and it was that of maybe-boyfriend. I made moves to rush in but something in his voice prickled my skin and halted me. Involuntarily, I found myself holding back, going no further than the living-room side of the kitchen door. Maybe-boyfriend then said *something something* 'Dammit, fuckit. Fool! Big fool! Buck idjit! Didn't see that comin', didn't know what I was thinking, chef, what I was doing . . . Stupid . . . Should have realised they . . .' with chef murmuring something about maybe-boyfriend shutting up and turning his head to the right. Gently I pushed the part-open door another bit part-open and looked through the join where I spied maybe-boyfriend sitting at the kitchen table on one of his kitchen chairs. He had his back, not quite, but almost turned towards me and something was wrong for he was holding a dripping-wet dishcloth up to his eyes. He had covered both eyes with this cloth and chef was standing nearby with a bunch of lint or gauze, with other cloths under one arm while pouring some surgical liquid from a bottle into a baking bowl of water sitting on the table. Also on this table, or thrust point downwards into the table so that it stood completely upright from it, was one of chef's long kitchen knives. It had blood on it. Again my instincts stayed me. I didn't believe for one moment that this wasn't human blood, that instead perhaps it was stains from some recently prepared *'Roasted beetroot and Roma tomatoes'*, or *'Celebration red cabbage in port and red wine'*, or *'Platter of edible red with further red and splashes of more red with extra startling red splatters to follow'*. No. This was blood. There was more blood too — a load of it — on chef's shirt, red streaks on the floor and reddish-brown stains on the table. Little splotches, I then noticed, were dripping from maybe-boyfriend himself. Strangely, still I remained where I was, as if something ever so strong had placed an invisible hand on my arm and firmly was staying me, ordering me, commanding me, warning me. There was none of that expected behaviour of a maybe-girlfriend, supposedly moments before full of regeneration and instant cure, rushing to her maybe-boyfriend's house, totally resolved to see him, to be upfront with him, explain her newfound freedom from restriction to him. There was no gasp, scream, no concerned dash to take hold of the maybe-beloved with a cry of, *'What happened? My God! What has happened?'* Instead I remained where I was, with neither chef nor maybe-boyfriend aware I was half in and half out of the room.

Maybe-boyfriend started up again, something about '. . . fucker. Sneaky wee bastard. What a bastard-bastard blasted bastard!' And now I gathered — for maybe-boyfriend had used those terms before whilst having a go at his *'no harm like but'* neighbour, the one who'd started off the supercharger-flag rumour which had then led to the informer rumour. 'We're going to hospital, longest mate,' said chef with maybe-boyfriend saying, 'No way. I'm in enough trouble with this flag-tout thing, supposedly now too, for being cocky enough to elbow in on yon renouncer's love interest' — meaning me as the 'love interest' — which was shocking for he hadn't said it kindly — had said it unkindly — had said it derisively. Had things soured that much between us then, that this was my actual maybe-boyfriend before me right now? But hold on, I thought, he's just been stabbed or beaten up and something's wrong with his eyes but then I thought, well, I myself have recently been poisoned, then hardly an hour earlier I'd been in the chip shop accused of being an accessory-to-murder, then there was himself on the telephone accusing me too of being mistress, as even now, behind my back, he was accusing me still of being mistress, yet you don't see me sitting down in a corner with longest friend from primary school criticising and having a go at him. Still, I thought again, he has been injured. Still, I thought again, he hadn't said it kindly. This, I suppose, was the perfect lesson instantly delivered as to why people shouldn't listen at doors. 'No, chef,' reiterated maybe-boyfriend, for chef again was bringing up the hospital. 'They'd definitely have me as an informer if they find out I've gone to the hospital.' He said then that his eyes would be fine and for chef to stop fussing, that soon they'd clear and become as they were before. 'We don't know that,' said chef. 'We don't know what they threw at you, what he threw at you, and you're saying it doesn't hurt but still, you can't open them so we're going to the hospital. Who knows,' he then added, 'maybe we'll bump into *"no harm like but"* down there as well.' 'I suppose they weren't expecting a fight,' said maybe-boyfriend, not heeding chef's last remark but instead following his own train of thought completely. As for me, listening to them, it seemed obvious there'd been another fight, and as usual over chef's fruitiness. But I realised that wasn't the case by maybe-boyfriend's next comment. 'I mean, seein' as I was on my own like,' he said, 'outnumbered, then he chucked that stuff and I couldn't see, and even after I heard you run up, chef, still we were out-numbered. So how'd you do it? How'd *you* — the poof, the dolly, never to be taken seri-ously — how'd you, all by yourself, scare the lot of them away?' Chef shrugged, which maybe-boyfriend didn't see, and he said, 'Ach,' and it was an evasive 'ach' or maybe a dismissive 'ach,' indicating this was weary-ing as a topic of conversation. His gaze though, which also maybe-boyfriend couldn't see, had wandered to his knife. It was still bloodied, still standing upright, still stuck in the table, but then chef quietly removed it from the table and placed it, still quietly, into the sink. He made moves then to take the wet cloth away from maybe-boyfriend's eyes but maybe-boyfriend resisted. He scraped his chair round, elbowing chef out of the way. 'Clear off, chef,' he said. 'Leave it. It's fine. They're not hurting,' but chef insisted he have a look for himself. I wanted to see too, because did he need the hospital or did he not need the hospital? Was he my maybe-boyfriend or wasn't he my maybe-boyfriend? Some invisible presence though, even now, stayed me still.

Mostly so far, during their exchange, my attention had been on maybe-boyfriend because why wouldn't it be on maybe-boyfriend? But now I glanced at chef and instantly got a shock. The expression on his face — intense, uncouched, for he believed himself unobserved, therefore no reason for couching — was one of love. This was not a 'best friend' look of love, or a dispassionate, 'concerned for all mankind' look of love. There was no 'maybe' category about this look either. I had never — certainly not for my maybe-boyfriend — seen such a look on chef's face before. Then again, I had not often looked at chef, not at his face, not really. This was just chef, the bent guy, the harmless guy, the one to be protected by the other guys; the one also to be condescended to, amused by, especially during the times he went into one of his food fits. At bottom, I'd supposed that chef was to be felt sorry for, and again not a proper sorry but one of those 'it must be awful to be him so I'm glad I'm not him' type of sorries. Not really to be regarded, not perceived as on the same level. Now though, it seemed to me, I was seeing this person for the first time. I understood now that this was why my instincts had stayed me, had prevented me from making my presence known. I'd even had premonition shudders, second time now to have had them without Milkman being involved. And now chef was removing the dishcloth and, as he did so, that look on his face increased and shocked me further. He brought his hand over to maybe-boyfriend's face — and maybe-boyfriend let him. This was no 'Let me have a look then' rough male fumble. Wasn't even to maybe-boyfriend's injured eyes that he brought his hand. He had placed it on his cheek. Then he stroked the cheek, once, bringing his hand down, then shifting it gently, slowly, over to the other cheek. Again maybe-boyfriend let him, keeping his own eyes, all the time, closed. I saw then that the blood from earlier, those splotches, hadn't been from maybe-boyfriend's eyes but were coming from his nose. He brushed chef's hand aside at that moment to wipe at them. Then he pushed chef's hand away again, then again, which was what I would have expected him to have done right away. At this point there was no speaking, just that gentle hand-removing and quiet hand-replacing, one set of eyes closed, the other open, maybe-boyfriend on the chair, chef beside him, leaning over him, standing up.

Maybe-boyfriend then said, 'Stop. Stop, chef. We can't do this. We can't keep doing this.' Then, in support of his words, his hand came up and again pushed chef's hand away. So he pushed, but *he* returned, then maybe-boyfriend pushed again, not strongly. Then he halted. There was no cursing, no *'Fuck off, chef. What are you doin'? I'm not like that.'* No surprise either between them, the surprise and unexpectedness at what was happening in that kitchen between those men was turning out to be only so for me. And now maybe-boyfriend, after pushing chef off, stopped and he took hold of this other man's arms and with his own eyes still closed, he held them. He leaned into them, into chef's middle, with chef bending over till his face was in maybe-boyfriend's hair. One of them then moaned, then there was, 'Leave it. It's over, chef, leave it,' but when chef released his grip to step away, perhaps to leave it, maybe-boyfriend turned his own face up and pulled him down towards him yet again.

This was when I pulled round into the living room, for no, I thought. I knew what was coming and this was not for my eyes to see or my ears to hear. Hold on, I then thought. What do you mean not for your eyes and ears? This is your maybe-boyfriend, maybe-boyfriend too, of the oh-so-recent *'you confound me, maybe-girlfriend, always hard to second-guess, impossible to connect with'*. But how long? How long have them two . . . ? I seemed to slip into a state of incomprehension whilst fully comprehending at the same time. And now they'd stopped murmuring which I guessed meant, though I dared not look, the second Gaultier kiss of the night was in process. After that, the murmuring started up once more. 'Wrong person,' said maybe-boyfriend — again meaning me — and chef said, '. . . for you, all for you, did it for you because . . .' 'Afraid. Risky. Too risky . . . What an idjit! . . . What a scared idjit! . . . If they'd killed you! If those lot . . . You could have died and never would I have been able —' This last could have been either chef or maybe-boyfriend. I wondered if my legs would get me to the front door. Meanwhile, I carried on standing, slumping, against the wall to the side of the kitchen in maybe-boyfriend's living room where the front door had been busted. And why it had been busted, why his compulsive hoarding had been interrupted, I no longer knew nor cared. As for the telephone fight, our recent fight — *given that now he and chef . . . that he and him . . . that they . . .* — what had that telephone fight really been about? So much for thinking maybe-boyfriend unstudied, uncomplicated, free from deception, the man who eschewed protections for his heart when here he was, confirming to chef, and to myself, that he too, had been a 'settler', had chosen some safety-net wrong person instead of the right person. What an idjit me, I thought, and I meant in thinking I'd protected myself, believing myself safe from the wrong-spouse category by staying in the maybe-category when it now turns out a person can be done to death in the maybe-category as well. The truth was dawning on me of how terrifying it was not to be numb, but to be aware, to have facts, retain facts, be present, be adult. It was while in the middle of maybe-boyfriend's continued declaration of being an idjit and of my berating myself also for being an idjit, that chef returned the three of us to the moment by demanding the hospital once more.

His tone had changed. Sharp, stern, commanding. Even when maybe-boyfriend said, 'It's nearly back, nearly normal. See, m'eyes are coming back. I can see a bit already,' chef still said, 'We're going, but give me a minute till I throw on another shirt.' I panicked, for with chef about to enter the living room to head upstairs — *He keeps his shirts here? Well, of course he keeps his shirts here!* — he'd discover me, and that frightened me because chef now did frighten me, not being the man I'd thought until now he was. But then, who had I thought him? I hadn't considered him. Hadn't found him particularly friendly, but nor had that bothered me because in the whole hierarchy of importance, he hadn't been in that hierarchy. But not harmless. This man, I could now see, was not harmless. Considering how proprietorial he got around food, what on earth would he be like over rights in a man? Then I thought of the knife, his knife, bloody, in the sink, still bloody. Thought too, that I might faint even though never in my life had I fainted. But I was light-headed, warm, oozy. There was a buzzing, insect-type swarming going on around me or within me, and by now, of course, those new familiars, the shudders, were firmly running up and down my lower spine and legs. There came further sounds then, intimate, from within the kitchen, moans suggestive of, at the very least, further Gaultier behaviour. One of them then said, 'Husband,' then there was, 'Let's chuck this. Why are we here anyway? Let's go to South America. We'll go to Buenos Aires — Cuba! Let's go to Cuba. I like Cuba. You'll like Cuba,' with me thinking, *Husband! Cuba! Let's!* — when me and him couldn't make it beyond a maybe-relationship or get as far as down the road to the red-light street.

I went unseen, across the haphazard room, out the busted door, down the path and away along that meander-cut-through. They never knew I'd been there, though as I went, I played out in my head what would have happened *if.* What if, to keep this ordinary, to make it normal, to cancel it out, I were to sneak out the front door only to make a noise of going back in again? They'd think I was turning up for the first time. I'd notice the busted door, shout immediately for ex-maybe-boyfriend. Ex-maybe-boyfriend and chef in the kitchen would have time then, physically to draw apart. They'd compose themselves and quickly do couching and editing before I entered. Ex-maybe-boyfriend would shout, 'In here, in the kitchen, maybe-girlfriend,' and I'd go in and there they'd be, two friends, knife in sink, out of sight, no longer calling for explanation. Ex-maybe-boyfriend's eyes and the blood though, would remain as before. Chef would demand hospitals and ex-maybe-boyfriend would reject hospitals. Nothing intimate, nothing tender, none of that intensity of look or of their touching. I would gasp, maybe scream, rush over, take hold of ex-maybe-boyfriend. 'What happened, maybe-boyfriend? Oh God! What happened?' and they'd explain, or let me infer, that homophobes in the area had again set upon chef which meant we'd get through it, we'd improvise, we'd keep it vague and dishonest. There'd be nothing of contradictory sentiment, nothing irreconcilable. Just chef getting attacked and then protected as usual. What neither would say, what certainly I would not say, as I hadn't, would be, 'Perhaps it's time we three had a talk.'

So it hadn't been a fight, not another hauling of reckonings, decrying of insufficiencies, mutual accusing. No shouting, no sulking. I knew though, that I wouldn't see ex-maybe-boyfriend, or step into his house, again. As I walked along in the night, heading, it seemed, to the taxi rank, and just as when I'd left the chip shop earlier, I couldn't feel my legs. I could see my legs, see the ground, but impossible it was to get a connection with them. Reaching my hands to my thighs, purposely I felt them, pressed them, doing so unobtrusively, however, because as usual now with me, I had that feeling of being observed.

But no anger. I didn't feel angry. I knew though, that in there, underneath the numbness, the anger must exist. At ex-maybe-boyfriend. At chef. At first brother-in-law for inception of the stories, then for spreading of his stories, including the latest of how foolish I was to cheat on Milkman in broad daylight with that boy from across town my own age. Anger also at the gossips, for embellishing brother-in-law's stories, for fabricating their own stories. At the sycophants who resented me and the chip-shop keepers and all those general storekeepers, who in time would feel pressured to present to me anything of their wares they thought I might like to have. It was missing, gone away, this anger, and, as with the legs which I could see but couldn't feel, and the ground I knew was there but above which I seemed to be floating, it was as if I had no right to be angry because if I'd managed this differently it wouldn't now be my fault. If only I'd done such and such instead of such and such, gone there instead of there, said that and not that, or looked different, or hadn't gone out that day with *Ivanhoe* or that night or that week or anytime during the last two months when I'd let him catch sight of me and want me. Here I stumbled and it was then the white van drew up alongside me. The passenger door opened and that sensation of *'not going freshly into that place of terror'* settled upon me once more.

I got in as if it was natural, as if this was not the first time of van, of this nondescript, played-down, most-important vehicle. Before I myself could do so, he leaned over and, close as millimetres, without touching, without looking, pulled the door to at my end. He had shifted some long-lens camera from the passenger seat, placing it in the roomy compartment bit of the van between us. Also in this compartment were a few small medicine bottles holding many of those shiny black pills with the white dots in the middle of them, one of which was still in my handbag. After closing my door, he leaned back into his seat and started up the engine. Then together, as a proper couple, we moved off. It was strange though, that after that whole build-up, after the last bastion of *'mustn't get in his vehicles',* of being warned, not just by myself but by longest friend from primary school, *'that whatever you do, no matter what, friend, do not get in his vehicles',* once I did step over that threshold, I would have imagined — two months earlier certainly I would have imagined — that doing so would have produced much more tumult and emotion than this. There was no tumult. No emotion. Here was this thing that happened for always I knew it was going to happen, for it had been telling me for ages that it was coming and that it was going to happen. And now it was beginning. What was there then, to get emotional and tumultuous about? What remained was to get in, to get it over. And it wasn't that consciously I thought, *may as well have me 'cos he knew all along he was going to have me and I can't stop this, can't stop him from having me;* or that here I was, journeying now to have done to me what I should have accepted long ago was going to be done to me. Instead it was that by this time of van, I'd been adapted into some hypnotised, debilitated state. Ex-maybe-boyfriend himself had said, 'Don't know, maybe-girl, but . . . look at your face and it's as if your sense organs are disappearing or as if they've already disappeared.' Some things stick. That stuck. I wished he had not commented on the dispossession of my face.

Looking ahead as always, Milkman said, 'That's that done. Taken care of.' His voice was quiet, unhurried, not pleasant. Then, with his next words, he sounded appreciative, even surprised. 'That was a turn-up. Bet they didn't reckon on yon squireman with his knives. But that'll stop it. They'll leave it now, leave him now. As for the other, the one with the cars — the erstwhile attachment — he'll be fine. No consequence of flag or of informership will come upon him. It was that you misesteemed him, didn't you? A maybe-boyfriend, wasn't he? No worries, princess. We won't have to concern ourselves there anymore.'

He drove me home without another word, and still without looking at me, until we reached my ma's front door. His not speaking during the journey was clever, but then Milkman had been clever. This was the perfect build-up, the creation of the optimal best atmosphere in which I was to hear and take in his last words. We drove out of ex-maybe-boyfriend's side of town, down into town, out the other side of town, keeping to the right geography and passing all my personal landmarks. After that it was more interface roads, then into my own area where as a properly established couple we

502

parked outside my mother's front door. And I knew it was that I should have been shocked, should have been revolted, should have been at least astonished instead of not even surprised that here I was in this notorious vehicle, sitting inches from this notorious man. But there was no choice. It was that there was no more alternative. Ill-equipped I'd been to take in what everybody else from the outset easily had taken in: I was Milkman's *fait accompli* all along.

Still in his van, in the dark, he turned off the engine, turned too, in his seat towards me. Finally I felt the gaze, the long, slow gaze, upon me, because now he could look, could allow himself to look. Here was success, completion, property. In contrast, I was the one who remained this time looking ahead. He took off his gloves and said, 'Very good. Excellent,' though I think more to himself than that it was calculation I should hear it. He leaned over then and lifted his fingers to my face. They paused in mid-air, very still, very close. Then he changed his mind and withdrew them. He sat back in his seat. Then came his last words. He said that I was beautiful, did I know I was beautiful, that I must believe I was beautiful. He said he'd made arrangements, that we'd go somewhere nice, do something nice, that he'd take me to a surprise nice place for our first date. He said I'd have to miss my Greek and Roman but that he was sure I wouldn't mind missing my Greek and Roman. Besides, he said, did I really need all that Greek and Roman? Something for us to decide, he said, later on. He said then that for as long as I remained living in the family home, he'd call up to my door but wait outside and that I was to go to him. He said then he'd call at seven the following night in one of his cars. 'Not this,' he added, dismissing the van, mentioning instead one of those alpha-numericals. For my part — here he meant what I could do for him, how I could make him happy — I could come out the door on time and not keep him waiting. Also I could wear something lovely, he said. 'Not trousers. Something lovely. Some feminine, womanly, elegant, nice dress.'

SEVEN

Three times in my life I've wanted to slap faces and once in my life I've wanted to hit someone in the face with a gun. I did do the gun but I have never slapped anybody. Of the three I've wanted to slap, one was eldest sister when she rushed in on the day in question to tell me the state forces had shot and killed Milkman. She looked gleeful, excited, that this man she thought was my lover, this man she thought had mattered to me, was dead. Openly she scanned my face to see how I would take it and even in my obstinacy — which had taken me, in opposition to Milkman and to the rumours about me and Milkman, to a deeper, more entrapped place than ever I had been in — still I could see how unconscious of herself she was at this point. She thinks this will teach me a lesson, I thought. Not because of the political scene and of what he had represented in it. Not because of what his

505

killers represented. That was nothing. This was everything to do with her not wanting me to have what long ago she had stopped allowing herself. Like her, I must be content, must make do, not with the man I desired as she thought, with the man I had loved and lost as loved and lost she had, but with some unwanted substitute who might now, after Milkman, come along. She continued to look transported, far from that state of grief she'd been walking about in for ages. She was not though, going to have her transports at my expense. Stop being happy, that's not to make you happy — *slap!* — was how my thinking went. For actual response, even as she awaited my reaction, I kept my face, as was usual now with me, nearly-remote and almost-inaccessible. Then, with a hint of feigned emotion, just enough to convey that for a moment, for one tiny moment, I was pointing out some mildly diverting curiosity, I said, 'You look like you're having an orgasm now.'

Her glee — not so much either, that sickening triumphant glee that some people get who certainly deserve to have faces slapped, but the glee of someone who finds herself alive for an instant in all the awfulness when her usual condition was to feel completely dead — well, that glee ceased, as I knew it would, for I had got her where I wanted her, where I had intended to get her, right at her centre. That's where I would have been got had she, or anybody, said those words to me. She slapped my face then, a recoil reaction, because I had got in where I'd no right to get in and even though in the moment I considered myself of every right, I did not, could not, slap her back. After the initial satisfaction of shocking her, of shaming her out of her victory, already I was regretting my words. So enough. I wanted her to go now, to take herself and her make-do husband, and his dirty slanders which had started everything, and to go now. Things were not gentle, not ever, then.

She went, loaded with grief again, standing at the foot of the cross again, and as for glee, I had not felt any of that. I wasn't happy he was dead, not glad — or maybe I was, for really, why should not I be? What I did know was that relief was coursing through me with an intensity I had not ever in my life felt before. My body was proclaiming, *'Halleluiah! He's dead. Thank fuck halleluiah!'* even if those were not the actual words at the forefront of my mind. What was at the forefront was that maybe I'll calm down now, maybe I'll get better now, maybe this'll be the end of all that *'don't let it be*

Milkman, oh please don't let it be Milkman', no more having to watch my back, expecting to turn a corner to have him fall into step with me, no more being followed, being spied upon, photographed, misperceived, encircled, anticipated. No more being commanded. No more capitulation such as the night before when I got beat down enough, had become indifferent to my fate enough as to have stepped inside his van. Most of all there would be no more worry about ex-maybe-boyfriend being killed by a carbomb. So it was, while standing in our kitchen digesting this bit of consequence, that I came to understand how much I'd been closed down, how much I'd been thwarted into a carefully constructed nothingness by that man. Also by the community, by the very mental atmosphere, that minutiae of invasion. As for his death, they had ambushed him late morning as he pulled up in that white van outside the parks & reservoirs, which meant that after six false starts, they had got their man at last. Before Milkman, they had shot a binman, two bus-drivers, a road sweeper, a real milkman who was our milkman, then another person who didn't have any blue-collar or service-industry connections — all in mistake for Milkman. Then they shot Milkman. Then they played down the mistaken shootings while playing up the intended shooting, as if it had been Milkman and only Milkman they had shot all along.

Certain parts of the media, however, critical of the state, were not prepared to let them away with it. Headlines such as 'MILKMAN SHOT IN MISTAKE FOR MILKMAN' and 'BUTCHER, BAKER, CANDLESTICK-MAKER — WATCH OUT' had already begun to appear. These were followed by newsreel and further print-runs, reminding the state of its other blunders, its perversions, its secret army outfits, its drive-by shootings, its very own dishevelled status of extra-special beyond-the-pale. Eventually the state responded by admitting that yes, it had precision-targeted a few accidental people in pursuance of intended people, that mistakes had been made, that that had been regrettable, but that the past should be put behind, that there was no point in dwelling. Most of all, in spite of target error and the unforeseen human factor, it reassured all right-thinking people that they could rest easy, now that a leading terrorist-renouncer had permanently been got out of the way. 'Not to get into equivocation or rhetorical stunts or sly debater tricks or savage glee,' said their front-of-shop man, 'but we consider this a job well done.' No display, therefore, of gloating, of one-upmanship, of triumphalism because triumphalism was not the path to go for public presentation packages. Not just *public* presentation packages. On hearing the news, and even in the privacy of the subtext of my own mind where nobody but me could witness me being me, also out of fear of being judged in the area some traitorous, cold-hearted bad person, I myself was trying not to be happy. But I kept thinking of my narrow escape from whatever he had planned for me that coming evening and I was happy — happy too though, that no mocking, exposing media spotlight was being shone that moment upon me.

So his death hit the headlines but that wasn't all that hit the headlines. After they shot him, and the six unfortunates who'd got in the way of him, it was revealed, along with his age, abode, 'husband to' and 'father of', that Milkman's name really was Milkman. This was shocking. 'Can't be right,' cried people. 'Far-fetched. Weird. Silly even, to have the name Milkman.' But when you think about it, why was that weird? Butcher's a name. Sexton's a name. So is Weaver, Hunter, Roper, Cleaver, Player, Mason,

Thatcher, Carver, Wheeler, Planter, Trapper, Teller, Doolittle, Pope and Nunn. Years later I came across a Mr Postman who was a librarian, so they're all over the place, those names. As for 'Milkman' and the acceptability or not of 'Milkman', what would Nigel and Jason, our guardians of the names, have to say about that? Not just our Nigel and Jason either. What of equivalent clerks and clerkesses protecting against names proscribed in other renouncer areas? Even Roisins and Marys guarding against opposing forbidden names in 'over the road' defender-run areas? Alarmists, meanwhile, continued to debate over the provenance of the Milkman name. Was it one of ours? One of theirs? Was it from over the road? Over the water? Over the border? Should it be allowed? Banned? Binned? Laughed at? Discounted? What was the consensus? *'An unusual name,'* everyone, with nervous caution, after great deliberation, said. It broke bounds of credibility, said the news, but lots of things in life break bounds of credibility. Breaking credibility, I was coming to understand, seemed to be what life was about. Nevertheless, the news of this Milkman name unsettled people; it cheated them, frightened them and there seemed no way round a feeling of embarrassment either.

511

When considered a pseudonym, some code-name, 'the milkman' had possessed mystique, intrigue, theatrical possibility. Once out of symbolism, however, once into the everyday, the banal, into any old Tom, Dick and Harryness, any respect it had garnered as the cognomen of a high-cadre paramilitary activist was undercut immediately and, just as immediately, fell away. People consulted phonebooks, encyclopaedias, reference books of names to see if anyone, anywhere in the world had been called Milkman. Many were left stranded, uncomprehending, with nothing for it but to grow speculation, both in the media and in the districts, over just who exactly this Milkman person was. Had he been the chilling, sinister paramilitary everyone here had always believed him to be? Or was it the case that poor Mister Milkman had been nothing but another innocent victim of state murder after all?

Whatever he had been and whatever he'd been called, he was gone, so I did what usually I did around death which was to forget all about it. The whole shambles — as in the old meaning of shambles, as in slaughterhouse, blood-house, meat market, business-as-usual — once again took hold. Deciding to miss my French night class, I

512

put on my make-up and got ready to go to the club. This was to the brightest, the busiest, the most popular of the eleven drinking-clubs existing in our small area and as for going: drinking-clubs were the exact places you would go, exactly what you would do, when both hyper and deadened and in need of alcohol.

Not long after I arrived, I left my drinking-friends to go to the toilets. I hadn't spoken of the shooting to these friends and they had said nothing of it to me. This was normal. There were friends for drinking with and friends for revealing to. I had one friend for revealing, but full-on drinking-sessions weren't really longest friend from primary school's scene. I pushed open the toilets door and as I did so, that man who was really a boy, Somebody McSomebody, pushed in behind me. By now in our non-relationship relationship he had dropped his amateur stalking and instead, like the other lickspittles in the area who had believed me mistress, had moved to bowing and scraping and pretending to like me. Ma though, about him, continued to get it wrong. 'Such a nice wee boy,' she said. 'Sturdy. Reliable. Right religion — and there's those nice love letters he's for-putting for you through our letterbox so would you not date him? Would

you not think of marryin' him?' But my
mother, desperate to get us wed, to anybody,
before the old age of twenty, knew nothing
because she was still in her day with her
people, not realising it was now my day with
different people, but the nice wee boy,
Somebody McSomebody, pushed into the
toilets and shoved me up against the sink.
He was holding a handgun and it was stuck
in my breast so then I knew — for already I
had suspected — that the death of Milkman
wouldn't mean, for me, the end of Milkman. Because of their stories; because they
thought Milkman had gained ownership;
because of my haughtiness; because my
protection was now dead; because it was
now being put about I'd tried to evade
retribution for cheating on him with a car
mechanic; because after any significant
death that was communal rather than personal always there was allowed that extra
bit of anarchy — because of all these be-
causes, perhaps it suited the more extreme
in the area to push the rumour out completely and have it be me and not that state
death squad who'd orchestrated the killing
of Milkman all along. Even at the outer
limits of absurdity and contradiction people
will make up anything. Then they will
believe and build on this anything. It was

true that, given the time and place, I might have been scary, walking around, terrorising the neighbourhood with 'How Ivan Ivanovich Quarrelled with Ivan Nikiforovich', but it wasn't just me. In their own idiosyncratic ways, an awful lot of other people were pretty scary here as well.

And now, returning to his former stalking personality, it seemed McSomebody was taking advantage of the dead Milkman situation to nip in quick and get his own back. To my surprise, he was now intermingling his stalk-talk with a dollop of anti-stalk-talk — perhaps to wrest back pride and control after being flouted twice by me as well as feeling compelled to genuflect with *'Here, Your Majesty, have this, Your Majesty'* every time I, as one of Milkman's possessions, walked by. Easier on the mind perhaps, to have me now the intemperate one, doggedly determined in my pursuit of him. 'Just leave us alone!' he cried. 'All we ever wanted was for you to leave us alone. Stop following us. Stop entrapping us. What are you planning to do to us? Get off us. Why can't you take on board you're not wanted, that your advances are not to be accepted, that it's thanks but no thanks? You mean nothing to us, we don't even think of you and another thing, you can't just act with impunity, carrying on as if it didn't happen, as if you didn't start this, as if you didn't stir things up. You're a cat — that's right, you heard us, a cat — a double cat! We don't think you're up to the level of even being a cat. But don't you push us so far because this is aggravated harassment.' He was right. It was aggravated harassment. Before Milkman, he'd sent a letter — one of those love letters ma in her ignorance had referred to his putting through our letterbox. In it he'd threatened to kill himself in our front garden only we didn't have a garden. In a second letter, this was amended to 'outside your front door'. Now, at this encounter in the toilets, his written threat of suicide seemed to have got turned into my written threat of suicide. In my hand-delivered missive to him apparently I'd warned I was going to take my life outside his door to make him feel guilty for not wanting me. This set me wondering if his words were shadow-speak for him planning to kill me right now inside these toilets by this sink. Clearly then, he was still attracted. Equally clearly, he was furious about it. If there was one thing McSomebody could never be accused of amongst all the things he could be accused of, that would be of not thinking complexly. Meantime I was at a loss on how to respond to his words.

'This is not the sort of place, you sub-cat,' he began, but then he ran out of words, too suffused with rage, I suppose, to complete on what he'd set out to convey to me. Not necessary though, for it was easy to read between the lines. He meant this drinking-club, this district, was not the sort of place into which you strolled without letters of introduction, without seals of approval; nor was it a place in which the harmonious tended to happen — the temptation to be animal, to be elemental, often overpowering in times of bloody conflict for the more as-censional side of a person to prevail. He was saying that anything went here, that I should know anything went here given I was from here. As he spoke my mind was rac-ing, thinking, this boy is stupid but he's dangerous stupid, and he wants to fuck me and he wants to beat me and from the look of things might even now want to shoot me. But then, already he'd made up his mind. I knew he wanted revenge, that for a long time he'd nursed revenge — even from before the era of Milkman. He'd made his decision because I was supposed to have been a nice girl and further, his nice girl, but some mistake had occurred which confused him and insulted him but because of Milkman setting his sights, he'd been forced to retreat and keep resentment in check. He could not then have called for justice. But now he could call for justice. Indeed, he could administer the justice. With Milkman out of the way, with everyone just getting on with it, what was there, who was there, to stop him after all?

'Do you think anybody here gives a fuck if we teach you a —'

Not sure, unsure, of all he was to say next 'cos he never got saying it. I snapped the gun off him, getting it by the barrel, the muzzle, the end, whatever that bit was called. He wasn't expecting that and before I did it, neither was I. Again that long-ago phrase — *a recklessness, an abandonment, a rejection of me by me* — had returned to me. I was going to die anyway, wouldn't live long anyway, any day now I'd be dead, all the time, violently murdered — and that, I now understand, gave a certain edge. It offered a different perspective, a freeing-up of the fear option. That was why too, I wasn't freshly in that place of terror that he thought, with his gun, he had just put me in. So I grabbed it and I hit him in the face with it, I mean the balaclava with it, with the handle, the butt, whatever that bit was called. It wasn't though, a satisfying crunch of metal on bone, of someone having their head broke open which until that moment I wouldn't have thought I'd be so bloodthirsty for. It was a clumsy feeble hit and before I could gather myself to have another go he punched me and grabbed the gun off me. Then he hit me in the face with it. I wasn't wearing a balaclava. After that, he pulled me up the wall and dug the gun in my breast as before.

That was all he was able to do because something else he hadn't reckoned on, hadn't overhauled his blueprint on, was women, particularly women in toilets, these women, in these toilets. These women took it upon themselves to jump McSomebody which was then what most of them did. The gun fell out of the scrum, then a second gun fell out also. Nobody seemed bothered by the guns and I too, glancing at them, wasn't bothered by them. They seemed cumbersome and irrelevant, or maybe just irrelevant. This called for bare hands, stilettos, booted feet, flesh-on-flesh, bone-on-bone, hearing the cracks, causing the cracks, venting all that pent-up anger. The guns were ignored therefore, not wanted, kicked about during the kicking of McSomebody. Meanwhile, I watched this new development keeping well to the side of the sink where he had shoved me. Had to. The pile of women, with him somewhere in amongst them, at that moment was blocking the only door.

So they beat him up. And it was for his behaviour that they beat him up, not for the irritation of guns, for wearing a balaclava when everybody knew who he was anyway; not for threatening me either, a woman, one of their soul sisters. No. It was for being a man and coming into the Ladies unannounced. He had shown disrespect, been dismissive of female fragilities and delicacies and sensibilities, had shown no courtesy, displayed no chivalry, no gallantry, no honour. It was that he had no manners basically. If he chose to walk in on them while they were applying lipstick, adjusting hair, sharing secrets, changing sanitary towels, then so be it, there would be consequences. And here they were, those consequences, happening now. After the current consequences, after they told their men which they were going to do in a minute, there would be further consequences. Just as that state task force then, hadn't killed Milkman to do me a favour, this rescue too, hadn't been so planned. Help was help though, no matter from what quarter. This meant that once again, twice in one day, I'd been handed a gratuity, a perquisite, some residual but much appreciated side effect; fortunately also, I'd been handed it at just the right moment in time.

So he was done in by them. Then he was done in by their boyfriends. Then next I heard — without asking, because never I asked, because always I would be minding my business when these things would come at me — he was had up at a kangaroo court. 'Courts happened. They just did. This one had confusion to start with over what exactly to charge him with. Then someone piped up with the charge of one-quarter rape.

And that was what they did. Amongst themselves, and while stringently codifying into a range of pernickety, encyclopaedic, rather impressive though obsessive hierarchies, our renouncers divided and subdivided all possible crimes and misdemeanours, all anti-social behaviours that could be committed by us as transgressors, miscreants and contemptible scoundrels of the area, until in the end they had what could only be described as an owner and user's guide. With their preciosity and overfine distinctions, they proved themselves schoolmasters and fusspots in this area — except when it came to women's issues.

Women's issues were baffling, demanding, awful bloody annoying, not least because anybody with an ounce of clergy could see that women who had issues — as evidenced by our sample grouping who still met weekly in that backyard shed — were completely off their heads. In those days, however, with times achanging, with the approach of the Eighties, it was getting that women had to be cajoled, had to be kept in with. What with female-orientation and female-amalgamation and women-this and women-that, also with talk of the sexes now being equal — seemed you could easily spark an international incident if you didn't walk out your door and at least make polite gesture to some of their hairbrained, demented ideas. That was why our renouncers tormented themselves and bent over backwards, trying their damnedest to please and to include into the discourse our beyond-the-pale women. At last they considered they'd done so by coming up with the invention of rape with subsections — meaning that in our district there could now be full rape, three-quarter rape, half rape or one-quarter rape — which our renouncers said was better than rape divided by two — as in 'rape' and 'not rape' which, they added, were the acceptable categories in most fiefdoms as well as in the burlesque courts of the occupiers. 'Streaks ahead therefore we are,' they maintained, and they meant in terms of modernity, of conflict resolution and of gender progressiveness. 'Look at us,' they said. 'We take things seriously.' Rape and all that jazz was practically what it was called. I'm not making this up. They made it up. Excellent, they said. That'll do for them, meaning women, meaning justice for the women with the issues as well as for women without issues because not all women had issues. With that, one-quarter rape became our district's default sexual charge.

And Somebody McSomebody was charged with it, for peeking about in women's toilets, even though none of the women from the toilets had mentioned rape or demanded to have it admitted that that was what it was. This was serious, declared the renouncers, and they wanted to know what McSomebody had to say for himself. But it was a game — more toy soldiers on toy battlefields, more toy trains in the attic, hard men in their teens, hard men in their twenties, hard men in their thirties, in their forties, with the mentality being toys even if it was far from toys these men were playing with. So with this toys outlook they were steeped in, and with the usual rumours everyone was steeped in, I didn't care what they charged him with. I didn't care what they did to him, what they did to each other. I had sought none of this, did not want any of it, had not asked for information or ever wanted to know. In the end I wasn't vouched to warrant which was fine by me as I wouldn't have warranted anyway, wouldn't have gone anyway, would not — least not voluntarily — have taken part. I heard finally that, as none of the women who'd beaten him up seemed bothered, the coterie sitting in judgement upon McSomebody quietly dropped the quarter-rape charge which had had a random *'oh, how about we just say it was this'* quality to it anyway. Instead they charged him with taking guns unauthorised from dumps to use for getting dates with girls purposes, which was not, they admonished, what guns were supposed to be used for.

Never heard, wasn't interested in what happened to Somebody McSomebody after that kangaroo-court judgement upon him, except that probably it involved him re-jigging his archetype of women's private rooms and of women. As for me, I went back to walking. Not to reading-while-walking. Also I picked up my running. Coming home from work the day after Milkman's death to put on my gear to go call on third brother-in-law, I opened the front door and there were wee sisters standing on the stairs, dressed up. They were in my clothes, my shoes, my accessories, my jewellery, my make-up, plus extra makeshift garments made out of our downstairs back-room curtains. Also they had added garlands, daisy-chains, amateur flounces and once more that premature tinsel from the Christmas box, all improvised too, I supposed, by themselves. I was about to start in because I'd warned them before about messing with my belongings. At that moment though, the three of them in their finery — my finery — were busy on the telephone. They were perched together on the staircase, holding the receiver between them and speaking in unison. 'Yes. Yes. Yes,' they replied. After a pause they said, 'She's here now. We'll tell her.' Then came the usual 'Goodbye', 'Goodbye', 'Farewell', 'Farewell' — also telephone kisses — until painstakingly the call was concluded and everyone had rung off. 'That was mammy,' they said. 'She says you're not to go gallivanting until you make us dinner. She can't because she's busy with the milkman.' They meant real milkman, and they didn't mean either, any innuendo of milkman, though it was evident something other than the platonic was going on round the corner between those two in real milkman's house. Before he'd discharged himself — again characteristic in his contrariety to the hospital's wishes — ma had been spending most of her time down at the hospital and now that he was discharged, she was ever in his house, bringing him cakes, feeding him soup, tending his wounds, checking what she looked like in the mirror, also reading books and newspapers to him, all day long — and all night long too.

'Goodbye,' sang youngest sister and I lifted her up and said, 'It's okay. The telephone call's over.' 'I know,' she said. 'I'm just making sure.' She wrapped her legs round my waist then, touched my black eye and said, 'Did you get that from waltzing? We got these from waltzing,' then the three stuck out their limbs to display scratches and bruises, strongly identical scratches and bruises, strongly aligned too, on their bodies, not quite, but almost, in the same place. 'These contusions were sustained,' explained eldest of wee sisters, 'whilst playing the international couple.' Ah, I thought, so *that*'s what all that prancing in the street's about. Here was the answer to a puzzle that had been playing around the fringes of my mind because all the little girls had taken to dressing up and dancing about, not just in our street but in every street of the area — even across the interface road in defender areas, for I'd had a peek in and noticed them one day as I was walking and reading my way into town. All these little girls — 'our side', 'their side' — were dressed in long clothes and high heels and were falling over as they played the international couple, proving this couple — ex-maybe-boyfriend's parents — meant very much more here than mere ballroom-dancing champions of the world. They had achieved that outstanding status of straddling the sectarian divide, a feat probably meaning nothing outside the sectarian areas in question, but which inside equated with the most rare and hopeful occurrence in the world. At first I hadn't paid attention, for the usual reason of wee kids doing wee kid things, but it got to the point where there were so many of them — dressed-up, paired off, dotted about, waltzing, getting in everybody's way, getting on everybody's nerves, falling over, getting up, dusting off and waltzing off again — that the phenomenon could not but encroach into the most thickest of thick-skinned minds. And now wee sisters were explaining the joy that was to be had from playing Mr and Mrs International. 'It's brilliant,' they confided, 'only it nearly was spoilt because of those wee boys.' They meant the little boys of the area for the little girls of the area had been trying for ages to complete the aesthetic by roping in the little boys to play ex-maybe-boyfriend's internationally waltzing father while they themselves played the star of the show, his mother, but that had gone no-where as the little boys hadn't wanted to play. Instead they wanted to continue throwing miniature anti-personnel devices at the foreign soldiers from the country 'over the water' any time a formation of them appeared on our streets. No matter the scolds, the cajoleries, the tears from the little girls, the little boys stubbornly refused to take part. This left the little girls no choice but to double-up and take turns at being both ex-maybe-boyfriend's glamor-ous, super-beautiful mother as well as his not-so-glamorous, or interesting — least not to the little girls — boringly dressed famous father and that had been the procedure until it became clear none of the little girls wanted to be him at all. Every one wanted to be her, to be ex-maybe-boyfriend's amaz-ing championship mother, so they dispensed with the father, either pairing off themselves as two supremely costumed waltzing women, or else just pretending to have a male prop dancing partner, 'for that way,' explained wee sisters, 'you get to dress up and be *her* every time'. This explained the colour — for there had been an explosion of colour — plus fabric, accessories, make-up, feathers, plumes, tiaras, beads, sparkles, tassels, lace, ribbons, ruffles, layered petticoats, lipsticks, eyeshadows, even fur — I had glimpsed fringed fur — high heels too, which belonged to the little girls' big sisters and which didn't fit which was why periodically the little girls fell over, sustaining injuries. 'But the thing is,' reiterated wee sisters, 'and you don't seem overjoyed by this, middle sister, *you get to be her every time*!' Wee sisters hammered this home, hammering home also, though unconscious of it, that for me this was to be one long getting-over of ex-maybe-boyfriend. Seemed I was to have reminders of him before I even walked out my door. After walking out the door there were further reminders: his parents plastered on billboards, his parents mentioned in every news item, lauded in magazines, praised in newspapers, interviewed on radio stations, imitated by little girls throughout the world and, not least, dancing and looking fabulous on wall murals and on every channel of every TV.

That was why they couldn't possibly take off my garments, wee sisters said, not till they'd played the international couple. They were all set to go and play too, just as soon as I gave them something to eat. Okay, I said, but after I came back from my run they'd better be home and had taken all my stuff off. As it was, they couldn't be allowed my high heels. 'Gimme them,' I said. 'You'll spring them,' and I took them from them, knowing full well they'd just go get them again as soon as I'd gone from the house. I said then, 'And you'd better not have been at my underwear drawer.' 'That's not us,' protested wee sisters. 'That's mammy. Mammy goes there heaps now, just as soon as every day you go to work.'

And yeah. She did. I had been through this too, with her, warning that she was not to mess with my stuff, especially not my underwear, warning also that she was to stay completely out of my room. Ever since her turnaround, this falling in love with real milkman — or not pretending anymore not always to have been in love with real milkman — she kept looking in the mirror and not liking what she saw. She had taken to frowning, holding her breath, pulling her stomach in, then letting her stomach out when she had to because she'd needed to breathe again. Then it was sighing and scrutinising every physical detail and I thought, she's fifty. Far too old to be behaving like that. And there were my clothes. She was rooting in them, though first, said wee sisters, she was rooting in her own belongings, turning every stitch she owned, they said, inside out. She was very sad, they said, because her garments, also every accessory she had, was dowdy, not of the moment, which was why she waited, they said, until after I'd gone to work. That was how the raids started. I caught her at it myself one day just after real milkman came out of hospital. I came home early from work and there she was in my room, sampling away. My wardrobe was open, my chest of drawers was open, my shoe boxes open, my jewellery box open, my make-up case empty with all its contents on her face or else dumped out on my bed. As well as that, she had moved half my stuff into her room and not just my stuff but some of second sister's stuff because, in her banishment, on having to leave in a hurry, second sister hadn't had time to pack and take her gear as well. It was not only me and second sister though. Ma had also gone to visit first and third sisters — tellingly at a time when she knew neither of them would be there. With first sister it was on the pretext of wanting to see her grandchildren, and with third sister it was on the pretext of chivvying as to why there weren't yet grandchildren. In reality though, it was with the intention of raiding their stuff as well. The husbands let her in, and they thought nothing of it, still thinking nothing when she went upstairs ignoring them, coming down later and staggering out their doors with her arms piled high with their wives' stuff. She came home laden, said wee sisters, so all us sisters were finding this real milkman affair revolutionary. As for her long-term pace-praying, her clock-praying, all that fierce virtuous competitive chapel-praying, according to wee sisters, 'She puts Leo Sayer and "When I Need You", and "I Can't Stop Loving You", and "You Make Me Feel Like Dancing" on the record-player instead.' So I came home from work and there she was, fretting over belts, handbags, scarves, mostly though, over how her own body had betrayed her. Without blushing either, or having the grace to look guilty at being caught red-handed, she said, 'Would you never think, daughter mine, to buy high heels with a lesser heel?' Right away I intended anger, to point out her violation in rummaging in what didn't belong to her. How would she like it, I'd ask, if I were to reveal that on setting off for chapel to do her praying, or round to the neighbours to do her gossiping, wee sisters were straight off up to her room? They were in her bed, in her nightclothes, reading her books, doing play-praying, play-gossiping and pretending to make up herbal charmes and harmes and other concoctions, taking turns as often they did, at being her. Because of her panic though, and because she seemed now to have entered some vulnerable, regressed, strange transition period, I found myself handing her a pair of low slingbacks and saying, 'Try these on, ma' instead.

Matters had moved on too, it seemed, throughout the whole of the area regarding real milkman. Even I paid attention to the latest talk of the great gang of pious women — now demoted, ex-pious women — and to that old love rivalry between them being once more stirred up. After first entreating God to spare the life of real milkman and then, when this supplication had been granted, imploring God further for the full recovery of real milkman, some of these women discovered that while they were in chapel, eyes closed, hands clasped, wearing out the pew with piety, invocations and kneecaps, others had taken advantage of their fervent, protracted devotions temporarily to minimise their own devotions to rush to the hospital to see real milkman first. Upon this discovery, everyone became in a hurry. Prayers, when they happened, happened on the hop. The ex-pious women apologised beforehand to God, assuring Him that, of course, this was provisional, that it was only ever going to be provisional, that soon they'd get back to full-on, normal-formal praying but meantime, if it was all right with Him, they'd foreshorten and abridge all items on the prayerlisting — this time not to fit in more prayers but to lessen the prayer-duration by temporarily subtracting most of them from it for now. So it wasn't that they'd completely forgotten the Presence. It was more that they too, like ma, were baking pies, decorating cakes, feeding soup, trying on daughters' clothes, daughters' make-up, daughters' jewellery and springing daughters' heels as they rushed to and from the hospital. Later, when real milkman was out of hospital, still they rushed and were busy, this time to visit him in his house to see how he was settling in back there.

Ma, however, had got the start on them

after receiving the tip-off from Jason. Thanks to Jason, who was in love with Nigel, her own husband, so not at all interested in *that* way in real milkman, ma, on hearing of the shooting, was able to reach the hospital first. Immediately she was pounced upon by the police and taken to some little hospital cupboard-room for questioning. Why did she want to see this man, this terrorist, whom they'd just shot as enemy-of-the-state, they asked? Of course they were seen to be trying their hand, this police, wondering if it might be possible to turn this middle-aged girlfriend of a middle-aged wounded paramilitary into an agent for them. Might they get her to reveal covert renouncer identities for them? planned covert renouncer activities for them? help them displant that diabolical enemy for them? The thing was though, that fast on the heels of ma to the hospital came three further possible middle-aged girlfriends of the same wounded paramilitary. Then another four also turned up. The police ran out of little impromptu hospital cupboard-rooms into which to spirit this potential supergrass demographic. That meant they had to transfer them to the police barracks which, given the growing girlfriend numbers, would no longer keep the situation as stealthy as they, the police, would have liked. This state-security force, stalking the hospital corridors, then intercepted a further two middle-aged girlfriends who also had to be taken in for questioning. By this stage the law must have been scratching its head. 'How many has he? What sort of philanderer is he? Exactly when, in between these love trysts, does Valentino here manage to fit his terrorist activity in?' Before they could attempt an answer it happened again, and the number of middle-aged female informers from our small no-go area was rumoured to swell from ten to eighteen. Frankly, it was unworkable, but not just for the police was it unworkable. The renouncers-of-the-state in our district, faced with the prospect of eighteen ex-pious women whom they knew would have to be psycho-evaluated to uncover if any of them had been flipped as informers, also found the situation unworkable. Not just unworkable — ridiculous. Not just ridiculous — perturbing. And not only in terms of the political situation was it unworkable, ridiculous and perturbing, but also on the more private footing of these women being the district's traditional wives and mothers as well.

'Something's missing. Do you not think something's missing?' one renouncer was said to have asked of another renouncer. The area had become eerily quiet, saturated with quietness. Ghostly, palely quiet it was, as if one hadn't realised just how unquiet it had been until all that undercurrent of persistent rosary-bead clicking and muttering of prayers had stopped. 'It's those pious women,' said another renouncer. 'Ex-pious women. They've stopped that awful murmuring, that persistent low-level pace-praying, that enervating, "teeth on edge" clock-praying, that bursting into hymn without provocation, all this stopping too, owing to the shooting of yon wanker, the one who doesn't love anybody, the one who shouts at children, the one who came home from that country "over the water" after the death of his brother and threw our weapons out into the street that time.' 'We shouldn't have tarred and feathered him,' said another renouncer. 'We should have spirited him to some impromptu little grave, then shot him.' 'Yeah,' said another. 'Then again,' said yet another, 'we must not be hard on ourselves.' This renouncer reminded the others of their fledgling days, also reminding that it had been these self-same women who'd intervened on their 'court proceedings twelve years earlier by turning up and camping right outside their safe-house door.

This had been after the man who didn't love anybody had strewn their guns, had shouted at the children, shouted at his neighbours, with the renouncers then showing up and taking him, along with their rapidly collected arsenal, to the safe house straightaway. In the main, they'd been for killing him, not just for disturbing their belongings, but for strewing them so matter-of-factly into the middle of broad daylight. If that young spotter hadn't acted fast and rushed to warn them of what had happened, any auld military helicopter — come to hover over the area as often they came to hover — most certainly would have caught view of their weapons right away. So they were for killing the man who didn't love anybody except they couldn't because of the women who were in love with him. Ordinarily, these women were obliging, supportive of the efforts of the renouncers. They'd turn out in numbers with binlids, with whistles and they'd warn everybody, including the renouncers, of the approach of the enemy; all for billeting the renouncers too, for tipping them off, for stopping the curfews, for transporting weapons and, of course, there was the expertise of their homespun medical corps. Any renouncer worth his salt would agree there was nothing like getting shot but retaining enough lifeforce to run the warren of side streets and back entries to make it into one of those women's houses — to have your bullet extracted, to have your skin pulled together, to have yourself sewn up or, if no time for sewing, to be held in place with enough nappypins to give you time to outrun the military house-searches which would by now be going on. So you couldn't invent that loyalty. But he'd strewn their guns, which was why they'd taken him to the safe house which wasn't a house really, but one of the chapel's hutments and they did this, not really either, to go through some pro-tracted kangaroo-court procedure, but to get him in there quickly and to shoot him in the head. Barely had they got him over the threshold than those women appeared, strangely kicking up no fuss as they did so. Instead these women set up camp on the street right outside the very hutment door. In silence, they faced the hutment. They looked at the hutment, and not a few — God forbid — even pointed at the hutment. Before long it became clear to the renouncers what those women were about. They knew, and they knew that the women knew they knew, that it would only take one single helicopter to do its flyover and to catch sight of this crowd of women sitting pointing outside a renouncer-run chapel hutment for that hutment then to be earmarked and ransacked by the state. So it was blackmail, even at the same time as it was human inconsistency. Undeniable it was to the renouncers that these women meant their loyal binlids and their loyal whistles, also their loyal sewing-up of arteries. But it was only undeniable to the same extent that they also meant their threatened betrayal of the renouncers should the man who didn't love anybody not be released at once. So everything was unspoken but what wasn't unspoken, for the spokesperson for the women eventually went to the hutment door and banged on it to shout it in at them, was that the man who didn't love anybody was to be released alive. There was to be no corpse, she shouted, but instead their friend was to be fully intact and breathing. When it came to it though, they didn't get all they were after because to save face the renouncers' final judgement was that this milkman of the area had proven another district resistant with anti-social behavioural tendencies not consistent within a standard perimeter of conformability, meaning he qualified as another member of our community's woebegone beyond-the-pales. As such, he was not all there — here they tapped their heads — which meant the death penalty could be eschewed in the interests of being decent to a district mental vulnerable. However, the man who didn't love anybody would not get off scot-free. He was to receive a light-to-moderate beating followed by a tar and feathering, also a warning that next time he endangered them and their weapons, and no matter how many people were in love with him, he would not be treated so very leniently as he was being treated this time. 'But we were too lenient,' they now said, twelve years on from the spirit of that former occasion. And now they were facing, in times remarkably similar, this very same or almost same women ultimatum once more. 'Hadn't they been told not to go to the hospital?' they said. 'They were warned, ordered, commanded, and look, they followed him into the horse's mouth and now have got themselves lifted.' 'But what do they see in him?' 'Yeah. And at their age too, for some aren't young.' 'Not just some. None of them are young. So-and-so's ma's definitely not young and the scouts have informed us that she too, has just been spirited from a hospital cupboard and is now down at the police barracks.' 'So has so-and-so's ma.' 'And so-and-so's ma.' 'And my ma,' confessed a renouncer. 'Sorry, but I didn't know, and neither did my da, until today when she rushed off and got herself arrested.' After a pause, some of the others admitted to the deplorable situation of their own mothers' involvement with the man who didn't love anybody too.

As for the police flipping the ex-pious women into informers or the renouncers chasing down the ex-pious women to see if they had been flipped as informers, nothing came of it. Women numbers had by now increased. The women with the issues — *'Oh no, not them!'* cried all military and paramilitary personnel — had also appeared and had rushed to the hospital out of support for real milkman. He was the only one in their area, they said, who fully comprehended and respected them and their cause. After that came the media, including that small but irksome hostile segment, that even now, without proof, were publishing a 'MILKMAN REALLY MILKMAN!' taunting lunchtime news headline, declaring the state again had got it wrong. The state, on discovering this was correct, that they had got it wrong, decided to call closure over the whole affair which they announced on the next television news bulletin. Meanwhile, the renouncers, worried as they had been about having to sit in 'court and pass stern and impartial judgement upon possible informants most likely to be their own mothers, watched this television bulletin of the state calling for closure and, for the first time ever, agreed with their adversaries, concurring that in this case they'd be happy to call it a day as well.

Ma and seventeen women then, were released by the police and let alone by the renouncers. They rushed immediately back to hospital and straight to Intensive Care. There, they were told that real milkman's condition was 'stable' but that none of them, for now, would be allowed in to see him. 'Sorry, but you're not family,' said the hospital, and apparently 'spouses on all but offer' didn't count either in this case. Some of the spouses went home then, to gather reinforcements, to foster plans and contingencies. This was when ma came in our door in the dark and revealed the ancient drama of herself, of Peggy, of real milkman and of those other women; also, of course, of that other issue, the wrong-spouse issue, that had been unmentionable all through their married life between herself and da.

Now here she was, nearly two weeks on from when I'd been poisoned but before I'd gone to the chip shop, trying out my sling-backs, briefly calmed because she could see they suited her. Her sense of insecurity though, was still heightened and already was roving round to the next thing. This turned out to be her 'rear' as she called it, for this rear had gotten bigger since last time she'd looked full-on at it in a mirror. That had been years previously. How many years, she didn't want to say. But she looked, she said, and saw that it had gotten bigger, and she knew this, she said, not only by the fact of looking at herself frontwise in the mirror and seeing that *that* part had gotten bigger, which followed that the back of her must commensurably have gotten bigger, she knew as well, she said, because incremen-tally she'd had to increase her dress size and also she knew, she said, by that experi-ence she'd had of that chair in the front parlour that time. I must have looked blank for she added, 'Talking rearward, daughter. That chair I don't sit in anymore, well, my rear is the reason why I don't sit in it. You were probably wondering —' 'No, ma,' I said. 'Wasn't wondering — and what chair? I haven't noticed any chair.' 'Of course you have,' she said, 'the wooden one with the armrests in the front parlour that used to be one of your Great-Great-Granny Winifred's chairs. Well, I used to sit in it. Now and then I'd sit in it, and do knitting, or talk to Jason, or to some of the other women, or have a cup of tea by myself in it or with the man *who really is a milkman'* — she looked at me here but I didn't rise to the occasion — 'sometimes I'd just sit,' she said, 'and think, or listen to the wireless, and that was fine. I'd sit in that chair without complexity, without any sense of consciousness even, that there I was, sitting in it. It was just a chair; not notable to be registered as tormenting to the psyche. I'd lower myself in, then, when done, I'd higher myself out of it. All normal. Not now, daughter. Now, there's a searing mental pain anytime I have doings with the chair because *slightly* my rear brushes the armrest of one side as I'm lowering myself in or highering myself out of it, or else my rear brushes similarly the armrest of the other side. These armrests aren't capable of articulation,' she stressed. 'They're stuck fast to the body because it's a one-piece chair and of course the chair itself can't have gotten smaller which means my rear's gotten bigger but it's gotten bigger without the concomitant modification to a new way of negotiating furniture and instead is still acting from the retention of the memory of how smaller in the olden days it used to be.' I opened my mouth, not sure, to say something — or maybe just to have it hang open. 'But understand, daughter,' went on ma, 'I'm not saying my rear cannot now fit in the chair because the chair's become too tight for it. *It can still fit in.* It's just that now it encompasses a certain amount of extra inches or fractions of inches to which it has never acclimatised and which in the old days didn't used to be.'

I knew now, of course, what she was driving at, though unsure still how to respond. Here seemed a sensitive, painful, microscopic depiction of ma's view of the growth of her behind, with nothing brash or crude or dumbed-down or of popular culture in the description either. My response therefore, should be comparable to her own words, should be of like tone and weight in order to acknowledge and to respect her older status, even her originality in delineating the depth of her rear condition in relation to the chair she was speaking of. I was also aware, of course, given this turnaround she was undergoing concerning herself and real milkman, and the rivalry between herself and the ex-pious women regarding real milkman, that ma, with this chair minutiae, might instead be cracking up. As for the chair, I was prevented having to give response by wee sisters calling to me from downstairs. They'd run out of the bedroom at the start of this talk to dash down to the front parlour to drag the chair in question out into the hallway. 'Middle sister! Middle sister!' they shouted and both ma and I went out to the landing and looked over the banisters and there was the chair down below in the hall. It was just that old chair from the front room, the old-fashioned, high-backed wooden one with armrests which looked harmless enough but apparently in terms of mental torture, were anything but harmless. 'Here it is, middle sister! This chair! It's this chair here!' wee sisters clamoured while ma, averting her eyes and putting her arm out against it, cried, 'Oh, do not remind me! Take it from me, littlest daughters.' So they tugged and struggled and dragged Great-Great-Granny Winifred's offending chair back into the front parlour then they rushed upstairs and we carried on.

And now it was her face. It had 'declined', she said. Then it was lines and age-spots and wrinkles. 'This one here' — she came close for me to note a particular wrinkle. I noted. It was a wrinkle. Amongst others. At the top of her cheek. On her face. 'That one started first,' she said. 'It was slight, rather ghostly, and I had to strain really hard, almost hurting my eyes one day to discern it in the public toilets downtown by the City Hall in my early thirties. I knew what it meant, but after an initial twinge of anxiety I dismissed it, daughter, because you see, I couldn't help it, there were still years yet.' Then it was her thighs. 'They died,' she said. 'Felt as if they'd died. Looked as if they'd died. That's how they look still, no longer any springiness to them.' Then it was knobbles in knees, gristly sounds in knees, a thickened waist, that rear that had also declined as well as amassing extra inches or fractions of inches. The arch of her lower back, she then said, because of all these downward slopings, was not as shapely arched as in the old days it used to be. 'I used to be gazelle-like in my movement, like your third sister. I even got pictures of me being it. This too. Do you see this? This red mark here? Do you see it? Well, it used to be up there and before that I didn't have it.' Wee sisters whispered that ma had been going on like this for hours and that they were worried. They wanted me to say what was wrong with her and to fix it, to do something, so a few times, though futilely, I tried to intervene. I attempted to reassure ma, because I'd noticed, even if she hadn't, that a side-benefit to real milkman getting shot but crucially not dying, was that ma was dropping years off her, though in correlation to this, it seemed she was losing a lot of confidence, becoming adolescent, giving off the belief she didn't stand a chance against those ex-pious women who also seemed to be dropping years off them but who again, and in correlation, also were developing self-esteem issues of their own. Ma, however, wouldn't let herself be comforted. There was a lot of *'Yes but'* interruptions no matter what I attempted to bolster her with. These *Yes-buts* were coming out before I'd even managed to utter the first phrase of the first bolster, and now it was armpits, arms, shaking of arms, the backs of upper arms which women her age shouldn't do if they didn't want to torment themselves. Then it was gaps in teeth, more declensions around breasts, joints clicking, bones catching, clunkings in the digestive system, problems with the bowels, with her eyesight going fuzzy as well as starting to take on that little-old-lady eye that little old ladies went about with. Also, her hair was going grey, she said, with new hair growing on her body, particularly — this as a whisper — *masculine hair* on her face. 'I could go on,' she said. And she did. She continued to be insecure about things which, until recently, and given her age, I shouldn't have believed she'd consider, let alone give a care about. Then again, there was that sense of her getting younger even if she didn't believe she was getting younger. So I suppose in that back-to-front way that happens in life, it was fitting that fears of growing old should assail her now in her new psychic age of sixteen. It was at this point, and as if letting me know that if I thought up until then I'd been witnessing utter defeat and dejection, what followed was utter defeat and dejection. Glancing again in the mirror, this time because she was sure her height had gotten smaller because her bones were crumbling, she let out the biggest sigh so far. This was more to herself than to me or wee sisters. She said, 'What's the point anyway? None of it matters anyway, not now, when there's that poor woman to consider, the mother of the four dead boys and of that poor dead girl, also the widow of her poor dead husband.' This was when she moved on to nuclear boy's ma.

Nuclear boy's ma was also, of course, Somebody McSomebody's ma, also the mother of the favourite sibling who'd been killed in that bomb explosion, the mother of wee tot too, who'd fallen out the window that time. This woman, however, mostly came to be known as nuclear boy's ma because nuclear boy had made much more of an impression on people's consciousness owing to his dramatic if incomprehensible nucleomitophobia — not to mention that suicide letter. None of the others in that family, alive or dead, had drawn anywhere near the same attention to themselves as he had. Indeed, apart from Somebody Mc-Somebody, all remaining family members came to be described solely in reference to him. There were nuclear boy's remaining six sisters. There were nuclear boy's various cousins and aunties and uncles, nuclear boy's etcetera and in this case, I now realised, ma was referring to nuclear boy's ma. Initially when she started in on this, again I could only stare, not knowing what she was intending by it. Ma said, and as if in conclusion for it seemed already she'd been grappling with this, 'I suppose I'm going to have to let her have him,' which was when I asked her to explain. She said the ex-pious women, in friendly unison, had come to our door the day before to appeal to her conscience about poor nuclear boy's mother. They put it to her reasonably, she said, that given *'POOR POOR POOR POOR'* (as they stressed it) nuclear boy's mother had suffered more personal political tragedies in her life quantitatively-speaking than had any of them in the area suffered personal political tragedies in their lives, would it not be more noble, spiritual and altruistic, they said, to stand aside and let real milkman be for her? Well, the penny dropped immediately for me but before I could start in on 'God's strength, ma, can't you see the trick o'them? And anyway, it doesn't work like that,' she herself was delineating the facts. Counting off on her fingers, she compared the tragedies, again quantitatively-speaking and in accordance with her hierarchy of suffering, that she herself had undergone with those of nuclear boy's mother. 'That *POOR POOR POOR POOR* woman,' she said. 'She's had a husband and four sons and a daughter die, all of them politically, whereas I've had a husband and one son die and no daughters — dead I mean, and yes' — she held up her hand to stop me — 'it is true that second son died politically, but your father — *good man! oh such a good man! and a good father, and a good husband*' — and here she'd veered off, now into compliments about da rather than her usual criticism, which I guessed meant another bout of guilt had as-

552

sailed her for having repressed for so long her *'I'm not in love because I'm already married so how can I be in love!'* love for real milkman so that now she was over-compensating with a feeling badness for marrying the wrong person — 'your father,' she said, veering back, 'died ordinarily from illness, God love him, so that meant he didn't die politically. So I suppose they're right and I'm going to have to bow out and do the lofty thing and hand real milkman over to her.'

By this time I was staring *and* speechless, then I was jumping up and down at ma's obtuseness in this matter. Could she hear herself? Why couldn't she see what those wily expious women were intending? If this were the case — if they were correct in their so-called high principles and sound reasoning of *'only one son dead and a husband, no daughters, therefore don't qualify'* — if this really were how these things proceeded, how many of us would have to be killed and in our graves politically before she'd consider going out on a date? Even acceding too, to *that* evaluation — that of her hierarchy of suffering, of her absolutist criteria of who gets most points for the sorrow and the grieving — even then, here she was, misperceiving what she termed 'the facts'. It was

553

down to me to adopt the pedantic approach and to iron out these misperceptions for her. Firstly, I said, poor nuclear boy's mother had lost only two of her sons through the political problems, not three sons, only two, even if others in the area were saying that nuclear boy should perhaps — regardless of America and Russia — be counted in there also. I couldn't afford to count him in as ma by now was heading into critical self-sabotage stage. So I said about the one son, the favourite, the one who'd died politically while crossing the road owing to that bomb in the street going off. And I said about the eldest renouncer son and one renouncer daughter and of course, the husband also dying politically. Then there was that poor dog of theirs that had had its throat cut up the entry by the soldiers that time. Second, I said it could be argued, even if feebly, that ma herself had lost, through banishment — which meant also through the political problems — one of her daughters. And it could be argued, again if feebly, that she was suffering the loss of another son, namely, fourth son, the on-the-run son, even if, though she loved him dearly, he wasn't her son really, not really — even if, too, he was still alive and living over that border somewhere. I pointed out also, that it was unlikely — given the doomed state of poor nuclear boy's mother — that that woman would be on the look-out for any sexual romantic interest. 'Come on, ma,' I said. 'You've seen her. At least you saw for yourself before she stopped coming out her door how daily that poor woman was deteriorating, how nobody now can do anything for her, how people have become frightened of her and are even considering slotting her, owing to this fear they have of her, into the death-row category of our district's beyond-the-pales. When did you last see her?' I asked. 'When did anybody last see her? They're saying she doesn't wash, doesn't eat, doesn't get out of bed, has abandoned the rest of her family. Forget nuclear boy's ma, ma,' I said, 'as someone in the running for trysts with men at "dot dot dot" places.' Ma winced and made a motion of covering her ears with her hands. 'You're brutal, child,' she said. 'You're harsh. You're so cold. There's always something so terribly cold about you, daughter.' And you're slow-off-blocks, ma, was what I thought to say but didn't otherwise we'd be back to another of those *gee-whizz* moments, then another fight, with us again in our old angers at each other. Also I didn't say, least not directly, 'Are all your friends trustworthy?', echoing back her reproving words to me during that night when she purged me of the poison. Instead I said the same thing indirectly, by bringing up the sly, devious handiwork of the other party involved.

'Your pals, ma,' I said, 'your praying pals, the ex-pious women. Is it likely, do you think, that they themselves are saying, "Oh, we must, simply must, step back and let her have him," meaning nuclear boy's mother? You think they'll be for giving up real milkman, for handing him over, for renouncing their possibilities with him, for her? Soon as you're out the road, ma, got out the door, easily too, by their emotional blackmail, that poor woman will be trampled under their first horse and carriage careering by. They'll regroup too, reconfigure and plot, this time to oust the next amongst them, after you, of real milkman's affections. But first it's you, ma,' I said. 'You're the highest in the running for the heart of real milkman, which is why you've had this nuclear-boy-mother card played so deftly and almost successfully upon yourself.' 'Away you on!' said ma. 'It can't be me that's first highest —' And here she broke off, this time making deprecating motions with her hand. 'It *is* you, ma,' I said. 'It's you he's interested in, you

556

he comes to visit for tea, always with extra pints of milk and special dairy products that I'm sure he doesn't hand out to everybody.' Again there were disbelieving motions, though less vehement, more half believing, more hopeful, with the hand. Definitely ma was out of practice and dearly needed bolstering. That meant I had to be charitable, no, had to be pragmatic, because in truth I hadn't noticed whether real milkman was interested in ma or nuclear boy's ma or in any of them others. They were too old to be paid notice. It was that I didn't want her giving up right at the very start. Of course there was the possibility that real milkman might decide, in spite of his apparent desire now for personal coupledom, that he didn't want this coupledom with any of them, or that he might revert back to broad, universal kinship just as soon as he was properly mended. That was too dispiriting for ma, or for the ex-pious women, or even for me to script into this scenario at this time. So we didn't. This meant I bolstered with lies which, when all the facts were in, might not have been lies really. I said, 'You're the strongest contender, ma. Always sayin' to me, he is, that he likes you, to tell you he's askin' about you.' 'Is he? Am I?' 'Yes,' I said, though he'd only ever done this on passing. Then again, in that one proper conversation in his lorry when he took me home and took care of the cat's head for me, real milkman had been concerned about ma one hundred per cent. So I wasn't lying really, and I told her this too, about the hundred per cent, to give a boost with high-sounding numbers to her confidence. 'It's okay, ma,' I said. 'Just keep the nerve, hold the faith, be on your mettle, attend bit by bit and obtain by quiet manoeuvres. Bear in mind too, what those women were like with Peggy. Their appetency and voraciousness that burst forth after Monk Peggy. You said yourself you were angry at them, yet here they are, doing the same again. Cunning women,' I added, thinking of how they were tricking ma, washing her brain, taking advantage of her inner conflict. It had been a long time, I could see, since she'd involved herself in blindside or flank movements. 'What canny, manipulative, crafty female men-of-all-seasons —' 'Middle daughter!' cried ma. 'These are your elders! Do not speak of the ex-sanctities in adjectives like that.'

I had gotten through to her though, for she began to be on her dignity. A certain 'how dare they exploit my conscience' was growing upon her which was encouraging but events were moving quickly for another by-product, I found out, of real milkman getting shot, probably the main by-product of his getting shot, was that getting shot did seem to have catalysed him out of his long-term 'not getting over Peggy' reclusion. His self-imposed exile from personal romantic and passionate love and settling instead for mere unconditional *agape* appeared now to have come to an end. Before he'd even left hospital, and setting aside that gunshot unpleasantness, and in spite too, of his stern and ascetic side trying its utmost to reassert sternness and asceticism, incongruously he found he was having a nice time. Ma told me that he told her that at first while lying in hospital, some aberrant insurrectionary sense had come upon him, wanting deeds of goodness to be done unto him instead of him always having to be the deeder of the goodnesses. This was in contrast to last time twelve years earlier, during the prime of his great self-sufficiency when, although he'd needed help, all the help he could get and subsequently received after that beating then that tar and feathering, his heart then, in contrast to his heart now, hadn't opened a jot to personal love or romance. So he was undergoing his own revolution, coming out from behind all that common good and self-sacrifice. Instead he wanted to be the recipient of personal love, and of sex, and of affection this time around. All this he was fully open to, ma said, also saying that he said that, as if on cue, as if by a miracle, deeds of goodness — with possibilities for personal attachments — were poured forth upon him, in that women started to appear almost at once. They turned up in droves at the hospital, he said, and it was mostly those traditional, pious women of the area. Then came the issue women. Also some men — a few neighbours unafraid of being implicated with someone constantly raising his head above the parapet — they showed at the hospital too. And of course there was ma, his longest friend. So they came, he said, and that was nice. Here he took and held ma's hand. She said that he said that the new deeds of goodness being done unto him sat comfortably within his newfound peaceful personality. When he was out of hospital, still people came to visit him and still the deeds sat comfortably. Ma though, experiencing a mixture of ecstasy at having her hand held and of being spoken to intimately by real milkman, was also feeling annoyance because she understood now, regarding those other women, what it was I'd been trying to draw her attention to all along.

Apart from her complaint then, as to her agedness, ma's other complaint was about the ubiquity of these ex-pious women. She had stopped haranguing me about marriage — itself another welcome fringe of real milkman getting wounded — also desisted in her words about my taking up with dangerous married people. Simply she hadn't the time. 'They're forever round there,' she cried, 'at his house with their sly moves, bringing him turnips. I saw them with their gifts of carrots and parsnips, their homemade soups, their cakes and aromatic waters of rose and their charmingly packaged, gift-wrapped potatoes sticking out of their pockets. Such deceit! It's hardly imaginable.' 'I know, ma,' I said. 'It's hardly not.' 'Dressing up too, daughter,' she went on, 'though goodness knows they're no spring —' This of course was when she remembered, courtesy of *Yes-but,* that she too was no spring — Again I hurried to intervene. I stressed that, owing to a reversal of the lifeforce inside her, she was blossoming, losing that *'life's over, I'm finished with life, past it, just eking out what's left'* older person's perspective that usually she went about in and that I hadn't noticed she'd gone about in until of late when she'd stopped going about in it. Instead she'd sprung to life, bursting with green shoots and — '. . . competitiveness and rivalry,' concluded *Yes-but* which was not how I would have concluded myself. 'I'm too old to be jealous,' said ma. 'Not used to it. I thought I had all that over with. You know, daughter, I think it was easier back then for me to pray to God for Peggy to have him than to pray to God for me to have him — I mean, because of the jealousy, the backlash I'd get from them others. I think too, it would have been easier to have been jealous of one of them getting him than for me to have got him and to have had to deal with their jealousy.' Just as with Great-Great-Granny Winifred's chair then, I sensed we were now in for another microscopically observed advanced discussion, this time on jealousy — a subject which not only I had never heard ma speak of, but which I myself didn't speak of, didn't want to admit to, mainly lest it bring on my own version of *Yes-but* and *Terror Of Other People And Not Just On Difficult Days.*

So *Yes-but* had resurfaced to counter all my attempts to uplift my mother. Every compliment I initiated by way of encouragement, *Yes-but* got in there with its negatives and shot it down. When *Yes-but* wasn't yes-butting, ma was looking in the mirror and sighing. All the same, she seemed as an electric light. One minute she was switched on, then switched off, then on, then off, down to death she'd go, then up she'd rally. At this point some thought occurred and I saw her frown, go down, get annoyed.

'It's all right for some,' she said, 'to gallivant the world over, ballroom-dancing, looking fabulous, with no conscience to speak of. Did you know that woman who wins those ballroom competitions on the TV is nearly the same age, daughter, as me? Well, she is! But we could all look like that. Oh, it would be easy to look like that — top of the world, dolled-up, flashy smiles, sparkling clothes, with bodies that move like reigning champions even before they've stepped onto the dancefloor. We could all be that, daughter, if we did what she did, for do you know what she did? She abandoned her six newborn babies on the settee to manage best they could with only a few Farley's Rusks sprinkled between them — all so she could funster off and have the most passionate, eventful career in the world. What behaviour's that? What mother would do that? Even for the glory of becoming best, most best, or even to be one of those selfless souls who help foster peace and cohesion in a place with a long history of hatred and violence. Dancing and acclaim and renown and prestige and credit and fame and looking like that isn't everything. You wouldn't see me abandoning my duty, leaving my children,' which brought her back to the common round and daily task once more.

And now she was sighing and falling down deeper with her electric light off. Then it was back to 'Can't believe I'm trying to do this, far too old to be doing this. Can't wear your clothes. They're wee girl clothes, not advanced lady clothes,' and to slumping on the edge of the bed at not being able to do it, at being jealous of maybe-boyfriend's ma for being able so magnificently to do it. This was when it came clear to me that I couldn't carry this off. I couldn't hold this up for her. Didn't have the right facilitation within me. Couldn't be the one to rally her for she took no heed of me, didn't rate my opinion, paid more attention to *Yes-but*'s opinion. Plus I had my own worries. Still I was being stalked by Milkman at this point. Not only was he not yet dead, he was well into having stepped up and closed in on foreplay predations. In the case of ma though, I needed reinforcements and that meant, could only mean, first sister had to be called. She'd know what to do, I thought, what to suggest, how to bolster ma out of her defeatism and negativity. Eldest sister wouldn't brook either, any *Yes-but* interruption. *Must fetch first sister, fetch first sister* then became my prioritised thought.

So while ma and *Yes-but,* with heads in hands on edges of beds, were, out of low morale, reverting back to being selfless and doing the right thing by yielding real milkman to nuclear boy's mother, and with wee sisters trying valiantly to coax them out of it, I went downstairs and picked up the telephone. I was wary of ringing first sister because of all that tension that existed now between us. It had reached breaking point and both of us, without doubt, were well aware of that. Aware too, we were, that unless I renounced Milkman, gave up and stopped my immoral, red-light involvement with Milkman, and unless she stopped falsely accusing me of having an affair with Milkman, pretty soon this tension would erupt in either physical violence between us or, even worse, verbal violence in unforgivable nasty words. That meant I must preface the call. I must let her know immediately before she could launch her next offensive, that I was ringing, not for me, not for her, not for Milkman, and not for her horrible husband. Ma was in trouble. She needed help, first sister's help. Needed it now, I'd say. If sister did launch into Milkman, for it seemed to be her number one compulsion-fixation with me, and if I responded in anger, which I would, given that was my number one compulsion-fixation with her, then one or other of us, most likely, would hang up. I wouldn't like that. Knew I'd hate that. But it did feel a risk that in the moment I had to take. So I picked up the receiver and, as usual, checked for bugs, also as usual not knowing how to recognise what I was checking for. Then I rang her. As the ringing tone sounded I had the thought of her husband answering and so debated hanging up only he didn't answer. First sister answered, which was when I remembered it wouldn't have been him. First brother-in-law was in bed, recovering from a recent paramilitary beating-up.

To stop instant altercation, I launched into my preface as planned. 'It's me, eldest sister. This is about ma,' and immediately I got into explanations. '. . . and so she needs help . . . That's right, her friend, the man who doesn't love anybody . . . Ach aye yeah . . . Ach aye no . . . It turns out, sister, she doesn't want to be just friends . . . She thinks she can't have him because the ex-pious women have sown seeds of guilt, saying — What? . . . Yeah . . . Uh-huh . . . Well, that's right. That's what I've been telling her but . . . Ach aye yes, I said that too, but she doesn't listen to me . . . I know that, sister, but don't forget, her nerves are gone and it's not as if she's experienced. She hasn't had doings with any of this since da.' Here I left out the whole wrong-spouse situation, given first sister herself might be tender in that area. 'So it's probably been years and years,' I hurried on. '. . . What? Oh, I didn't think of that but it's no good anyway, because *I* can't get through to her . . . That's what I've been trying to tell her but it's yes-but and yes-but and getting into dejection over her clothes, her body, some chair she can't fit into . . . That's right, chair. No. *Chair*! I did say "chair"! . . . I'm not shouting! And no, sister, I'm not exaggerating. Listen. Cannot you hear her moans and sighs for yourself?' At this, I held the receiver up the stairs where extreme expressions of mental anguish were issuing down clearly from ma in my bedroom. Also coming were the brave attempts of wee sisters to reassure her, telling ma she looked exactly as she should look which, given ma's state of mind, was probably not the thing to say at this point. Wee sisters were alternating these attempts at comfort with rushing downstairs to hear what was happening at our end of the telephone conversation, then back up again to re-attempt assurance and to witness the latest insecurity being birthed up there. 'See?' I said, placing the receiver back at my ear. 'So will you come, sister? She needs help. She needs you. You're the only one who can turn this around and get through to her, talk to her, help her, do something with her confidence and her outfits. I can't, not me, you can. So will you come? Can you come? Cannot you come? Now?'

So that was what I said, deliberately too, employing 'the man who didn't love anybody' instead of 'real milkman'. Any mention of 'milkman' — any milkman — would definitely have caused *frisson* at this point. Sister didn't pause. She said she'd be there in 'fifteen minutes and ten minutes' which meant twenty-five minutes which was understandable, the ten-minute area being so bleak and eerie that nobody liked to include it in with their normal time. 'I'll tell her,' I said, then I said, 'Thanks, sister,' and we did goodbyes, not as protracted and exhausting as ordinarily they would have been had that underpinning of tension regarding Milkman not still been going on between us. The fact though, we did a few goodbyes more than just one goodbye or no goodbye meant some sign of tentative repair of sisterhood had taken place. So telephone call over, and with no big fight, no slaps in face, no words spoken that both of us would regret but be unable to take back after, she was coming. Thank God, in fifteen minutes and ten minutes she'd be here to sort ma out. I replaced the receiver then, not caring overduly if those ear-wiggers from the state had or had not been listening. I sighed relief also, then braced myself out of habit to face ma again upstairs.

Sister did turn up in fifteen minutes and ten minutes as promised. She had brought clothes and accessories appropriate to person and occasion; also her three youngling twin sons and one daughter, leaving her husband in their house to nurse his rough-justice wounds alone. Immediately she took charge as I knew she would and as it was proper she should, for she was more in accord with ma, had always been of like mind, in harmony, more a soul energiser than I for ma would ever be a soul energiser. Unerringly also, she was accurate as to what was wanted, so she set about roping in me, wee sisters and her own wee tots as gofers while she herself calmed and reassured ma. *Yes-but* was banished, indeed left of its own accord rather than attempt any battle with sister. The rest of us got involved and fetched and carried and were glad to do so for ma's sake. Ma, meanwhile, perked up, became relieved and very, very trusting. First sister also perked up, becoming less sad and less grieving. So with ma pleased, first sister pleased, wee sisters pleased, wee tots pleased and me pleased, I said after a bit that while they got on with it, I'd go downstairs and put the teapot on.

And now, two whole weeks on from tablets girl poisoning me, also from her murder, and from ma with her love and insecurity issues kicking in regarding real milkman; two days on too, from chef and ex-maybe-boyfriend and their South American adventure plans, and from Milkman being dead, and from Somebody McSomebody nursing bruises and regretting things, here I was, with ordinary life once again going on. I was in the kitchen, making dinner for the girls. This was before they were to head out to play the international couple and before I was to put on my running gear and, for the first time since being poisoned, go to third brother-in-law's house down the road. Wee sisters were saying it would be good if I'd hurry up, that they were all set to go, all ready to play, just as soon as they'd eaten and as usual it was Fray Bentos they wanted. 'With chips,' they added. 'Or Paris Buns,' they added. 'With chips,' they added. Or 'bananas with chips', or 'soft-boiled eggs with chips', or 'shop-bought pies with chips', and they carried on, with everything with chips even though already I'd explained they couldn't have chips, one reason being that I didn't know how to make them and felt sure that although it had not been proven by actuality, I'd burn the house down if ever I should try so never would I try. Another reason was I couldn't face returning to the chip shop even though Milkman was dead — probably more so because he was dead. Those shopkeepers who'd capitulated even though I hadn't made them capitulate would most likely now exhibit their grudges openly, with it only a matter of time before they wanted their money, as well as revenge, back. So it wasn't over, this business of me and Milkman. Then again, I knew all along it wouldn't be over. With these sorts of things you have to take each day, each person, each reprisal, at a time. Instead of chips, I said wee sisters could have whatever they liked by way of Fray Bentos, Opal Fruits, liquorice allsorts, ice-cream, those communion wafer flying-saucer confection sweetmeats in edible paper pouched with strong fizz which explode on the tongue which I knew they loved having, and boiled beet-root. 'Whatever,' I said. 'Just not with chips,' which half delighted and half disappointed but in the end, they settled on variations of those same baby treats I'd daydreamed about whilst recovering from being poi-soned. So I prepared their tea, which meant basically getting it out of the cupboards. All the time though, it was, 'Middle sister! Please hurry. Will not you hurry? Modest amounts please. But cannot you be more instanter than that?'

I gave it to them and they ate up, then rushed out to play the international couple. Looking out the window on my way upstairs to change for running, I could see this international couple had really taken off. Little girls were falling over everywhere. It seemed the whole district of them was out, playing, flouncing, and at first glance they appeared mainly to resemble chandeliers with added lusciousness such as golden brocade and embossed wallpaper. By the time I did go out, all the streets were over-run with them: beribboned, besilked, bevel-veted, behighheeled, bescratchy-petticoated and in pairs or else alone but pretending to be in pairs, waltzing and periodically crashing over. Meanwhile, the little boys, oblivious of the little girls, temporarily too, suspending operations against that army from 'over there' — owing, probably, to the current absence of that army from 'over there' — were taking turns at being good guy in their new play of the latest martyr killed recently in the political problems: Renouncer Hero Milkman, shadowed, set upon, then gunned down in their usual cowardly fashion by that murder squad spawned by a terrorist state.

'Fuckin'. Fuckin'.'

I knew he knew I was there, that it was me, but he carried on with his back turned, in his garden, in his gear, doing his usual mutters while warming up. He didn't look at me, no acknowledgement as I arrived and leaned over to open his little house's little gate. Still sulking then, I guessed, and I meant over that telephone call, the one he'd had a while back with ma about my missing our run sessions. Because of this, also because he'd been sceptical of my earlier complaint of legs losing power, body losing coordination, balance tipping, starting to stumble, starting to tumble, I thought it best silently to fall into stretching beside him rather than attempt any further explanation. So that then, was what I did. After a bit he said, still without looking, 'Thought you'd given up running.' 'No,' I said. 'That was just poison.' 'Well, days and days went by,' he said, 'and it didn't seem to me like you were coming running.' 'Attempted murder, brother-in-law.' 'That's what they all say, sister-in-law. It's one thing to say' — and here brother-in-law's voice was tense, edgy, wounded — ' "No, not twelve miles, thirty miles," for that would be contrariness. But to say — *or to get your mother to say* — "No, not running, never again going running," that's just bad play, that is.'

Still not looking at me, he moved on to his hip flexors. I knew I had to salvage the situation, acknowledge his grievance, pat down his hurt heart. Best way to do that was to have him goad me into browbeating him, which at least in the moment, for his part, he was attempting to do. It was down to me then to say, 'Right, that's it. I've had enough. We're doing twenty miles today.' But I was in too much doubt of my recovery, of my stamina, to manage twenty miles. I was unsure of ten miles, even five miles, didn't know really, though my legs were returning, if I was ready at all yet for running. I supposed I could throw out some speculative number of miles we were not

574

running but, 'We're doing twelve miles today,' he announced, opening the bidding before I got a chance. 'We are not doing twelve miles,' I said. 'Not eleven either,' which did the trick for then he sounded — which was to him, a button — pacified and shocked at the same time. 'Surely not *not* eleven,' he cried. 'That's right,' I said. 'Not eleven. Not nine either, or eight.' 'All right then,' he said, 'we'll do nine.' 'No,' I said, 'I said not nine. Not seven, or six, maybe five — we'll do six miles.' 'Six miles isn't much!' he cried. 'Six miles! Six miles and not any more than six miles? How about six twice, sister-in-law, or six miles with another three miles or . . .' Of course I could have replied, 'Look listen, brother-in-law. You do more if you like. In fact, why don't we both just do what we feel like doing?', for it didn't matter that we should run together anymore, not now that Milkman was dead. I didn't admit this openly, I mean to myself, in case it spelled out to me that I had become that traitorous, cold-hearted bad person. But the fact was, after Milkman and his *'I'm male and you're female'*, and his *'you don't need that running'*, plus his subsoil *'I'm going to curtail you and isolate you so that soon you'll do nothing'*; after going from two months too, of stumbling, of legs strangely no longer working to legs soon to be magnificently working, I did feel safe again to run on my own. For the present though, or at least until brother-in-law should again go bananas with his next bout of *über*-addiction, I decided to keep on running my runs with him. 'Six miles only,' I pronounced, which eventually had brother-in-law conceding. 'All right,' he said, also saying he was in protestation about the six miles. He supposed he could make up the shortfall with skipping or extra squats and lunges later at the boxing club. So, 'I'm unhappy with this,' he said, but he didn't seem unhappy. He seemed happy, which I think meant we were friends once again. At this moment his wife, my third sister, appeared, along with her gang of mates, all of them with drink taken. They had extra bottles with them, plus shopping, lots of boutique and shopping-mall shopping, all from some retail-barcrawl onslaught they'd been on all day in town.

'God, we're plastered,' they said, and then they, including sister, fell over the ornamental hedge. Sister exploded into advanced asterisks, into percentage marks, crossword symbol signs, ampersands, circumflexes, hash keys, dollar signs, all that *'If You See Kay'* blue french language. Her friends, picking themselves up off the grass, plus their bottles and shopping, rejoined with, 'Well, we told you, friend. We warned you. It's rambunctious, out of control. That hedge is sinister. Get rid of it.' 'Can't,' said sister. 'I'm curious to see how it'll transpire and individualise.' 'You can see how it's transpired and individualised. It's transpired into day of the triffids. It's individualising into trying to kill us.' Then they left off hedge-disparagement and turned their attention to us.

Brother-in-law got it first.

'Hear you've been battering women down at the parks & —' This particular friend of sister couldn't finish her observation because brother-in-law fell out of his stretch just on hearing the opening words. 'What!' he spluttered. 'Who's been puttin' that about about me?' 'Stop,' said third sister to her friends. 'There, lamb.' She turned to him. 'Pay no heed. They're dark, dank weeds to your illumined sensitivity.' Although it would have been difficult to keep a straight face and refer to third brother-in-law as a high-strung ethereality — as seen by her friends bursting into laughter — in some under-the-skin way I did understand what sister meant. If any of us present were to be called forth as the most modest, the most easily shocked amongst us, I would say, and sister would say, even her friends in spite of their laughter would say, 'Oh well, if it boils down to it, we suppose that would be him.'

'Here!' said third sister, and she sprang over to her husband, which had me noticing, as ma had said, how lithe and graceful on her feet — when not falling over hedges — third sister was. 'You mean that's not true?' cried brother-in-law, slightly less shocked but still reeling from the accusation. 'Of course it's not true. The idea of you hitting a —' 'I don't mean *that*,' said brother-in-law. 'I mean it's not true that somebody's been puttin' it about about me?' 'Nobody's been puttin' it about about you.' And here third sister stretched up to give her husband a smacky, dramatic kiss on the mouth. 'No, stand off,' he said. He set her aside. 'I'm not in the mood to kiss you.' Then he turned to the others who had ruffled him, rocked him, and with an issue too, that shouldn't be treated as a joke and which he himself shouldn't have to put up with, especially not from the very sex from which he'd least expect mockery of such principles to come. 'Stop that accusing and maligning,' he said. 'It isn't funny. Puttin' things about about people, ruinin' good men's good reputations. You're not kids anymore, so act your age.'

No impact whatsoever. After that, they started in on me.

'Aye-aye, lookie here,' cried one, though all of them were looking already. 'Snap!' cried another, pointing back to third brother-in-law. 'You two off then, to the Annual Black Eye Convention?' which was when third brother-in-law turned and saw my black eye, also when I saw his.

Black eyes on brother-in-law were not frequent, but they were frequent in comparison with those on me not to be rare items. When I saw my own that morning in the mirror, the only way I could deal with it was by remembering that Somebody Mc-Somebody hadn't got off lightly himself. Must be counting at least twenty black eyes, I told myself — courtesy of those women, then their men, then the renouncers — all far blacker too, no doubt, than this here. 'That'll teach him,' I reassured my reflection, then I wondered whether to go to work. In the end I did, after patching up the eye with tons of make-up; not though — as I discovered immediately upon going out my door and encountering people — as successfully as first I had thought.

'So it's true,' said third brother-in-law. 'I heard a rumour but it was issuing from your first brother-in-law so I wasn't tended to mind it. But that Shitten McShite McSomebody did do that to you?' I shrugged, which meant, yeah, but it's old business and anyway, hardly he got away with it himself. 'Ach,' was what I did say which, depending on the context, can mean anything at all. In this context it meant, leave it, brother-in-law. It's been taken care of. Besides, I thought, relative to everything that had been happening — especially relative to what would have happened to me on the evening before if Milkman hadn't been killed and instead had had me meet him as he had foreplayed me to meet him — Somebody McSomebody and his whack with his gun hardly rated a consequence at all. 'Not pointful,' I said. 'Pointful to me, sister-in-law,' said brother-in-law. 'And what of principles? You're a woman. He's a man. You're a female. He's a male. You're my sister-in-law and I don't care how many of his family got murdered, he's a bastard and would've been a bastard even if they hadn't got murdered.' They hadn't got murdered. Only four had got murdered. The other two had been a suicide and an accidental death.

Brother-in-law was now seriously cross and I was touched by his crossness. Somebody McSomebody was wrong then. People in this place did give a fuck. But there was something else about brother-in-law, something linked to that strange, communally diagnosed mental aberration that he had around women. For all his idolatry, all his belief in the sanctity of femaleness, of women being the higher beings, the mystery of life and so on, he couldn't grasp any abuse towards them other than what *he* termed rape. Rape for brother-in-law wasn't categorised. It wasn't equivocations, rhetorical stunts, sly debater tricks or a quarter amount of something or a half amount of something or a three-quarter amount of something. It was not a presentation package. Rape was rape. It was also black eyes. It was guns in breasts. Hands, fists, weapons, feet, used by male people, deliberately or accidentally-on-purpose against female people. 'NEVER LIFT A FINGER TO A WOMAN' — if ever it had existed — third brother-in-law's teeshirt, to everyone's embarrassment, would have said. According to his rulebook — mine too, at least before the predations upon me by the community and by Milkman — the physical and verbal aspects could be the only aspects. That meant that what was not of *those* trespasses — stalking without touch, hemming-in, taking over, controlling a person with no flesh on flesh, no bone on bone ensuing — could not then be happening. So it came about that of everybody who had heard of the wooing of me by Milkman, third brother-in-law was the only one who, unquestioningly, hadn't considered it to have taken place.

Not seeing mental wreckage then, seemed one of his downsides. As for the black eye, he did see that. 'Why don't we just leave it, brother-in-law?' I said. 'He's been done in — *honestly* — by hundreds of thousands of people.' I added there'd been a synchronicity to it, a sense of providence, a deftness, some cosmic comeuppance easily to be described as pure alchemical process. 'So no further action needed,' I said, trying my best to drive this point home. It was that I was tired of the eye, tired of McSomebody, tired of rules and the district's regulations. As for principles, sometimes you have to say 'stuff principles', such as now when the energy for me was over on all that. 'So you don't need to,' I said, adding that his purposing to go back, and to take me back, would mean delay in getting on to the next thing — our run being the next thing. 'But thanks, brother-in-law,' I said. 'Don't be thinking I'm not grateful because I am grateful.' After a pause brother-in-law said he was going to beat him up all the same. 'Not necessary,' I said. 'Still,' he said. 'Ach,' I said. 'Ach nothing,' he said. 'Ach sure,' I said. 'Ach sure what?' he said. 'Ach sure, if that's how you feel.' 'Ach sure, of course that's how I feel.' 'Ach, all right then.' 'Ach,' he said. 'Ach,' I said. 'Ach,' he said. 'Ach,' I said. 'Ach.'

So that was that settled. We fell back to stretching which was when the others, amused by our little passage until they were bored by our little passage, pushed us out of this stretching. Sister came out with a final 'Oh, but you do lead an exciting life, middle sister,' which I didn't take offence at and even found funny, then all of them turned away and pressed themselves into third sister and third brother-in-law's ridiculously tiny house. Soon after, and through their living-room window, came the sound of bags crinkling, of exclamations on purchases, of the urgent business of drinks, glasses, ashtrays and Elvis. Meanwhile, we two resumed our stretching then brother-in-law said, 'Right? Are ye right?' and I said, 'Aye, come on, we'll do it.' As we jumped the tiny hedge because we couldn't be bothered with the tiny gate to set off on our running, I inhaled the early evening light and realised this was softening, what others might term a little softening. Then, landing on the pavement in the direction of the parks & reservoirs, I exhaled this light and for a moment, just a moment, I almost nearly laughed.

ACKNOWLEDGEMENTS

Thanks to:

Katy Nicholson; Clare Dimond; James Smith; Gerard Macdonald; Carlos Peña Martin; Julie Ruggins; Mia Topley-Ruggins; Belle Topley-Ruggins; Lisette Teasdale; Mike Teasdale; Katy Teasdale; Dan Teasdale; George Teasdale; Pat Thatcher; Sarah Evans; the Royal Literary Fund; Joe Burns; Catharine Birchwood; Maggie Butt; Jane Wilde; Judy Hindley; John Hindley; Brian Utton; Sally Utton; Liz Kay; Helen Colbeck; Virginia Crowe; Pat Vigneswaren; K. Vigneswaren; Ann Radley; Nigel Stephens; Tony Dawson; Russell Halil; Annie Drury; Mark Lambert; Archie; Selina Martin; Michaela Hurcombe; David Cox; Marianne Macdonald; Charles Walsh; Astrid Fuhrmeister; Vesna Main; Peter Main; Janine Gerhardt; my agent David Grossman; Louisa Joyner and the team at Faber; Ian

585

Critchley, copyeditor of *Milkman;* Hazel Orme, copyeditor of *Little Constructions;* Maureen Ruprecht Fadem; James Gardner, Joan Wignall, Terry Howell, Christine Tutt and John Shaw (the Committee) at Lewes District Churches HOMELINK; Newhaven Food Bank; Nicky Gray (formerly of Sussex Community Development Association at Newhaven); Hampton Allotment Charity; the Society of Authors; the Housing and Council Tax Benefit system; the Department of Work and Pensions system; the First-Tier Tribunal Social Entitlement Chamber (of HM Courts and Tribunals Service), Brighton, consisting of Dr R.D.S. Watson and Judge A.J. Kelly, also the gentle, soothing usher whose name, sadly, I never knew; Elizabeth Finn Grants.

There have been many gifts and much assistance offered to me with thoughtfulness and kindness by friends and strangers over the years. I look forward to throwing one hell of a party one day to say thanks to them all, but not yet, as they would have to pay for it.

Final thoughts:
Thanks to me.
Thanks to White Eagle Lodge for having

me on their healing list.
To Spirit: thank you.

ABOUT THE AUTHOR

Anna Burns was born in Belfast, Northern Ireland. She is the author of two previous novels, *No Bones* and *Little Constructions,* and of the novella *Mostly Hero. No Bones* won the Winifred Holtby Memorial Prize and was shortlisted for the Orange Prize for Fiction. She lives in East Sussex, England.

The employees of Thorndike Press hope you have enjoyed this Large Print book. All our Thorndike, Wheeler, and Kennebec Large Print titles are designed for easy reading, and all our books are made to last. Other Thorndike Press Large Print books are available at your library, through selected bookstores, or directly from us.

For information about titles, please call:
(800) 223-1244

or visit our website at:
gale.com/thorndike

To share your comments, please write:
Publisher
Thorndike Press
10 Water St., Suite 310
Waterville, ME 04901